5th Grade Technology Curriculum: Teacher Manual

FIFTH GRADE TECHNOLOGY

A COMPREHENSIVE CURRICULUM

Part Six of Nine of the SL Technology Curriculum

2024

Visit the companion website at Ask a Tech Teacher for more resources to teach technology

ALL MATERIAL IN THIS BOOK IS PROTECTED BY THE INTELLECTUAL PROPERTY LAWS OF THE USA.

No part of this work can be reproduced or used in any form or by any means—graphic, electronic, or mechanical, including photocopying, recording, taping, Web distribution or information storage and retrieval systems—without the prior written permission of the publisher

For permission to use material from this text or product, contact us by email at:

info@structuredlearning.net

ISBN 978-1-942101-27-7

Structured Learning LLC. ©All Rights Reserved

Introduction

The educational paradigm has changed—again. Technology is now granular to learning, blended into standards from Kindergarten on, like these standards rephrased from Common Core:

- Expect students to demonstrate sufficient command of **keyboarding** to type a minimum of one page [three by sixth grade] in a single sitting
- Expect students to **evaluate different media** [print or digital]
- Expect students to **gather relevant information** from print and digital sources
- Expect students to integrate and evaluate **information presented in diverse media** and formats
- Expect students to **interpret information** presented visually, orally, or quantitatively [such as interactive Web pages]
- Expect students to make **strategic use of digital media**
- Expect students to use **glossaries or dictionaries, both print and digital** ...
- Expect students to use information from **illustrations and words in print or digital** text
- Expect students to communicate with a **variety of media**
- Expect students to **use text features and search tools** (e.g., key words, sidebars, **hyperlinks**) to locate information

But how is this taught?

With the **Structured Learning Technology Curriculum**. Aligned with Common Core State Standards* and National Educational Technology Standards, and using a time-proven method honed in classrooms, students learn the technology that promotes literacy, critical thinking, problem-solving, and decision-making through project-based work. The purpose is not to teach step-by-step tech skills (like adding borders, formatting a document, and creating a blog). There are many fine books for that. What this curriculum does is guide you in providing the **right information at the right time**.

Just as most children don't read at two or write at four, they shouldn't be required to place hands on home row in kindergarten or use the Internet before they understand the risks and responsibilities. The Structured Learning curriculum makes sure students get what they need at the right age with proper scaffolding. The end result is a phenomenal amount of learning in a short period of time.

> "New technologies have broadened and expanded the role that speaking and listening play in acquiring and sharing knowledge and have tightened their link to other forms of communication. Digital texts confront students with the potential for continually updated content and dynamically changing combinations of words, graphics, images, hyperlinks, and embedded video and audio."
> —CCSS

> "Use of technology differentiates for student learning styles by providing an alternative method of achieving conceptual understanding, procedural skill and fluency, and applying this knowledge to authentic circumstances."
> —CCSS

If there are skills you don't know, visit our Help blog, Ask a Tech Teacher.com or visit the online companion resources at Structured Learning.net. It includes free videos to unpack each lesson, how-to's for curriculum skills, and more.

What's in the SL Technology Curriculum?

The SL Curriculum is project-based and collaborative, with wide-ranging opportunities for students to show their knowledge in the manner that fits their communication and learning style. Each grade level in the curriculum includes five topics that should be woven into 'most' 21st-century lesson plans:

- *keyboarding—more than typing*
- *digital citizenship—critical with Internet-based learning*
- *problem-solving—encourage critical thinking*
- *vocabulary—decode unknown words with technology*
- *publishing-sharing—to promote collaborative learning*

Here's a quick overview of what is included in the curriculum:

- *curated list of assessments and images*
- *articles that address tech pedagogy*
- *Certificate of Completion for students*
- *curriculum map of skills taught*
- *monthly homework (3rd-8th only)*
- *posters to visually represent topics*

- *Scope and Sequence of skills taught*
- *full lesson on keyboarding, digital citizenship and problem solving (at most grade levels)*
- *step-by-step weekly lessons*

Each weekly lesson includes:

- *assessment strategies*
- *class warm-up and exit ticket*
- *Common Core Standards*
- *differentiation strategies*
- *educational applications*
- *essential question and big idea*
- *examples, rubrics, images, printables*
- *ISTE Standards*
- *materials required*
- *pedagogic articles (if any)*

- *problem solving for lesson*
- *skills—new and scaffolded*
- *steps to accomplish goals*
- *suggestions to unpack*
- *suggestions based on digital device*
- *teacher preparation required*
- *time required to complete*
- *vocabulary used*
- *weekly how-to video (online)*
- *weekly real-time online question sessions*

Programs Used

Programs used in this curriculum focus on skills that serve the fullness of a student's educational career. Free alternatives are noted where available:

General		2-8	
Webtools	Drawing program	Word processing tools	Desktop publisher
Google Earth	Image editor	Spreadsheet tools	Presentation tools
	Keyboarding tool	Email program	

What's in the Sixth Edition?

In response to your requests, here are changes you'll find in the Sixth Edition:

- You'll learn how to unpack lessons whether you're the **grade-level teacher or the tech teacher**.
- Lessons can be delivered on all **popular digital devices**.
- The importance of **higher order thinking**— analysis, evaluation, and synthesis—is called out.
- The importance of **'habits of mind'** is included.
- Lessons note which **skills are scaffolded** from earlier lessons and which are new.
- Each lesson points out **academic applications** of technology.
- Students learn to **understand the process**, not just replicate a skill.
- **Collaboration and sharing** is often required.
- Teachers learn strategies to **meet students where they learn**.
- Each lesson includes a **warm-up and exit ticket**.
- A **Table of Images** and a **Table of Assessments** are included.
- **Scope and Sequence** includes CCSS references.
- **Curriculum Maps** shows which month topics are covered as well as which grade.
- Each grade-level curriculum includes **student workbooks** (sold separately).
- Each grade level has a **lesson on coding**.

Who Needs This Book

You are the Tech Specialist, Coordinator for Instructional Technology, IT Coordinator, Technology Facilitator or Director, Curriculum Specialist, or tech teacher—tasked with finding the right project for a classroom. You have a limited budget, less software, and the drive to do it right no matter roadblocks.

Or you are the classroom teacher, a tech enthusiast with a goal this year—and this time you mean it—to integrate the wonders of technology into lessons. You've seen it work. Others in your PLN are doing it. And significantly, you want to comply with Common Core State Standards, ISTE, your state requirements, and/or IB guidelines that weave technology into the fabric of inquiry.

You are a homeschooler. Even though you're not comfortable with technology, you know your children must be. You are committed to providing the tools s/he needs to succeed. Just as important: Your child WANTS to learn with these tools!

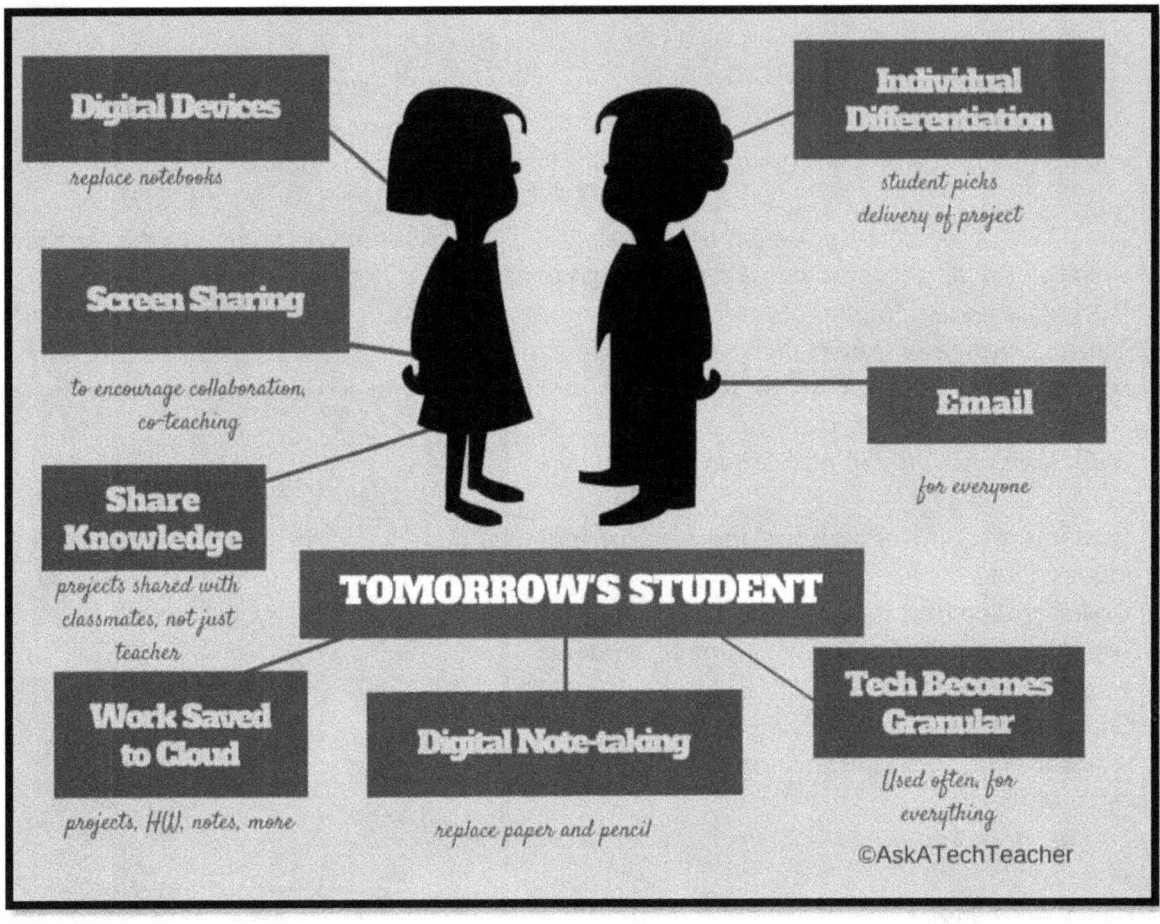

Figure 1—Tomorrow's student

How do you reach your goal? With this curriculum. Teaching children to strategically and safely use technology is a vital part of being a functional member of society—and should be part of every school's curriculum. If not you (the teacher), who will do this? To build **Tomorrow's Student** (*Figure 1*) requires integration of technology and learning. We show you how.

How to Use This Book

Figure 2a shows what's at the beginning of each lesson. *Figure 2b* shows what you'll find at the end:

- Academic Applications
- Assessment Strategies
- Big Idea
- Class Warm-up
- Essential Question

- Material Required
- Problem solving
- Skills
- Standards
- Steps

- Teacher Prep
- Time Required
- Vocabulary

Figure 2a-b—What's in each lesson?

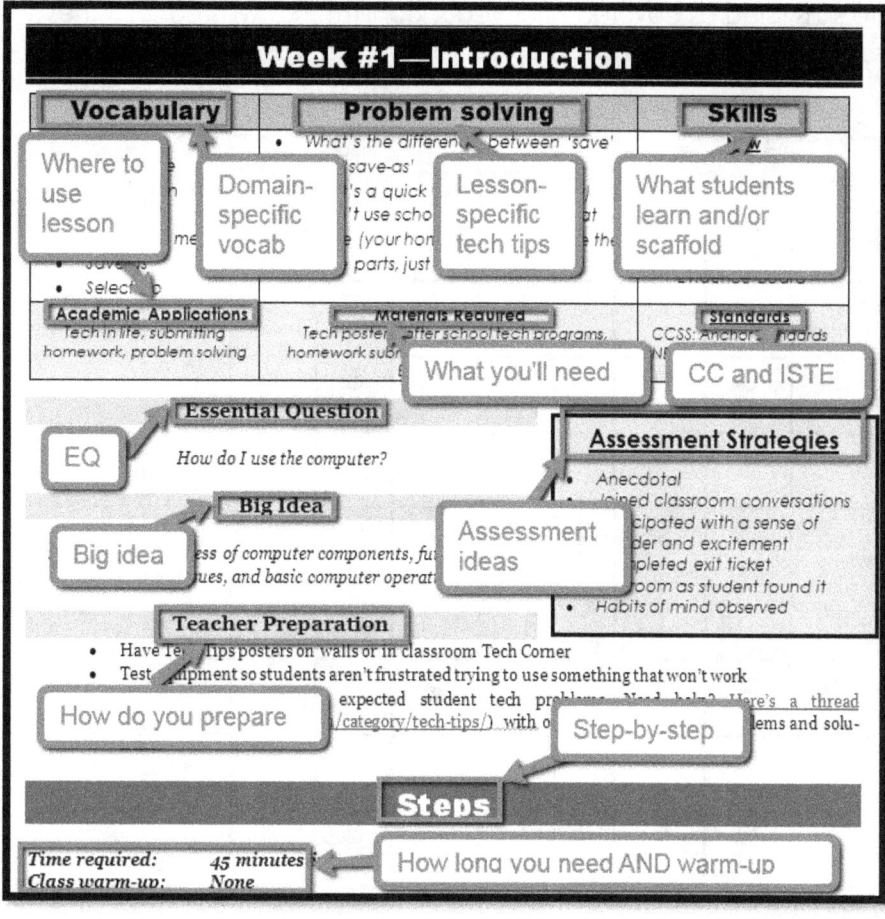

- *Class differentiation strategies*
- *Class exit ticket*

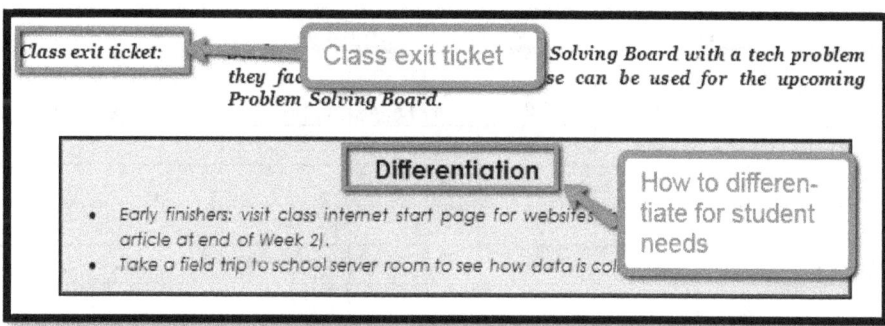

The curriculum map in *Figure 3* shows what's covered in which grade. Where units are taught multiple years, teaching reflects increasingly less scaffolding and more student direction. If you're the grade-level teacher, here's how to use the map:

- Determine what skills were covered earlier years. Expect students to transfer that knowledge to this new school year.

- Review the topics and skills, but don't expect to teach.
- If there are skills listed as covered prior years, confirm that was done. If they weren't (for whatever reason), when you reach lessons that require the skills, plan extra time.

Figure 3—Curriculum Map—K-8

	Mouse Skills	Vocabulary - Hardware	Problem-solving	Platform	Keyboard	WP	Slide-shows	DTP	Spread-sheet	Google Earth	Search/ Research	Graphics	Co-ding	WWW	Games	Dig Cit
K	☺	☺	☺	☺	☺					☺		☺	☺	☺	☺	☺
1	☺	☺	☺	☺	☺	☺	☺	☺	☺	☺		☺	☺	☺	☺	☺
2		☺	☺	☺	☺	☺	☺	☺	☺	☺		☺	☺	☺	☺	☺
3		☺	☺	☺	☺	☺	☺	☺	☺	☺	☺	☺	☺	☺	☺	☺
4		☺	☺		☺	☺	☺	☺	☺	☺	☺	☺	☺	☺		☺
5		☺	☺		☺		☺		☺	☺	☺	☺	☺	☺		☺
6		☺	☺	☺	☺	☺	☺	☺	☺	☺	☺	☺	☺	☺		☺
7		☺	☺	☺	☺	☺			☺	☺	☺	☺	☺	☺	☺	☺
8		☺	☺	☺	☺	☺			☺	☺	☺	☺	☺	☺	☺	☺

Figure 4 is a month-by-month curriculum map for this grade level. In the student workbook, students complete this themselves or as a group when they finish each lesson.

Figure 4—Curriculum Map—5th grade, month-to-month

	Sept Wk1-4	Oct Wk5-8	Nov Wk9-12	Dec Wk13-16	Jan Wk17-20	Feb Wk21-24	March Wk25-28	Apr Wk29-32
Blogs	x			x		x		
Class mgmt tools	x							
Coding		x						x
Collaboration						x	x	x
Communication	x							x
Computer etiquette	x							x
Critical thinking	x			x	x			x
DTP			x	x				x
Digital Citizenship	x							x
Google Earth						x		x
Graphics						x	x	x
Internet			x			x		x

Internet privacy	x					x		x
Keyboarding	x	x				x		x
Presentations								x
Problem solving	x	x	x	x	x	x	x	x
Publishing/sharing	x							x
Research		x						x
Spreadsheets					x			x
Visual learning		x	x	x	x			x
Vocabulary	x	x	x	x	x	x	x	x
Webtools	x	x				x		x
Word Processing	x	x				x		x

Some topics are covered every month. The strategy: spiral and scaffold learning until it's habit.

If there is a skill students don't get, circle back on it, especially when you see it come up a second or third time through the course of the K-8 curricula. By the end of 8th grade, students have a well-rounded tech toolkit that serves their learning needs and prepares them for college and/or career.

Here are hints on using this curriculum:

Figure 1--Student workbooks

- Get free curriculum-aligned resources at Ask A Tech Teacher or email askatechteacher at Gmail dot com with questions.
- Invest in student digital workbooks (sold separately), a companion to the teacher guide. Why?
    - *Projects are at student fingertips with full-color examples and directions (licensing varies depending on plan).*
    - *Workbooks can be viewed and annotated through a reader.*
    - *Students work at their own pace.*
- Once you've selected the program best for you, contact Zeke Rowe at structuredlearning.net for free start-up training.
- Teach lessons in the order presented in the book (grades K-5). They introduce, reinforce, and circle back on skills and concepts. Resist the urge to mix up lessons even if your perfect time for a particular project comes earlier/later than placement in the book. Some lessons can be taught any time during the year (like coding) or throughout the year (like keyboarding, digital citizenship, and problem solving).
- Don't expect to get through all lessons the first time you teach the curriculum. Lessons rely on scaffolded knowledge from prior years. Until students have built that foundation, they will move more slowly through activities. As students learn skills, expect more out of them.
- Personalize the skills taught in each lesson to your needs with 'Academic Applications'. These are suggestions for blending learning into your school curriculum.

- Most lessons start with a warm-up to get students back into tech and give you time to finish up a previous class. This is especially useful to the tech teacher and the LMS. Most lessons end with an Exit Ticket to wrap up learning.
- Some lessons offer several activities that will meet goals outlined in the Essential Question and Big Idea. Pick the activity (or activities) that work well for your student group. Alternatively, you can let students pick the one they like best.
- 'Teacher Preparation' often includes chatting with the grade-level team. Why?
    - *tie tech into their inquiry*
    - *offer websites for early-finishers that address their topics*
- Check off completed items on the line preceding the activity so you know what to get back to when you have time. If you have the ebook, use iAnnotate, Notable (Google for websites), or another annotation tool that works for your devices.
- The curriculum expects students to develop 'habits of mind'. Read more about Art Costa and Bena Kallick's discussion of these principles in *Figure* 6, and the article at the end of Lesson #1. In a sentence: Habits of Mind ask students to engage in their learning, not simply memorize.

Figure 6—Habits of Mind

- Sometimes the class is too excited about what they're learning to move on. Take an extra week. Most schools run 35-40 weeks. This book includes 32 lessons.
- Expect students to be risk takers. Don't rush to solve their problems. Ask them to think how it was done in the past. Focus on problems listed in the lesson, but embrace all that come your way. This scaffolds critical thinking and troubleshooting when you won't be there to help.
- Expect students to direct their own learning. You are a 'guide on the side', a facilitator not lecturer. Learning is accomplished by both success and failure. Don't expect free time while students work. Move among them to provide assistance, and observations on their keyboarding, problem-solving, and vocabulary decoding skills.

- Encourage student-directed differentiation. If the Big Idea and Essential Question can be accommodated in other ways, embrace those.
- If you need resources on specific topics, check Ask a Tech Teacher's resource pages.
- Always use lesson vocabulary. Students gain authentic understanding by your example.
- Look for these icons:

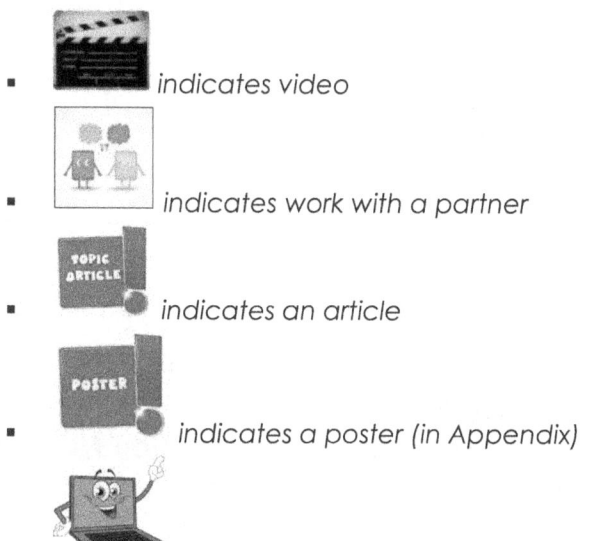

- Use as much technology as possible in your classroom—authentically and agilely--whether it's a smartphone timing a quiz, a video of activities posted to the class website, or an audio file with student input. If you treat tech as a tool in daily activities, so will students.
- **If you have the digital book, zoom in on posters, rubrics, lessons to enlarge as needed.**
- Every effort has been made to accommodate digital devices. If the activity is impossible in a particular digital device (i.e., iPads don't have mouses; software doesn't run in Chromebooks), focus on the **Big Idea and Essential Question**—the skill taught and its application to inquiry. Adapt instructions to the tool you use as you work through the steps.

Figure 7—Compatible digital devices

A desktop PC, iMac, laptop, MacBook, Chromebook, iPad, or smartphone

 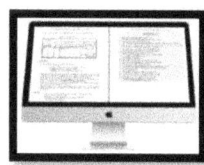     

- Throughout the year, circle back on concepts. It takes five times to get a skill (*Figure 8*)—
    - **First**: They barely hear you
    - **Second**: They try it
    - **Third**: They remember it
    - **Fourth**: They use it outside of class
    - **Fifth**: They tell a friend

Typical Lesson

Each lesson requires about 45 minutes a week, either in one sitting or spread throughout the week, and can be unpacked:

- In the grade-level classroom
- In the school's tech lab

In general terms, here's how to run a lesson in **the tech lab**:

- Post a **written schedule** for the day on the class screen:

    o Warm up
    o Main activity
    o Exit ticket

    This gives students a visual guideline. Add it to your class blog or website to serve those students who aren't present. Expect students to start with the warm-up when they arrive to class.
- **Warm up about 10 minutes,** often with typing practice.
- Complete student **Board presentations** (grades 3-8).
- If it's the end of a grading period, review skills accomplished with **Scope and Sequence**.
- If starting a **new project, review it.** If in the middle of one, use the balance of class to work towards completion. Monitor, answer questions, and help as needed.
- As often as possible, give **younger students two weeks** to finish a project—one to practice, one to save/export/share/print. This redundancy reinforces new skills and mitigates stress. If it's week two, start with the project and finish with typing so students have ample time to work.
- List age-appropriate websites on class Internet start page that **tie into inquiry** for students who complete the current project. Students know these websites can be used during free time.
- **Class exit ticket** might include lining up in arrays, answering a poll posted on the class screen, or simply have classmates verify that neighbors left their stations as they found it.
- **Use tech wherever possible.** Model what you ask of them.

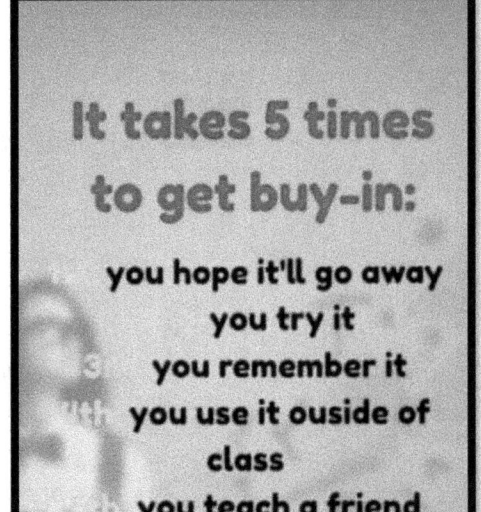

Figure 2--It takes 5 times...

Here's how to run the lesson in **the grade-level classroom**:

- Take the lesson pieces mentioned above and scatter them throughout the week. For example:

    o **3-10 minutes for the class warm-up**—at the start of the week
    o **10-15 minutes keyboarding practice**—any day
    o **10-15 minutes Board presentations**—any day
    o **15-35 minutes for the project**—any day
    o **2-3 minutes for class exit ticket**—to reinforce learning

- **Check off accomplished activities** so you know what remains each week.

Here are useful pieces to extend this curriculum, available from Structured Learning:

- *Student workbooks—allow students to be self-paced*
- *Digital Citizenship curriculum— if this is a school focus (sold separately)*
- *Keyboarding Curriculum— if this is a school focus (sold separately)*

Copyrights

You have a single-user license of this book. That means you may reproduce copies of material in this textbook for classroom use only. Reproduction of the entire book (or an entire lesson) is strictly prohibited. No part of this publication may be transmitted, stored, or recorded in any form without written permission from the publisher.

About the Authors

Ask a Tech Teacher *is a group of technology teachers who run an award-winning resource blog. Here they provide free materials, advice, lesson plans, pedagogical conversation, website reviews, and more to all who drop by. The free newsletters and articles help thousands of teachers, homeschoolers, and those serious about finding the best way to maneuver the minefields of technology in education.*

*Throughout this text, we refer to Common Core State Standards and a license granted to "...copy, publish, distribute, and display the Common Core State Standards for purposes that support the CCSS Initiative. Copyright 2010. National Governors Association Center for Best Practices and Council of Chief State School Officers. All rights reserved.

5th Grade Technology Curriculum: Teacher Manual

Table of Contents

Introduction

Curriculum Maps

Technology Scope and Sequence K-5

Table of Images

Table of Assessments

Table of Articles

Lesson Plans

1	Introduction		17	Spreadsheet Formulae
2	Digital Tools in the Classroom		18	More Spreadsheet Formulae
3	Keyboarding		19	Graphs
4	Student Blogs		20	Spreadsheet Summative
5	Organizing Ideas		21	Google Earth Tour
6	Problem Solving		22	Graphics in Word Processing
7	Graphic Organizers		23	Writing With Graphics
8	Word Processing		24	Image Editing I
9	Coding: Hour of Code		25	Image Editing II
10	Digital Citizenship		26	Image Editing III
11	Internet Search		27	Image Editing IV
12	Website Evaluation		28	Photoshop Tennis
13	DTP: Newsletter		29	Keyboarding and Science
14	DTP: Calendar		30	What Have I Learned
15	DTP: Trifold I		31	Hello Next Year Students
16	DTP: Trifold II		32	End-of-Year Challenge

Appendices

1. Homework
2. Certificate

Articles

1. 4 Things Every Teacher Must Teach 40
2. 5 Ways to make class keyboarding fun 67
3. 7 Word Tricks A Teacher Should Know 107
4. 9 Google Tricks A Teacher Should Know 108
5. 11 Ways X/Twitter improves education 120
6. 13 Ways Blogs Teach Common Core 79
7. Class Warm-ups and Exit Tickets 39
8. Habits of Mind vs. CC vs. IB 37
9. How Minecraft Teaches Problem Solving 94
10. How to Prepare Students for PARCC/SBA 69
11. How to Teach Students to Solve Problems 91
12. What is the 21st Century Lesson Plan 34
13. Which Class Internet Start Page is Best 57
14. Will texting destroy writing skills? 122

Posters

5th Grade Technology Curriculum: Teacher Manual

Table of Images

Figure 1—Tomorrow's student 7
Figure 2a-b—What's in each lesson? 8
Figure 3—Curriculum Map—K-8 9
Figure 4—Curriculum Map—5th grade, month-to-month 10
Figure 5—Student workbook 11
Figure 6—Habits of Mind 12
Figure 7—Compatible digital devices 13
Figure 8—It takes 5 times... 14
Figure 9—Technology rules 31
Figure 10a—Evidence Board; 10b—Badge 32
Figure 11—Problem-solving Board 32
Figure 12a—Parts of computer; 12b—iPad; 12c—Chromebook 44
Figure 13—How to hold mouse 44
Figure 14—Template for UN and PWs 45
Figure 15a—Notability; 15b—Acrobat; 15c—iAnnotate 46
Figure 16a—Class calendar in Google; 16b—Padlet; 16c—DTP 47
Figure 17—Class Internet start page 47
Figure 18a—Class start page in Symbaloo; 18b—Portaportal; 18c—LiveBinders 48
Figure 19—Student blog 49
Figure 20a—Homework dropbox; 20b—email etiquette 50
Figure 21a—keyboarding curriculum map; 21b—keyboarding hints 60
Figure 22a—Keyboarding posture; 22b—position 60
Figure 23—Keyboarding hand position 61
Figure 24—Keyboarding technique checklist 61
Figure 25—Grading scale for keyboarding 62
Figure 26—Why learn to keyboard 63
Figure 27—Important keys 63
Figure 28—Info for Problem-solving Board 72
Figure 29—Common computer problems 73
Figure 30—Common shortkeys 74
Figure 31—Avatar 75
Figure 32—Student blog 75
Figure 33—Blogging rubric 76
Figure 34—Keyboard keys quiz 82
Figure 35—Problem-solving board rubric 82
Figure 36—1st grade mindmap 83
Figure 37a—SpiderScribe; 37b—MindMaple; 37c—Bubbl.us 84
Figure 38a—How to outline in MS Word; 38b—Google Docs 85
Figure 39a—Outline in Word; 39b—Google Docs 85
Figure 40—How to save your file 86
Figure 41—Blank keyboard quiz 88
Figure 42—How to solve a problem 89
Figure 43—Problem-solving quotes 89
Figure 44a—iPad shortkeys; 44b—Chromebook shortkeys 90
Figure 45a-c—Graphic organizers in K-4 98
Figure 46a—Graphic organizer in Google Draw; 46b—in online tool 98

Figure 47—5th grade graphic organizer 99
Figure 48—Padlet embedded into class start page 100
Figure 49a-d—Projects in word processing 102
Figure 50a—MS Word; 50b—Google Docs 103
Figure 51a-b—What programming feels like vs. what it is 110
Figure 52a-d—Coding from previous years 110
Figure 53—How to create a macro 111
Figure 54—How to create a shortkey 112
Figure 55—Digital Citizenship topics 116
Figure 56—Legal use of internet media 117
Figure 57—Netiquette Rules 118
Figure 58—Digcit topic pyramid 119
Figure 59—Internet research 124
Figure 60a—Poll in Padlet; 60b—Google Forms; 60c—Google Spreadsheet 125
Figure 61—Parts of a website 127
Figure 62a-b—Tables in 3rd and 4th grade 128
Figure 63—Table of website extensions 129
Figure 64—Sample website eval tool 130
Figure 65—Presentation board sign ups in Google Calendar; 65b—Padlet 132
Figure 66—Google Earth Board notes 132
Figure 67—Sample Google Earth locations 132
Figure 68a-e—DTP project from 2nd-4th 133
Figure 69—Compare-contrast digital tools—incomplete 134
Figure 70—Compare-contrast digital tools—complete 134
Figure 71a—Newsletter in Publisher; 71b—in Google Docs 135
Figure 72a—Newsletter in PowerPoint; 72b—in Word 135
Figure 73—DTP newspaper 136
Figure 74—DTP app 136
Figure 75—Newsletter with webtool 138
Figure 76a—Calendar in Word; 76b—in PowerPoint 140
Figure 77a-b—Sample DTP calendars 140
Figure 78—Calendar embedded into start page 142
Figure 79—Keyboarding hints 146
Figure 80a-b—4th grade trifold 147
Figure 81a-b: 2 examples of 5th grade trifolds 147
Figure 82a—Trifold in Word; 84b—in Google Docs 148
Figure 83a-b: Story as plain text and formatted 148
Figure 84a-b—Trifold template 149
Figure 85a-b: Sample trifolds 149
Figure 86a—Keyboarding certificate; 86b—Speedsters 152
Figure 87a-b—Trifold templates 152
Figure 88a-d—Grammar vs. formatting 153
Figure 89a-c: Spreadsheet projects K-4 157
Figure 90a-b: Academic formulae 157
Figure 91—Compare/contrast digital tools 158
Figure 92—Arrays with spreadsheets 159
Figure 93—Automath with spreadsheets 159
Figure 94a-c: Deconstructing spreadsheet formulae 160
Figure 95—Spreadsheet project 163
Figure 96—Turn data into a graph 166
Figure 97a-b: Table vs. Graph 167

Figure 98a-b: Graph options in Excel and Spreadsheet 167
Figure 99a-b: Two types of graphs 167
Figure 100—Glossary in companion website 170
Figure 101—I can't find my file 171
Figure 102—Spreadsheet summative 171
Figure 103a-d: Google Earth projects in K-4 176
Figure 104—GE Tour 176
Figure 105—GE dialogue box 177
Figure 106a—GE placemark; 106b: GE tour 177
Figure 107a-c—Image editing in Word and Docs 181
Figure 108—Image editing in PicMonkey 182
Figure 109—Image with color block 182
Figure 110—Hand position for keyboarding 184
Figure 111—Citations 185
Figure 112—Collage of edited images 188
Figure 113a-b—Color adjustment 189
Figure 114a-b—Removing distractions from an image 189
Figure 115a-b: Touch up portraits 189
Figure 116a-b: Change color in car 190
Figure 117—Put individuals in different backgrounds 190
Figure 118—Definition of Photoshop 190
Figure 119—Real or a hoax? 191
Figure 120a-b: Add or remove pieces from a photo 191
Figure 121—Image editor dialogue box 192
Figure 122a-b—Drawing in an image editor 192
Figure 123a-c: 3 ways to crop 193
Figure 124a-c: Cropping 193
Figure 125a-d: Place individual in different backgrounds 193
Figure 126—How to clone 196
Figure 127a-c: Cloning 196
Figure 128a-c: Cloning from one picture to another 197
Figure 129a-b: Cropping or cloning 197
Figure 130—Card from an image editor 200
Figure 131a-b: Blurring an image 202
Figure 132a-c: Changing hue and saturation 203
Figure 133—Using the History brush 203
Figure 134a-e: Images with history tool 203
Figure 135a-c: Actions in image editor 204
Figure 136—Background layers 205
Figure 137a-b: Drill through background layers 205
Figure 138—Can you do each of these? 206
Figure 139—Scientific Method 210
Figure 140—Compare contrast software and online tool 211
Figure 141—Compare contrast digital devices 212
Figure 142a-b New 5th grade digital tools 214

Table of Assessments

1—Parts of the computer 52
2—Parts of the smartphone 53
3—Parts of an iPad 54
4—Chromebook parts 55
5—Keyboarding quiz 64
6—Important Keys 65
7—Blank keyboard quiz 66
8—Problem Solving Board rubric 73
9—Student blogging agreement 77
10—Blog grading rubric 78
11—Word processing summative (optional) 105
12—Word processing assessment 106
13—Google Earth Board rubric 133
14—Newsletter rubric 137
15—DTP Calendar rubric 141
16—Problem-solving Board quiz 143
17—Trifold Brochure rubric 155
18—Speak Like a Geek presentation rubric 170
19—Spreadsheet summative 173
20—Spreadsheet quiz grade curation 174
21—Google Earth tour rubric 178
22—Google Earth tour notes 179
23—Photoshop Tennis 208
24—End-of-year team challenge 220

5th Grade Technology Curriculum: Teacher Manual

K-5 TECHNOLOGY SCOPE AND SEQUENCE©

Aligned with ISTE (International Society for Technology in Education) and Common Core State Standards
Check each skill off with I (Introduced), W (Working on), or M (Mastered)

	Empowered Learner	K	1	2	3	4	5
	Students leverage technology to take an active role in choosing, achieving, and demonstrating competency in their learning goals, informed by the learning sciences.						
	Use technology and digital media strategically and capably (CCSS C&CR profile)	I	W	M	M	M	M
	Are familiar with the strengths and limitations of various technological tools and mediums and can select and use those best suited to communication goals (CCSS C&CR Profile)	I	W	M	M	M	M
	Strategize personal learning						
	Understand how inquiry contributes to creative and empowered learning	I	W	M	M	M	M
	Understand how technology contributes to classroom and personal learning	I	W	M	M	M	M
	Understand how higher order thinking skills are buttressed by technology	I	W	M	M	M	M
	Select between available options, choosing one best suited to learning	I	W	M	M	M	M
	Compare-contrast available tools, determining which is best suited to need	I	W	M	M	M	M
	Know what digital tools are available and how to use them for class and home (i.e., digital calendars, blogs, websites, and annotation tools)	I	W	M	M	M	M
	Know how to read digital books both online and through readers	I	W	M	M	M	M
	Be responsive to varied needs of task-audience-purpose	I	W	M	M	M	M
	Interact, collaborate, publish with peers employing a variety of digital media			I	W	M	M
	Develop cultural understanding by engaging with learners of other cultures			I	W	M	M
	Share a summative collection of work in a way that suits communication style	I	W	M	M	M	M
	Seek feedback to demonstrate learning						
	Add comments to class blogs, forums, discussion boards, webtools	I	W	M	M	M	M
	Work in groups collaboratively and productively	I	W	M	M	M	M
	Transfer knowledge						
	Scaffold learning year-to-year and lesson-to-lesson	I	W	M	M	M	M
	Transfer understanding of one digital tool or device to others	I	W	M	M	M	M
	Understand tools, toolbars, symbols, and how that knowledge transfers to many digital tools	I	W	M	M	M	M
	Use familiar tech tools (like Google Earth's ruler) to solve real-world problems	I	W	M	M	M	M
	Hardware						
	Know parts of digital devices and how to connect them	I	W	M	M	M	M
	Know parts of keyboard	I	W	M	M	M	M
	Understand difference between power buttons on monitor and tower	I	W	M	M	M	M
	Can troubleshoot hardware	I	W	M	M	M	M
	Operating Systems (PC, Mac, Chromebook, iPads)						
	Understand concept of Desktop or Home	I	W	M	M	M	M
	Know how to run a slideshow with the native slideshow tool	I	W	M	M	M	M
	Know how to log-on	I	W	M	M	M	M

5th Grade Technology Curriculum: Teacher Manual

		Know how to Open/Close programs	I	W	M	M	M	M
		Understand concepts of taskbar, start button, icons, drop-down menus	I	W	M	M	M	M
		Know how to find files, add more, and save to network file folder and/or cloud	I	W	M	M	M	M
		Know how to drag-drop (or copy-paste) within a doc and between folders					I	W
		Know how to use tool tips (hover over icon) and right-click menus				I	W	M
		Know how to access different drives					I	W
		Can troubleshoot operating systems	I	W	M	M	M	M
		Know how to use software installed on PCs and/or Macs	I	W	M	M	M	M
		**Online Tech for Classroom Management**
		Understand school technology			I	W	M	M
		Understand dropbox for homework				I	W	M
		Understand online tools like blogs, digital portfolios						I
		Understand Cloud for transferring school work to home						I
		Understand how to use class digital tools (digital devices, annotation, blogs, internet start page)	I	W	M	M	M	M
		Know how to use a website--back button, links, scroll bars, web address	I	W	M	M	M	M
		Understand website layout and where to click and where you shouldn't	I	W	M	M	M	M
		Know how to annotate a PDF or online document			I	W	M	M
		Know how to share out classwork (including homework)				I	W	M
		Know how to use online vocabulary decoding tools quickly and efficiently	I	W	M	M	M	M
		Understand internet basics (toolbar, tabbed browsing, home button)	I	W	M	M	M	M
		Know how to safely play online videos from a variety of sources	I	W	M	M	M	M
		Know how to legally copy-paste from internet for a project				I	W	M
		Know how to log onto webtool accounts			I	W	M	M
		**Mouse Skills**
		Know how to click, hold, drag, double-click	I	W	M	M	M	M
		Know how to hover	I	W	M	M	M	M
		Introduce right mouse button			I	W	M	M
		**Keyboarding**
		Know how to practice keyboarding on internet sites and software	I	W	M	M	M	M
		Strive to achieve grade-appropriate keyboarding speed and accuracy goal				I	W	M
		Type with hands on their own side of keyboard, curved, fingers on home row			I	W	M	M
		Practice touch typing				I	W	M
		Compose at keyboard by creating classroom-based projects				I	W	M
		Understand speed difference between handwriting and keyboarding				I	W	M
		Select shortkeys instead of toolbar tools when appropriate	I	W	M	M	M	M
		Use correct posture, elbows at sides	I	W	M	M	M	M
		Know parts of keyboard--keys, numbers, F keys, arrows, Esc			I	W	M	M
		Know escape, period key, shift key, spacebar, tab	I	I	I	W	M	M
		**Word Processing**
		Know when to use a word processing program			I	W	M	M
		Use principles of grammar, spelling when word processing on computer	I	W	M	M	M	M

©AskaTechTeacher

	Know basic page layout--heading, title, body, footer			I	W	M	M
	Know how word-wrap works			I	W	M	M
	Know how to highlight a word, sentence, line, select/deselect, doublespace			I	W	M	M
	Know how to add a watermark, bullet list, table, pictures, graphic organizer					I	W
	Know correct spacing after sentences, paragraphs		I	W	M	M	M
	Know how to use grade-appropriate heading on all Word docs				I	W	M
	Know how to use the thesaurus					I	W
	Know how to format a document			I	W	M	M
	Know to put cursor in specific location, i.e., for graphic			I	W	M	M
	Know how to Print Preview before printing			I	W	M	M
	Know how to select and then do--two-step process in editing, formatting			I	W	M	M
	Know how to compose at Keyboard			I	W	M	M
	Can use Ctrl+Enter to force a new page			I	W	M	M
	Know how to write a letter using digital tools	I	W	M	M	M	M
	Can troubleshoot word processing			I	W	M	M
	Google Earth						
	Display familiarity with tools for moving around world	I	W	M	M	M	M
	Know how to find a location, add a picture, placemark, save a picture				I	W	M
	Understand latitudes and longitudes				I	W	M
	Know how to use ruler to measure distances					I	W
	Run a tour of placemarks around the planet				I	W	M
2	**Digital Citizen**						

Students recognize the rights, responsibilities, and opportunities of living, learning, and working in an interconnected digital world, and they act and model in ways that are safe, legal, and ethical.

	Gather relevant information from print and digital sources, assess credibility of source, and integrate the information while avoiding plagiarism. (CCSS C&CR Writing Anchor Standards)				I	W	M
	Internet privacy and safety						
	Know how to configure privacy settings					I	W
	Understand cyberbullying, use of passwords	I	W	M	M	M	M
	Understand digital footprint and online presence				I	W	M
	Understand how online entities track student activity online				I	W	M
	Understand the appropriate use of the 'digital neighborhood'	I	W	M	M	M	M
	Legal use of online materials						
	Discuss copyright law			I	W	M	M
	Discuss plagiarism and how to cite sources			I	W	M	M
	Discuss 'fair use'			I	W	M	M
	Discuss 'intellectual property', the rights and obligations of using and sharing			I	W	M	M
	Digital Netiquette						
	Understand etiquette in the digital neighborhood	I	W	M	M	M	M
	Know to stay out of other file folders	I	W	M	M	M	M
	Digital Citizenship						

5th Grade Technology Curriculum: Teacher Manual

	Understand what a 'digital citizen' is		I	W	M	M	M	M
	Exhibit a positive attitude toward technology to support collaboration, learning		I	W	M	M	M	M
	Demonstrate personal responsibility for lifelong learning		I	W	M	M	M	M
	Exhibit leadership for digital citizenship--set the standard for classmates		I	W	M	M	M	M
	Interactions online							
	Address digital commerce							I
	Use safe, responsible, and ethical behavior on the internet		I	W	M	M	M	M
	Discuss social media						I	W
	Discuss digital rights and responsibilities		I	W	M	M	M	M
	Recognize irresponsible and unsafe practices on the internet						I	W	M
	Know how to leave a useful comment for a classmate						I	W	M
	Know how online comments follow same rules as speaking and listening						I	W	M
3	**Knowledge Constructor**							
	Students critically curate a variety of resources using digital tools to construct knowledge, produce creative artifacts and make meaningful learning experiences for themselves and others.							
	Use the internet to build strong content knowledge (CCSS C&CR profile)		I	I	W	M	M	M
	Use technology to produce and publish writing and collaborate (CCRA.W.6)		I	I	W	M	M	M
	Use technology strategically and capably (CCSS C&CR profile)		I	I	W	M	M	M
	Comprehend as well as critique. (CCSS C&CR profile)				I	W	M	M
	Value evidence (CCSS C&CR profile)				I	W	M	M
	Compare-contrast documents across digital media (CCSS Anchor Standards)				I	W	M	M
	Gather relevant information from multiple digital sources (CCRA.W.8)				I	W	M	M
	Assess credibility of digital sources used for research (CCSS Anchor Standards)				I	W	M	M
	Integrate and evaluate information from diverse media (CCRA.R.7)				I	W	M	M
	Make strategic use of digital media to express information (CCRA.SL.5)				I	W	M	M
	Use electronic menus and links to locate key facts (RI/)				I	W	M	M
	Effective online research strategies							
	Use screenshots to collect information				I	W	M	M
	Locate, organize, analyze, evaluate, and synthesize information from a variety of sources		I	W	M	M	M	M
	Evaluate and select information sources and digital tools based on task				I	W	M	M
	Read search results before clicking link and know how to identify reliable resources				I	W	M	M
	Guide inquiry by knowing how to choose links and menus		I	W	M	M	M	M
	Know how to search effectively and efficiently, limit search as needed, and use Ctrl+F					I	W	M
	Know how to effectively use LMS systems and the Cloud						I	W
	Technology as knowledge curator							
	Evaluate the accuracy, perspective, relevancy of information, media, data, or other resources.					I	W	M
	Curate information from digital resources using a variety of tools and methods that demonstrate meaningful connections or conclusions (such as outlines, mindmaps).					I	W	M
	Understand the difference between software and webtools and when/where to use each		I	W	M	M	M

©AskaTechTeacher

5th Grade Technology Curriculum: Teacher Manual

	Understand how parts make up a whole in, say, a puzzle or a divided picture	I	W	M			
	Know how to read digitally using both online websites and dedicated ereaders	I	W	M	M	M	M
	Know how to evaluate accuracy and relevance of websites					I	W
	Build knowledge by exploring real-world issues, developing ideas, and pursuing solutions.			I	W	M	M
	Online collaborative environments						
	Use blogs for journaling and tracking project progress						I
	Incorporate text, images, widgets to better communicate ideas						I
	Know how to use Discussion boards and forums					I	W	M
4	**Innovative Designer**						
	Use technology to identify and solve problems by creating new, useful, imaginative solutions.						
	Respond to varying demands of audience, task, purpose, and discipline (CCSS C&CR profile)	I	W	M	M	M	M
	Use glossaries or dictionaries to clarify meaning of key words and phrases (CCSS.L.K.4)		I	W	M	M	M
	Gather, comprehend, evaluate, synthesize, and report on information in order to answer questions or solve problems, (CCSS Key Design Consideration)			I	W	M	M
	Draw on information from multiple print or digital sources, demonstrating the ability to locate an answer to a question quickly or to solve a problem efficiently (CCSS. RI.5)				I	W	M
	Reason abstractly and quantitatively (CCSS. Math.Practice.MP2)		I	W	M	M	M
	Use appropriate tools strategically (CCSS. Math.Practice.MP5)	I	W	M	M	M	M
	Attend to precision (CCSS. Math.Practice.MP6)	I	W	M	M	M	M
	Design Process						
	Use planning tools such as mindmaps and brainstorming to organize ideas and solve problems				I	W	M
	Use presentation tools like graphic organizers, Infographics, screencasts, and videos to share in-depth topical ideas and solve authentic problems in a variety of creative ways				I	W	M
	Use templates and patterns to create new designs (like shapes, letters)	I	W	M	M	M	M
	Select and use digital tools (such as comics) to plan and manage a design process that considers design constraints and calculated risk	I	W	M	M	M	M
	Develop, test and refine prototypes as part of a cyclical design process			I	W	M	M
	Able to tolerate ambiguity, persevere, work with open-ended problems.	I	W	M	M	M	M
	Use established patterns and processes to solve common tech problems	I	W	M	M	M	M
	Recognize the part 'failure' plays in solving problems	I	W	M	M	M	M
	Know how to use tables, charts, and why				I	W	M
	Decision Making						
	Identify and define authentic problems and questions for investigation					I	W
	Collect, analyze data to identify solutions and make informed decisions	I	W	M	M	M	M
	Debug programs using sequencing, if-then thinking, logic, other strategies	I	W	W	W	W	W
	Able to evaluate which program is right for which task	I	W	M	M	M	M
	Students recognize digital designs in the world around them	I					
	Slideshows						
	Know when to use presentation tools			I	W	M	M

©AskaTechTeacher

		Know how to add/rearrange slides, auto-advance			I	W	M	M
		Know how to add a variety of backgrounds, animations, movies, transitions			I	W	M	M
		Know how to insert pictures from file, internet, clip-art			I	W	M	M
		Know how to insert text, images, slides, multimedia			I	W	M	M
		Understand how to deliver a professional presentation			I	W	M	M
		Can troubleshoot presentation tools		I	W	M	M	M
		Familiar with a variety of slideshow tools including software and online tools		I	W	M	M	M
		Graphics						
		Use drawing software and web-based tools efficiently		I	W	M	M	M
		Know how to insert images, clipart			I	W	M	M
		Know how to import from a file			I	W	M	M
		Know how to resize/move/crop /wrap an image			I	W	M	M
		Know how to mix text and pictures to convey unique message		I	W	M	M	M
		Know how to create and annotate screenshots to share information		I	W	M	M	M
		Desktop publishing						
		Can identify parts of the desktop publishing screen			I	W	M	M
		Know when to use a desktop publishing program to share information			I	W	M	M
		Know how to make a card, flier, cover page, magazine, trifold, newsletter			I	W	M	M
		Know how to insert a picture, blank page, text box, footer, border			I	W	M	M
		Know how to work with color schemes			I	W	M	M
		Know how to plan a publication				I	W	M
		Can troubleshoot publishing tools			I	W	M	M
		Know how to use greeting cards to reinforce writing and tech skills		I	W	M	M	M
		Screencasts, Videos						
		Know how to create screencasts and videos to share information						I
		Know how to upload screencasts and videos for peers						I
		Know how to use the design process to prepare screencasts						I
5		**Computational Thinker**						

Students develop and employ strategies for understanding and solving problems in ways that leverage the power of technological methods to develop and test solutions.

	Gather, comprehend, evaluate, synthesize, and report on information to conduct original research in order to answer questions or solve problems, (CCSS Key Design Consideration)	I	W	M	M	M	M
	Draw on information from multiple sources, demonstrating the ability to locate an answer to a question quickly or to solve a problem efficiently (CCSS. RI.5)	I	W	M	M	M	M
	Make sense of problems and persevere in solving them (CCSS. Math.Practice.MP1)	I	W	M	M	M	M
	Reason abstractly and quantitatively (CCSS. Math.Practice.MP2)	I	W	M	M	M	M
	Construct viable arguments and critique the reasoning of others (CCSS. Math.Practice.MP3)	I	W	M	M	M	M
	Model with mathematics (CCSS. Math.Practice.MP4)	I	W	M	M	M	M
	Use appropriate tools strategically (CCSS. Math.Practice.MP5)	I	W	M	M	M	M
	Attend to precision (CCSS. Math.Practice.MP6)	I	W	M	M	M	M
	Look for and make use of structure (CCSS. Math.Practice.MP7)	I	W	M	M	M	M

©AskaTechTeacher

	Look for and express regularity in repeated reasoning (CCSS.Math.Practice.MP8)	I	W	M	M	M	M
Critical Thinking							
	Understand how to identify, define authentic problems, questions	I	W	M	M	M	M
	Understand that class computer pod is just like the computer lab	I	W	M	M	M	M
	Know what digital tools are available and how to use them for class and home, including digital calendars, blogs, websites, and annotation tools	I	W	M	M	M	M
	Understand the part tools, toolbars, menus, taskbars, symbols play in unpacking digital tools	I	W	M	M	M	M
	Always attempt to solve a problem before asking for teacher assistance	I	W	M	M	M	M
	Know how to print to a physical or cloud-based location	I	W	M	M	M	M
	Know how to save work to a local drive and the cloud	I	W	M	M	M	M
	Know how to use programs not yet learned	I	W	M	M	M	M
	Know the difference between save and save-as				I	W	M
	Know the difference between backspace and delete				I	W	M
	Know how to use digital tools to compare-contrast		I	W	M	M	M
	Know why a particular digital tool is suited to a specific need		I	W	M	M	M
	Know how to analyze data digitally and represent data in various ways to facilitate problem-solving and decision-making.			I	I	W	M
Problem solving							
	Identify, define, and solve authentic problems, questions for investigation	I	W	M	M	M	M
	Know user name and password	I	W	M	M	M	M
	Know how to determine the date, undo	I	W	M	M	M	M
	Learn to use keyboard shortkeys as alternative solutions				I	W	M
	Know what to do if double-click doesn't work	I	W	M	M	M	M
	Know what to do if document or program disappears, or screen freezes	I	W	M	M	M	M
	Can visually compare own screen with instructors	I	W	M	M	M	M
	Follow established procedure when asking for help	I	W	M	M	M	M
	Know what to do when part of computer doesn't work	I	W	M	M	M	M
	Can use Alt+F4 to shut down frozen program				I	W	M
	Can use Task Manager to shut down locked program				I	W	M
	Know how to access work from anywhere in the school	I	W	M	M	M	M
	Know how to solve common hardware problems	I	W	M	M	M	M
	Know what to do if computer doesn't work				I	W	M
	Can trouble shoot a non-working program				I	W	M
	Can recognize and use up to 13 different problem-solving strategies	I	W	W	W	M	M
	Can break problems into component parts, extract key information, develop descriptive models to understand complex systems or facilitate problem-solving.				I	W	W
	Use graphic organizers to decode problems and automate solutions				I	W	W
Programming							
	Understand technology contributes to higher-order thinking in Habits of Mind, DoK, or another	I	W	W	W	M	M
	Understand the cause-effect relationship inherent in actions	I	W	W	W	M	M
	Understand If-then and conditionals in coding	I	W	M	M	M	M

5th Grade Technology Curriculum: Teacher Manual

		Understand sequencing, algorithms, loops, functions, and variables	I	W	M	M	M	M
		Eagerly experiment with programming tools	I	W	M	M	M	M
		Understand how automation works; use algorithmic thinking to develop a sequence of steps to create and test automated solutions. (i.e., timelines, brainstorming)			I	W	W	W
		Recognize that codes are simply another language			I	W	W	W
		Able to debug programs using sequencing, if-then thinking, logic, or other strategies	I	W	W	W	W	W
		**Scratch**
		Create/add/edit/broadcast sprites						I
		Add sound, text bubbles, backgrounds, movement						I
		Complete program task cards for most common skills						I
		Use models created by others; remix to develop unique Scratch video						I
		**Robotics**
		Contribute to project teams to produce original works or solve problems						I
		Build, program, debug a robot						I
		Trouble shoot simple problems						I
		Use sensors to monitor the environment						I
		Measure distances with robots						I
		**Spreadsheets**
		Process and sort data, report results by collecting data and reporting it				I	W	M
		Know how to add text, graphics, data, color			I	W	M	M
		Know how to use paint bucket fill--coordinate drawing			I	W	M	M
		Know how to add, subtract, multiply, divide formulas, and label x/y axis				I	W	M
		Know how to name a chart				I	W	M
		Know how to recolor tabs; rename worksheets				I	W	M
		Explore a business using models/simulations to study complex issues					I	W
		Know how to publish spreadsheet through a widget to blog and/or website					I	W
		Can troubleshoot spreadsheets				I	W	W
6		**Creative Communicator**
		*Students communicate clearly and express themselves creatively for a variety of purposes using the platforms, tools, styles, formats, and digital media appropriate to their goals.*
		Use technology and digital media strategically and capably (CCSS C&CR profile)	I	W	W	W	M	M
		Use technology to produce and publish writing and interact/collaborate with others (CCSS.ELA-LITERACY.CCRA.W.6)	I	W	M	M	M	M
		Explore digital tools to produce and publish writing (CCSS.ELA-Literacy.W)	I	W	M	M	M	M
		Explore digital tools to collaborate with peers (CCSS.ELA-Literacy.W)	I	W	M	M	M	M
		Use multimedia to aid comprehension (CCSS.ELA-Literacy.W)					I	W
		Ask and answer questions from information presented (CCSS.ELA-Literacy.SL)		I	W	M	M	M
		Include audio recordings and multimedia to enhance main ideas (CCSS.ELA-Literacy.SL)			I	W	M	M
		Integrate and evaluate information presented in diverse media and formats, including visually, quantitatively, and orally (CCSS.ELA-LITERACY.CCRA.SL.2)	I	W	M	M	M	M

5th Grade Technology Curriculum: Teacher Manual

		Use multimedia to organize ideas, concepts, info (CCSS.ELA-Literacy.WHST)	I	W	M	M	M	M
		Interact, collaborate, and publish with peers, experts, or others employing a variety of digital environments and media			I	W	M	M
	colspan="8"	**Vocabulary**
		Understand domain-specific vocabulary	I	W	M	M	M	M
		Communicate ideas effectively using variety of media, formats (CCSS Anchor Standards)	I	W	M	M	M	M
		Use digital tools to decode academic and domain-specific vocab			I	W	M	C
	colspan="8"	**Blogs**
		Interact, collaborate, publish with peers employing a variety of digital media						I
		Develop cultural understanding and global awareness by engaging learners of other cultures						I
		Contribute to project teams to produce original works or solve problems						I
		**Digital Tools**
		Communicate information, ideas effectively to multiple audiences using a variety of media and formats including visual organizers, infographics			I	W	M	M
		Use web-based communication tools to share unique and individual ideas			I	W	M	M
		Learn a variety of tools that address varied communication styles (from written to visual to video) by teaching them to classmates			I	W	M	M
		Know how to use models and simulations to explore complex systems and issues					I	W
		Simulate running a business to identify trends, forecast sales					I	W
		Interact, collaborate, and publish employing digital media including greeting cards for youngers	I	W	M	M	M	M
		Develop cultural understanding by engaging with learners of other cultures	I	W	M	M	M	M
		**Digital Storytelling, Quick Writes**
		Compose short stories, quick writes, letters, comics using online tools	I	W	M	M	M	M
		Collaborate and share stories in an online tool		I	W	M	M	M
		Use select digital tools to collaborate and publish with peers employing a variety of digital environments and media	I	W	M	M	M	M
		Participate in a virtual field trip that tells the story of a student's experience	I	W	M	M	M	M
		**Speaking and Listening**
		Engage in impromptu speaking such as the Evidence Board				I	W	W
		Present well-prepared presentations such as slideshows, knowing how to use multimedia props			I	W	M	M
		Engage in short presentations such as the Presentation Boards				I	W	M
7	colspan="8"	**Global Collaborator**
	colspan="8"	*Students use digital tools to broaden their perspectives and enrich their learning by collaborating with others and working effectively in teams locally and globally.*
		Understand other perspectives and cultures. (CCSS C&CR profile)	I	W	M	M	M	M
		Respond to the varying demands of audience, task, purpose, discipline. (CCSS C&CR Profile)	I	W	M	M	M	M
		Use digital tools to connect with learners from a variety of backgrounds and cultures, engaging with them in ways that broaden mutual understanding and learning	I	W	M	M	M	M
		Explore local and global issues and use collaborative technologies to work with others to investigate solutions	I	W	M	M	M	M
		Know what 'Cloud computing' is				I	W	M

	Collaborate with Others					
	Use digital tools like Padlet to collaborate with peers in projects			I	W	M
	Use collaborative technologies to work with others to examine issues and problems from multiple viewpoints.	I	W	M	M	M	M
	Contribute constructively to project teams, assuming various roles and responsibilities to work effectively toward a common goal.	I	W	M	M	M	M
	Use blogs, forums, Discussion Boards to collaborate and share					I	W
	Use programs like Google Apps to collaborate					I	W

©AskaTechTeacher

Lesson #1 Introduction

Vocabulary	Problem solving	Skills
• Back-up • Landscape • Orientation • Portrait • Right-click menu • Save-as • Select-do	• What's the difference between 'save' and 'save-as' • What's a quick way to ** (shortkey) • I don't use school email program at home (your home version will have the same parts, just in different places) • I have lots of problems (check PS board)	**New** Class rules Some posters **Scaffolded** Problem solving Evidence Board
Academic Applications Tech in life, submitting homework, problem solving	**Materials Required** posters, after school tech, homework submittal, class rules, Evidence Board, student workbooks (if using)	**Standards** CCSS: Anchor standards NETS: 1a, 1b

Essential Question

How do I use technology?

Big Idea

Develop an awareness of components, fundamental hardware issues, and basic operations of school digital device

Teacher Preparation

- Have Tech Tips posters on walls or in class Tech Corner.
- Test equipment so students aren't frustrated trying to use something that won't work.
- Know how to fix expected student tech problems.

Assessment Strategies

- Anecdotal observation
- [tried to] solve own problems
- Used good keyboarding habits
- Decisions followed class rules
- Joined classroom conversations
- Participated with a sense of wonder
- Completed exit ticket
- Left room as student found it
- Habits of Mind observed
- Engaged in higher order thinking

Steps

Time required: 45 minutes in one sitting or spread throughout the week
Class warm-up: None

_____Before anything else, explain to students what your expectations are for their time with you—what's the *21st Century Lesson Plan* (article at end of lesson).
_____Tour classroom. Show students tech. Review important posters, i.e., difference between 'backspace' and 'delete', Mulligan Rule, portrait and landscape, and 'select-do'. See full size examples in Appendix.
_____Collect rules from students to guide class actions, including:

- *No excuses; don't blame others; don't blame the computer.*
- *No food or drink around the computer. Period. Exclamation point!*
- *Respect the work of others and yourself.*
- *Keep hands to yourself. Feel free to help neighbors, but with words only.*
- *Try before asking for help.*

_____You may start with a list like *Figure 9*, from the prior year, and get student thoughts on updating, amending, and revising.

Figure 9—Technology rules

COMPUTER LAB RULES
- No Food or drink allowed
- Take responsibility
- Missed class? Make it up
- Wash hands to use equipment
- Respect
- Spelling must be correct
- Save early. Save often.
- Always save to network file folder
- Use the internet correctly
- No 4-letter words—can't won't
- Innocent until proven guilty
- Ignorance of the law is no excuse

Wherever you are, be there till you leave

_____If using workbooks, students can handwrite their suggested rules into the PDF.
_____Make sure this list includes class discussion guidelines such as 1) listening to others, 2) taking turns while speaking, and 3) waiting to be called on before speaking.
_____Let students know that you are open to alternative suggestions on tools to use for a class project. For example, if you suggest Wordle, a student can request Tagxedo. Approval will be granted if the tool fulfills class guidelines. Expect them to use **evidence** to build their case, **compare-contrast** their tool to your suggestions, and **draw logical conclusions**.
_____Offer a **Keyboarding Club** after school two days a week to accommodate students who can't do their homework at home. Limit it to 45 minutes.
_____Offer after-school help on those days for students who need assistance with a tech skill or a project involving tech. Request student volunteers who will assist classmates. You may collaborate with your school's STAR program, where students volunteer for activities as part of class requirements.
_____Review homework policy (homework in the back of this text): due at the end of each month. Students may submit homework via email, a dropbox, or Google Apps (discussed in next unit).
_____Discuss the evidence board (*Figures 10a* and *10b*):

Figure 10a—Evidence Board; 10b—Badge

_____This is a bulletin board that celebrates student transfer of knowledge from tech class to home, friends, or other educational endeavors. About once a month, students will have an opportunity to share how they use tech skills in other classes, at home, or with friends. They will fill out a badge (like *Figure 10b*) and post it on the Evidence Board by their class. By the end of the year, you want this collection to encircle the classroom.

_____Review Problem Solving corner of classroom—a bulletin board where you collect common tech problems students will be expected to solve wherever they use computers (see *Figure 11*). More on this in the Problem-solving lesson.

Figure 11—Problem-solving Board

_____Throughout class, check for understanding.

Class exit ticket: **Students tack a post-it on Problem-solving Board with a tech problem they faced in the last week. These can be used for the upcoming Problem-solving Board.**

Differentiation

- Early finishers: visit class internet start page for websites that tie into classwork (see article at end of Lesson 2).
- For more, read *"Class Warm-ups and Exit Tickets"* at the end of the lesson.
- For more on how to build a lesson, read *"4 Things Every Teacher Must Teach"* at end of lesson.
- Take a field trip to school server room to see how data is collected and curated.

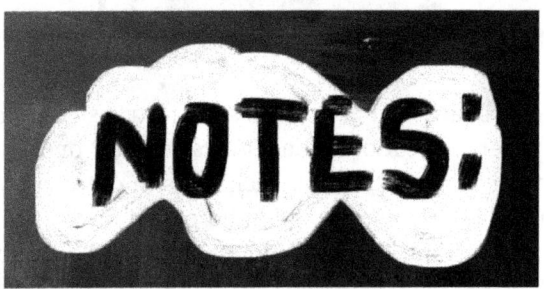

Article 1—What is the 21st Century Lesson Plan

What is the 21st Century Lesson Plan?

Technology and the connected world put a fork in the old model of teaching—teacher in front of the class, sage on the stage, students madly taking notes, textbooks opened to a particular chapter being reviewed, homework as worksheets based on the text, tests regurgitating important facts. Did I miss anything? This model is outdated **not because it didn't work** (many statistics show students ranked higher on global testing years ago than they do now), **but because the environment changed.** Our classrooms are more diverse. Students are digital natives, already in the habit of learning via technology. The 'college and career' students are preparing for is different so the education model must be different.

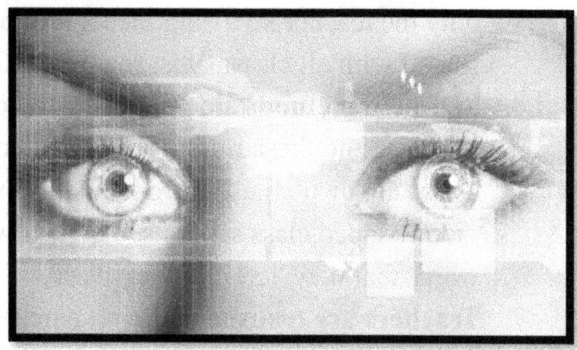

Preparing for this new environment requires radical changes in teacher lesson plans. Here are seventeen concepts you'll want to include in your preparation:

1. Students are graduating from high school unable to work in the jobs that are available. It's the teacher's responsibility to insure students **learn over-arching concepts** such as how to speak to a group, how to listen effectively, how to think critically, and how to solve problems. The vehicle for teaching these ideas is history, science, literature, but they aren't the goal.
2. To focus on the over-arching concepts above, make earning **platform-neutral**. For example, when teaching spreadsheets, make the software or online tools a vehicle for practicing critical thinking, data analysis, and evidence-based learning, not for learning one brand of software or a particular spreadsheet tool. Besides, what you use at school may not be what students have at home. You don't want students to conflate your lessons with 'something done at school'. You want them to apply them to their life.
3. **Morph the purpose from 'knowing' to 'understanding'.** Teach the process, not a skill. Students should understand why they select a particular tool, not just how to use it. Why use PowerPoint instead of a word processing program? Or a spreadsheet instead of a slideshow? Expect students to be critical thinkers, not passive learners.
4. **Transfer of knowledge is critical.** What students learn in one class is applied to all classes (where relevant). For example, *word study* is no longer about memorizing vocabulary, but knowing how to decode unknown academic and domain-specific words using affixes, roots, and context.
5. **Collaboration and sharing** is part of what students learn. They help each other by reviewing and commenting on projects before submittal to the teacher (Google Apps makes that easy). The definition of 'project' itself has changed from 'shiny perfect student work' to *review-edit-*

rewrite-submit. You grade them on all four steps, not just the last one. This makes a lot of sense—who gets it right the first time? I rewrote this article at least three times before submitting. Why expect differently from students? **Plus:** No longer do students submit a project that only the teacher sees (and then a few are posted on classroom bulletin boards). Now, it is shared with all classmates, so all benefit from every student's work.

6. **Self-help methods** are provided and you expect students to use them. This includes online dictionaries and thesauruses, how-to videos, and access to teacher assistance outside of class. These are available 24/7 for students, not just during classroom hours. This happens via online videos, taped class sessions, the class website, and downloadable materials so students don't worry that they 'left it in their desk'.

7. **Teachers are transparent** with parents. You let them know what's going on in the classroom, welcome their questions and visits, communicate often via email or blogs when it's convenient for them. That doesn't mean you're on duty around the clock. It means you differentiate for the needs of your parents. Your Admin understands that change by providing extended lunch hours, compensatory time off, or subs when you're fulfilling this responsibility.

8. **Failure is a learning tool.** Assessments aren't about 'getting everything right' but about making progress toward the goal of preparing for life

9. **Differentiation is the norm.** You allow different approaches as long as students achieve the Big Idea or answer the Essential Question. You aren't the only one to come up with these varied approaches—students know what works best for their learning and present it to you as an option.

10. The **textbook is a resource**, supplemented by a panoply of books, primary documents, online sites, experts, Skype chats, and anything else that supports the topic. This information doesn't always agree on a conclusion. Students use habits of mind like critical thinking, deep learning, and evidence-based decisions to decide on the right answers.

11. The **lesson plan changes from the first day to the last**—and that's OK. It is adapted to student needs, interests, and hurdles that arise as it unfolds, while staying true to its essential question and big idea.

12. **Assessment** might include a quiz or test, but it also judges the student's transfer of knowledge from other classes, their tenacity in digging into the topic, their participation in classroom discussions, and more.

13. **Vocabulary is integrated into lessons,** not a stand-alone topic. Students are expected to decode words in class materials that they don't understand by using quickly-accessed online vocabulary tools, or deriving meaning from affixes, roots, and context.

14. **Problem solving is integral** to learning. It's not a stressful event, rather viewed as a life skill. Who doesn't have problems every day that must be solved? Students are expected to attempt a solution using tools at their disposal (such as prior knowledge, classmates, and classroom resources) before asking for help.

15. **Digital citizenship is taught,** modeled and enforced in every lesson, every day, and every classroom. It's no longer something covered in the 'tech lab' because every class has as much

potential for working online as offline. Every time the lesson plan calls for an online tool or research using a search engine or a YouTube video, teacher's review/remind/teach how to visit the online neighborhood safely. It's frightening how students blithely follow weblinks to places most parents wouldn't allow their child to visit in their neighborhood. Just as students have learned how to survive in a physical community of strangers, they must learn to do the same in a digital neighborhood.

16. **Keyboarding skills are granular.** They aren't used only in the computer lab, but in every class students take. If students are using iPads, Chromebooks, laptops, or desktops for learning, they are using keyboarding—which means they must know how to do so efficiently, quickly, and stresslessly. Since keyboarding benefits all classes, all teachers–including the librarian–become partners in this effort. I go into classrooms and show students the broad strokes; the teacher reinforces it every time the student sits down at the computer.

17. **Play is the new teaching.** It is a well-accepted concept for preschoolers and has made a successful leap to the classroom, relabeled as 'gamification'. Use the power of games to draw students into learning and encourage them to build on their own interests. Popular games in the classroom include Minecraft, Mission US, Scratch, and others. If your school is new to this concept, clear it with admin first and be prepared to support your case.

When I first wrote lesson plans, it was all about aligning learning with standards, completing the school's curricula, ticking off required skills. Now, I must build the habits of mind that allow for success in education and home life and construct a personal knowledge base with students that will work for their differentiated needs. Like any lesson plan, this is only difficult the first time. After that, it seems natural.

Article 2—Habits of Mind vs. CC vs. IB

Habits of Mind vs. Common core vs. IB

Pedagogic experts have spent an enormous amount of time attempting to unravel the definition of 'educated'. It used to be the 3 R's—reading, writing, and 'rithmetic. The problem with that metric is that, in the fullness of time, those who excelled in the three areas weren't necessarily the ones who succeeded. As long ago as the early 1900's, Teddy Roosevelt warned:

""*C students rule the world.*"

It's the kids without their nose in a book that notice the world around them, make connections, and learn natively. They excel at activities that aren't the result of a GPA and an Ivy League college. Their motivation is often failure, and taking the wrong path again and again. As Thomas Edison said:

""*I have not failed. I've just found 10,000 ways that won't work.*"

Microsoft founder, Bill Gates, and Albert Einstein are poster children for that approach. Both became change agents in their fields despite following a non-traditional path.

In the face of mounting evidence, education experts accepted a prescriptive fact: student success is not measured by milestones like 'took a foreign language in fifth grade' or 'passed Algebra in high school' but by how s/he thinks. One curated list of cerebral skills that has become an education buzz word is Arthur L. Costa and Bena Kallick's list of sixteen what they call Habits of Mind (Copyright ©2000):

1. *Persisting*
2. *Managing impulsivity*
3. *Listening with Understanding and Empathy*
4. *Thinking Flexibly*
5. *Thinking about Thinking*
6. *Striving for Accuracy*
7. *Questioning and Posing Problems*
8. *Applying Past Knowledge to New Situations*
9. *Thinking and Communicating with Clarity and Precision*
10. *Gathering Data through All Senses*
11. *Creating, Imagining, Innovating*
12. *Responding with Wonderment and Awe*
13. *Taking Responsible Risks*
14. *Finding Humor*
15. *Thinking Interdependently*
16. *Remaining Open to Continuous Learning*

Together, these promote strategic reasoning, insightfulness, perseverance, creativity and craftsmanship.

But they're not new. They share the same goals with at least three other widely-used education systems: 1) Common Core (as close as America gets to national standards), 2) the International Baccalaureate (IB) program (a well-regarded international curriculum, much more popular outside the US than within), and 3) good ol' common sense. Below, I've listed each Habit of Mind with a brief explanation of what that means (in italics). I then point out connections to Common Core, the IB Program, and the common sense your grandma shared with you. The result is a compelling argument that education is less a data download and more a fitness program for our brains.

Persisting

Stick with a problem, even when it's difficult and seems hopeless.

Winston Churchill said, "Never, never, in nothing great or small, large or petty, never give in..." The same decade, Albert Einstein said:

"It's not that I'm so smart, it's just that I stay with problems longer."

The Common Core is not a curriculum, rather a collection of forty-one overarching Standards in reading, writing, language, math, and speaking/listening that shape a student's quest for college and career. Sprinkled throughout are fundamental traits that go beyond the 3R's and delve deeply into the ability of a student to think. The math standards require students learn to 'persevere in solving problems'.

The IB Program has twelve attitudes that are fundamental to every learner: *appreciation, empathy, commitment, enthusiasm, confidence, independence, cooperation, integrity, creativity, respect, curiosity, and tolerance.* Students exhibiting the attitude of commitment persist in their own learning, persevere no matter the difficulties.

Managing Impulsivity

Consider options. Think before speaking.

Among his endless words of wisdom, Benjamin Franklin said:

"It is easier to suppress the first desire than to satisfy all that follow it."

Common Core Standards tell us to 'Use appropriate tools strategically'.

Besides the twelve attitudes listed above, the IB Program names ten traits that profile a learner: *inquirer, knowledgeable, thinker, communicator, principle, open-minded, caring, a risk-taker, balanced, and reflective.* Students who are reflective give thoughtful consideration before acting.

For the rest of the article, search the title on Ask a Tech Teacher

Article 3—Class Warm-ups and Exit Tickets

Class Warm-ups and Exit Tickets

Warm-ups are given at the beginning of class to measure what students remember from prior lessons or know about a subject before jumping into a unit. They inform teachers how to optimize time by teaching what students need to learn, not wasting time on what students already know. They are a couple of minutes, can be delivered via a Discussion Board, blog comments, a Google Form, or many other methods. Exit tickets are similar, but assess what students learned **during** the lesson. In this way, teachers know if they should review material, find a different approach to teaching a topic, or students are ready to move on. Like Warm-ups, Exit tickets are a few minutes, and delivered in a wide variety of creative methods.

Here are a few examples:

Polls

Polls are quick ways to assess student understanding of the goal of your daily teaching. It measures student learning as much as lesson effectiveness. Polls are fast—three-five minutes—are anonymously graded and shared immediately with students. It lets everyone know if the big idea of the lesson is understood and if the essential questions have been answered.

These can be graded, but are usually used formatively, to determine organic class knowledge before moving on to other topics.

Tools: Socrative, PollDaddy, Google Forms
Time: a few minutes
Method: Formative assessment

Virtual Wall

Ask students a question and have them add their answer to a virtual wall.

Virtual walls are also great ideas for reviewing a subject prior to a summative assessment. Have each student post an important idea they got from the unit with significant required details.

Tools: Padlet, Linoit
Time: a few minutes
Method: Formative assessment

Article 4—4 Things Every Teacher Must Teach and How

4 Things Every Teacher Must Teach and How

Teaching technology is not sharing a new subject, like Spanish or math. It's exploring an education tool, knowing how to use computers, IPads, the Internet, and other digital devices to serve learning goals. Sure, there are classes that teach MS Word and C++, but for most schools, technology is employed strategically and capably to achieve all colors of education.

Which gets me to the four subjects every teacher must teach, whether s/he's a math teacher, science, literacy, or technology. In today's education world, all of us teach—

- *vocabulary*
- *keyboarding*
- *digital citizenship*
- *research*

They used to be taught in isolation—*Fridays at 8:20, we learn vocabulary*—but not anymore. Now they must be blended into all subjects like ingredients in a cake, the result—college or career for the 21st century student. Four subjects that must be taught—and thanks to technology, CAN be with ease. Let me explain.

Vocabulary

Common Core requires that:

> ***Students constantly build the transferable vocabulary they need to access grade level complex texts. This can be done effectively by spiraling like content in increasingly complex texts.***

Does that sound difficult? Think back to how you conquered vocabulary. As an adult, you rarely meet words you can't understand—unless you're chatting with William F. Buckley—and if you do, you decode it by analyzing prefixes, suffixes, roots, context. Failing that, e-dictionaries are available on all digital devices.

Teach your students to do the same:

- first: try to decode the word using affixes, root, context
- second: research meaning

You might think that will grind the academic process to a halt, but truth, in age-appropriate texts, there are likely less than five unknown words per page. What you don't want to do is have students write down words for later investigation. That becomes a chore, cerebral excitement leeched like heat to a night desert sky. Much better to stop, decode, and move on.

As students work on a project in my classes, I see neighbors ask for help with a mysterious word (students are welcome to chat during class about academic topics), screens light up as students use the online dictionary to discover meaning, and words appear on the class screen as part of the backchannel X/Twitter stream. Seconds later, a definition will appear—someone's contribution. If it's wrong, invariably a student will correct it. Rarely, I jump in.

Don't believe this works? Try it out.

Keyboarding

For years, I taught keyboarding as a separate activity. We warmed up class with 10-15 minutes of keyboarding augmented by 45 minutes a week of keyboard homework. I've revised my thinking. Since keyboarding benefits all classes, I make all teachers—including the librarian—my partners in this effort. I go into classrooms and show students the broad strokes of keyboarding posture, good habits, skills that will enable them to type fast and accurately enough to eventually—maybe third or fourth grade—use the keyboard without slowing down their thinking. That's a big deal and worth repeating—

To be organic, students must be able to keyboard without thinking of their fingers, fast enough that they keep up with their thoughts.

That's about 25 words per minute. *Really?* Yes really. Sure, we think fast, but ruminating over a class question, essay, report is much [much] slower. 25-35 words per minute suffice.

I start students with mouse and keyboard familiarity in kindergarten and 1st grade, introduce the concept of hands and fingers in 2nd, and start speed and accuracy in 3rd. By 5th grade, they're good. This works because now, keyboarding is integrated across all classes, anytime students use a digital device with a keyboard. Now, all teachers pay as much attention to HOW students use the keyboard as WHAT is produced, focusing on:

- good posture
- hands on home row (by 3rd grade)
- elbows at sides
- paper (if using one) to the side of keyboard
- eyes on screen (by 4th grade)
- no flying fingers or hands
- paced rhythm

Parents, too, are my partners. I communicate the same requirements to them with the hope they'll reinforce these at home. A reminder that assessments are often online gets their attention.

Digital Citizenship

It's frightening how much time students spend in an online world they consider safe, following links like blind streets to places most parent wouldn't take their child. Just as students have learned how to survive in a physical community of strangers, they must now learn to do the same in a digital neighborhood. Parents and teachers can't be everywhere, and hiding children from danger doesn't teach them survival skills, so we must teach them how to live in this wild new online world.

Likely, most kindergartners arrive to your classroom familiar with parent smartphones and IPad apps. That means, you start by discussing the 'digital neighborhood', 'stranger danger', 'personal privacy'. Do this every time students use the Internet. Sure, it'll take longer to get to Starfall Math, but students must know the right way to use online sites. Like with keyboarding, make other teachers and parents partners. Let them know what you've taught about digital citizenship and ask them to reinforce it.

Here's the hard part: You must be diligent. Until safe Internet use becomes a habit, you must discuss it every time students cross the threshold of the World Wide Web. There are endless resources—use all of them. Eventually, Internet use will be a safe place to access the innumerable volumes of wonderful resources.

Research

Expect students to use text features and search tools (e.g., key words, sidebars, hyperlinks) to locate information)

I added 'Research' as a fourth blended topic in response to the wealth of misinformation that bombards us daily. It used to be students learned from a trusted textbook that had been vetted and approved over time. Now, textbooks have been replaced with a panoply of books, online sites, experts, Skype chats whose information doesn't always agree. How are students to choose between the opinions of their parents or an astrophysicist who Skyped with the class?

No room for uninformed choosing. Students must research—find truthful, valid information about topics that concern them.

Introduce this concept with a discussion on government. American Democracy thrives on the loud and often messy sharing of diverse opinions. That is to be applauded, not stamped out. But with the demise of trustworthy news interpreters (like the Evening News with Walter Cronkite taken as fact by tens of thousands every evening) comes the rise of primary sources. Thanks to the Internet, finding original documents is doable. Ask students to read, interpret, and share their evidence-based thoughts. No one's right or wrong. We're merely investigating how many shades of 'truth' there are.

There you have it. Four topics that must be included in every lesson. If you covered nothing else but these, you'd have a good year.

Lesson #2 Digital Tools in the Classroom

Vocabulary	Problem solving	Skills
• Benchmark • Blog • Bounce back • Ctrl+F • Digital portfolio • Email • Log in • Peripheral • Protocol • Shortkey • Warm-up	• I forgot log in (where did you record it?) • I gave my log-in to a friend • Email bounced back (resend from 'sent' file after checking address) • How do I search (Ctrl+F) • Can't remember where a tool is (use shortkey) • I forgot to do the Exit Ticket • Computers don't work? How have you solved this problem in the past? • Dropbox didn't 'send' (it shares)	**New** Student blogs Class calendar Student dropbox **Scaffolded** Digital citizenship Digital portfolios Email Class website Screenshot
Academic Applications All classwork that requires digital access	**Materials Required** speed quiz, log-in sheets, hardware study guide, digital tools, student workbooks (if using)	**Standards** CCSS: W.5.6 NETS: 1b, 4b

Essential Question

How do I use the computer?

Big Idea

Develop an awareness of digital tools that enhance education

Teacher Preparation

- Have log-ins to keyboard program (if required).
- Have student digital portfolios available (if required).
- Talk with grade level team to tie into their inquiry.
- Verify required links are available.
- Know if you need extra time to complete lesson.
- Have hardware assessment guides available.
- Integrate domain-specific tech vocabulary into lesson.
- Know which tasks weren't completed last week.
- If you're the tech teacher, visit students in the classroom. Remind them tech lab rules apply in classroom. See article, *"Take Tech into the Classroom"* at end of lesson for ideas.
- Collect vocabulary for Speak Like a Geek presentations. Use a physical Vocab Wall (i.e., a bulletin board) or a virtual wall like Padlet (Google for address).

Assessment Strategies

- Completed speed quiz
- Annotate workbooks (if using)
- Completed hardware guide
- Filled in UN/PW list
- Joined classroom conversations
- [tried to] solve own problems
- Completed exit ticket
- Decisions followed class rules
- Left room as student found it
- Higher order thinking: analysis, evaluation, synthesis
- Habits of mind observed

Steps

Time required: 45 minutes either in one sitting or spread throughout the week
Class warm-up: None

_____Review computer parts. *Figure 12a* is a generic desktop. Find the listed parts on your school devices (full-size copies at the end of the lesson to use for a study

guide and testing) in preparation for assessment in two weeks. For example, if you use iPads, ask students where the 'headphones' are on this device? Or the mouse? How about the USB Port (there is none)? Ask students where the iPad microphone is (see *Figure 12b*) on, say, the PC or Chromebook (*Figure 12c*). How about the charging dock? Smartphones—see assessment at end of lesson:

Figure 12a—Parts of computer; 12b—iPad; 12c—Chromebook

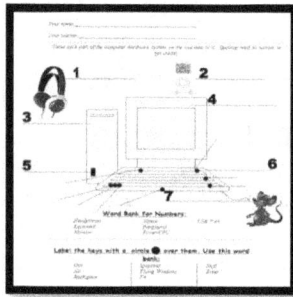 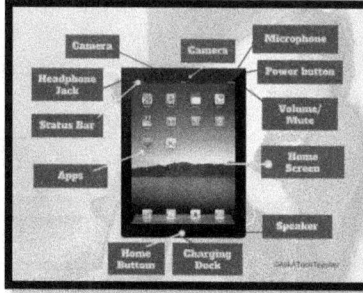 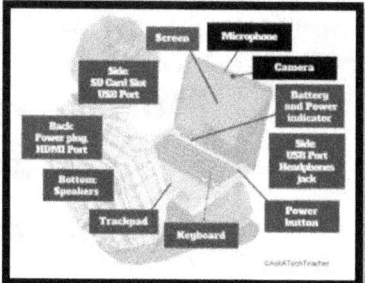

_____If students are using the workbooks, they can write the answers into the assessments as a study guide. If not using workbooks, upload Hardware Quiz to class website so students can study at home.
_____Discuss how understanding hardware helps to solve tech problems.
_____Reinforce the importance of students solving their own problems. This will be discussed in depth in the Problem-solving lesson.
_____Have neighbors check each other's mouse hold (see *Figure 13*):

Figure 13—How to hold mouse

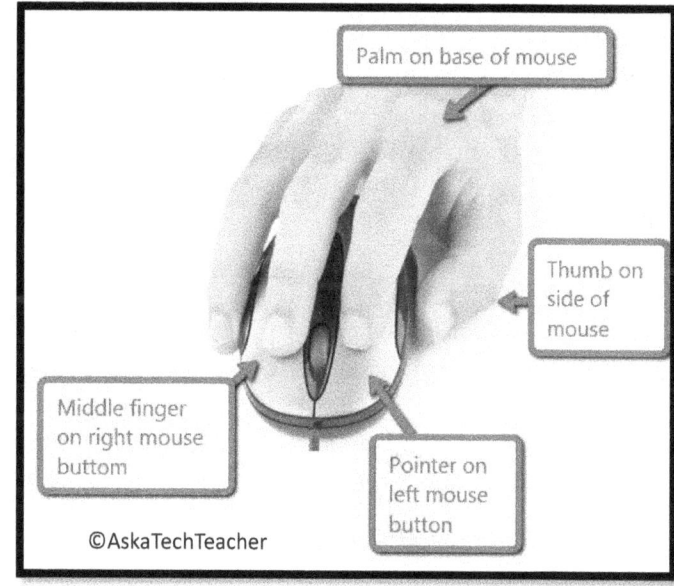

_____Make a digital copy of *Figure 14* (or comparable) available on student digital devices to annotate with an annotation tool. Other options:

- *Keep a physical copy by the student's seat or in their personal binder.*
- *Take a snapshot of it to keep on their digital device for quick reference.*

Figure 14—Template for UN and PWs

User Name/Passwords		
PROGRAM	**UN**	**PASSWORD**
Keyboard program		
Math program		
Computer		
Class wiki		
Add'l		
Add'l		

_____Discuss **digital citizenship**. You cover it in depth in the dedicated Lesson Plan and circle back on topics throughout the year. If it's a class focus, use the SL K-8 Digital Citizenship curriculum (available on our website) that's a companion to this tech curriculum (not included in this package).

_____Discuss the following:

- annotation tool
- class calendar
- class Internet start page
- class website
- digital portfolios
- email
- Google Apps
- journaling
- student blogs
- student dropbox
- student workbooks
- vocabulary decoding tools

_____Adapt them to your digital devices (Chromebooks, PCs, iMac, iPads, or other).

Student workbooks

_____If using the PDF student workbooks that go along with this tech curriculum, introduce them to students now. Show how to open them from their digital device, access links, find rubrics and project samples, and take notes using the annotation tool. Students can circle back to review concepts or forward to preview upcoming lessons.

5th Grade Technology Curriculum: Teacher Manual

Annotation Tool

_____If using student workbooks, show students how to annotate their copy with a note-taking tool such as iAnnotate (*Figure 15a*), Notability (*Figure 15b*), Adobe Acrobat (free—*Figure 15c*)) or another tool available in your school.

Figure 15a—Notability; 15b—Acrobat; 15c—iAnnotate

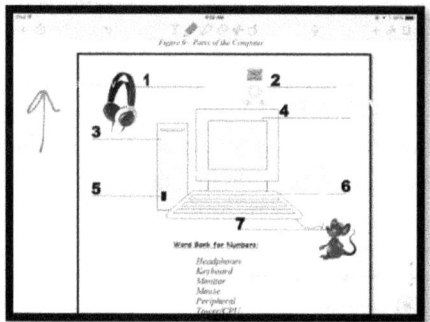 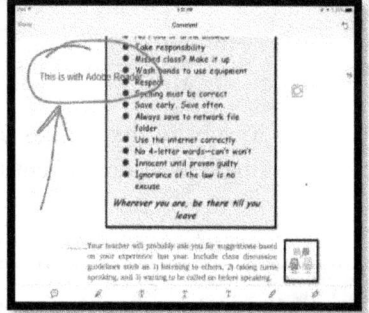 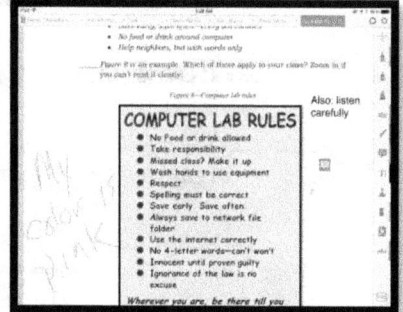

_____If students share the PDF with other students (for example, it's loaded on a class computer that multiple classes visit), show how to select their own color that's different from other students.
_____Include a discussion of screenshots. Students can annotate their workbooks, save a screenshot to their digital portfolios. Depending upon your digital device, you'll use a screenshot tool like:

- **Windows**: *the Snipping Tool*
- **Chromebook:** *hold down the control key and press the window switcher key*
- **Mac**: *Command Shift 3 to do a full screenshot and Command Shift 4 to take a partial*
- **Surface tablet**: *hold down volume and Windows button at the same time*
- **iPad**: *hold Home button and power button at same time*
- **Online**: *a screenshot tool*

_____Review options available in the annotation tool you use, such as:

- *highlighting*
- *text*
- *note*
- *freeform*

Class Calendar

_____Have a class calendar to track due dates, class events, and other information. This can be Google Calendar (*Figure 16a*), Office 365, Padlet (*Figure 16b*), or an option of your choice. If possible, embed it into the class website or have students embed it into their blogs (it'll auto-update).
_____Demonstrate how to edit calendar by adding homework.
_____Assign a student each month to be responsible for adding events to the class calendar. Start with next week's Hardware quiz. Or, allow all students to enter events. Encourage students to contribute responsibly to class calendar.
_____For Google Calendar training, search YouTube for how-to videos. These can be self-directed by students or as a class activity.

Figure 16a—Class calendar in Google; 16b—Padlet; 16c—DTP

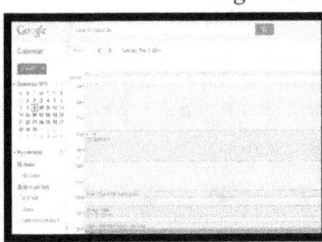

Class Internet Start Page

_____A class Internet start page is a website that comes up when the student opens the Internet. It organizes critical content in a single location and curates links students will use.

Figure 17—Class Internet start page

_____Include what students visit daily (i.e., guidelines, calendar, 'to do' list, typing websites, research locations, sponge sites, calculator) as well as info specific to current project. Mine includes interesting pictures, rss feeds, weather, a graffiti wall, and class pet. Yours will be different.

_____When you set up page, include student start-up tasks for each class (ToDo list) so students can enter class and begin work while you wrap something else up.

_____I used Protopage.com (Figure 17), but you can use Symbaloo (Figure 18a), Portaportal (Figure 18b), LiveBinders (Figure 18c), class Diigo account, or Evernote (Google names for address or visit Ask a Tech Teacher's resources pages for *Class Management>Internet Start Pages*).

Figure 18a—Class start page in Symbaloo; 18b—Portaportal; 18c—LiveBinders

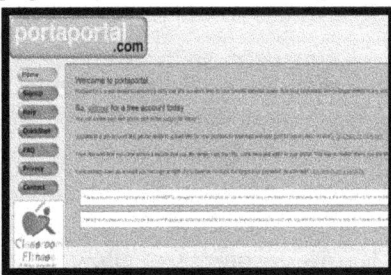

_____Remind students that any time they visit the Internet, they must do so safely and legally. If you didn't discuss digital citizenship in K-4, take time right now to review it.

Class website

_____A class website is a great way to track activities, keep parents in the loop, and share projects. If your school doesn't have Google Apps, free websites can be created at Weebly, Wix, or a blog account like WordPress (Google for address or visit Ask a Tech Teacher's resources pages for websites).

Google Apps

_____Google Apps for Education has more than 20 million educational users. The suite includes:

- *Gmail (for email)*
- *Google Drive*
- *Cloud storage (in Google Drive)*
- *Google Calendar*
- *YouTube*

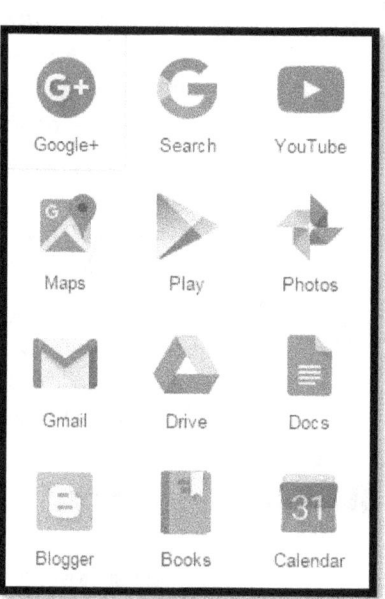

_____Google Apps files are backed up instantly in the Cloud. Importantly, it enables collaboration and sharing—two cornerstones to Common Core and ISTE. This facilitates a shift from software-based, print-centric programs to a more open, equitable and green approach to education (Microsoft now has their version called Office 365).
_____Google Apps training—at Edutraining.
_____Show students how to use student accounts—log in, use Drive, share documents with others, more. Demonstrate similarity between Google Docs/Sheets/Presentation and Office.

Journaling

_____If students will be journaling, introduce them to online tools that make that possible (i.e., Penzu, a word processing program, or by using blog entries). Show where it can be found and give a quick run-through.
_____Expect students to figure this tool out by using it.

Student blogs

Figure 3--Student blog

_____Student blogs (*Figure 19*) teach writing skills, how to use evidence in arguments, and perspective-taking. They are student-directed, but you will approve all posts and comments until students get used to the digital citizenship rules that apply to online conversations.
_____Blogs reflect student personalities with colors, fonts, widgets. Encourage creativity. What students include will help you better understand their interests, how they learn, and how to reach them academically.

_____You might ask students to theme their blog to something bigger than themselves.
_____In general, student blogs require:

- *titles that pull reader in*
- *articles that review, provide evidence, and summarize content*
- *tone/voice consistent throughout all articles—conversational, knowledgeable, friendly*
- *working linkback(s) to evidence that supports statements*
- *at least one media to support each article (picture, video, sound)*
- *display an understanding of audience. How are readers different from X/Twitter?*
- *display an understanding of writing purpose. How is blog goal different from tweets? Essays? Poetry?*
- *citations—authors name, permission, linkbacks, copyright*
- *occasional teamwork*

_____Occasionally (several times during grading period), assess blogs based on the above criteria.
_____See lesson on 'Student Blogs' for more detail.

Student digital portfolios

_____Discuss how students use **Digital Portfolios** (also known as digital lockers or digital binders):

- *store work (in Cloud) required in other classes or at home*
- *interact, collaborate, and publish with peers, experts, or others*
- *contribute to project teams*
- *edit or review work in multiple locations*
- *submit class assignments*

_____There are a variety of approaches to digital portfolios that satisfy some or all of the above uses: 1) folders on school network, 2) fee-based programs from companies such as Richer Picture 3) cloud-based storage like Dropbox or Google Apps, and 4) online collaborative sites like Google Classroom or PBWorks (Google names for addresses if you're interested).
_____Have students practice by uploading something to their digital portfolio.

Student dropbox

_____A homework or assignment drop box can be created through the school Learning Management System (LMS), email, Google Apps (through 'share' function)—even a Discussion Board.
_____If your school has this option, review so students are comfortable.
_____If you have Google Apps, create a Homework drop box like *Figure 20a*:

- *Each student creates a folder called 'Homework' that is shared with you.*
- *To submit work to you, copy it to that folder so you can view and comment.*

Figure 20a—Homework dropbox; 20b—email etiquette

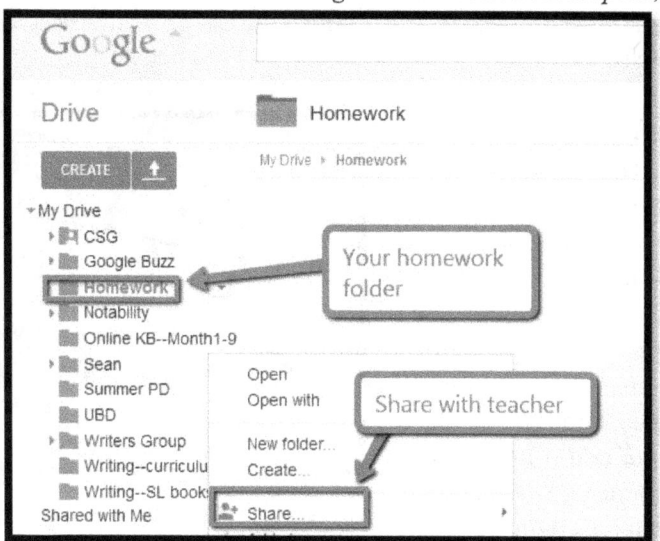
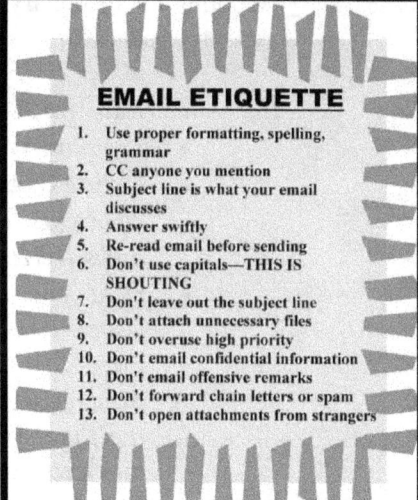

Student email

_____Review how to email (if your fifth graders are using email):

- If you are a Google school, Gmail comes with this for your students. Review where to find it and how to use it.
- If students are using their home-based email account or their parents, review this. Ask them all to send you an email that evening so you can verify their address. Keep a list in case students forget theirs and need it for a project. Alert parents so they know this is a school-sanctioned email.
- If students used email last year, have one student or a group review basics— *To, cc, subject line, body of email, attachment, urgent.*
- Discuss rules on **email poster** (*Figure 20b* is a thumbnail; full-size in appendix). Do students have other suggestions?
- Discuss how email can be used to back-up important documents (by emailing a copy to themselves or creating a draft email with doc attached and stored in 'Draft' file).

_____It is student responsibility to 1) spell address correctly, 2) notice when email 'bounces', and 3) resend if necessary. Ask them what they should do to verify that their email was delivered.

Vocabulary Decoding Tools

_____Show students how to access the native apps or webtools on their digital devices that can be used to decode vocabulary students don't understand. Depending upon the device, these will be on the homepage, the browser toolbar, a shortkey, or a right click. Show students how to quickly look up words from any of their classes rather than skipping over content that includes the word.

Let them practice with several of the words in this lesson's *Vocabulary* list.

_____ Options for dictionary tools include (Google names for address or visit Ask a Tech Teacher's resources pages for *Research*):

- *Kids Wordsmyth*
- *Merriam-Webster for Kids*
- *Picture Dictionary*
- *right click on a word in MS Word and select 'Look up'*
- *right click in Google Apps (i.e., Google Docs) and select 'research'*
- *dictionary created by students in prior years—they find a word they don't understand, add it with a definition to a webpage you've set up for that purpose (maybe on the class blog or website)*

_____ Throughout class, check for understanding.

Class exit ticket: ***Send an email to the teacher listing the top three digital tools the student is excited to use.***

Differentiation

- Added hardware quiz to class calendar.
- Add next week's keyboarding quiz to class calendar.
- To help students learn to check email on a regular basis, send fun emails like:
  - Ask them to take a silly picture using Photo Booth and email it to you
  - See who is the first to reply to and forward an email from the teacher
  - Send link to an online educational game (like ProdigyGame) and have students email you their best score
  - Send students on a campus scavenger hunt to look for specific items

"A printer consists of three main parts: the case, the jammed paper tray and the blinking red light"

Assessment 1—Parts of the computer

HARDWARE—PARTS OF THE COMPUTER

Name each part of computer hardware system Draw your own lines for the key names. Spelling must be correct to get credit

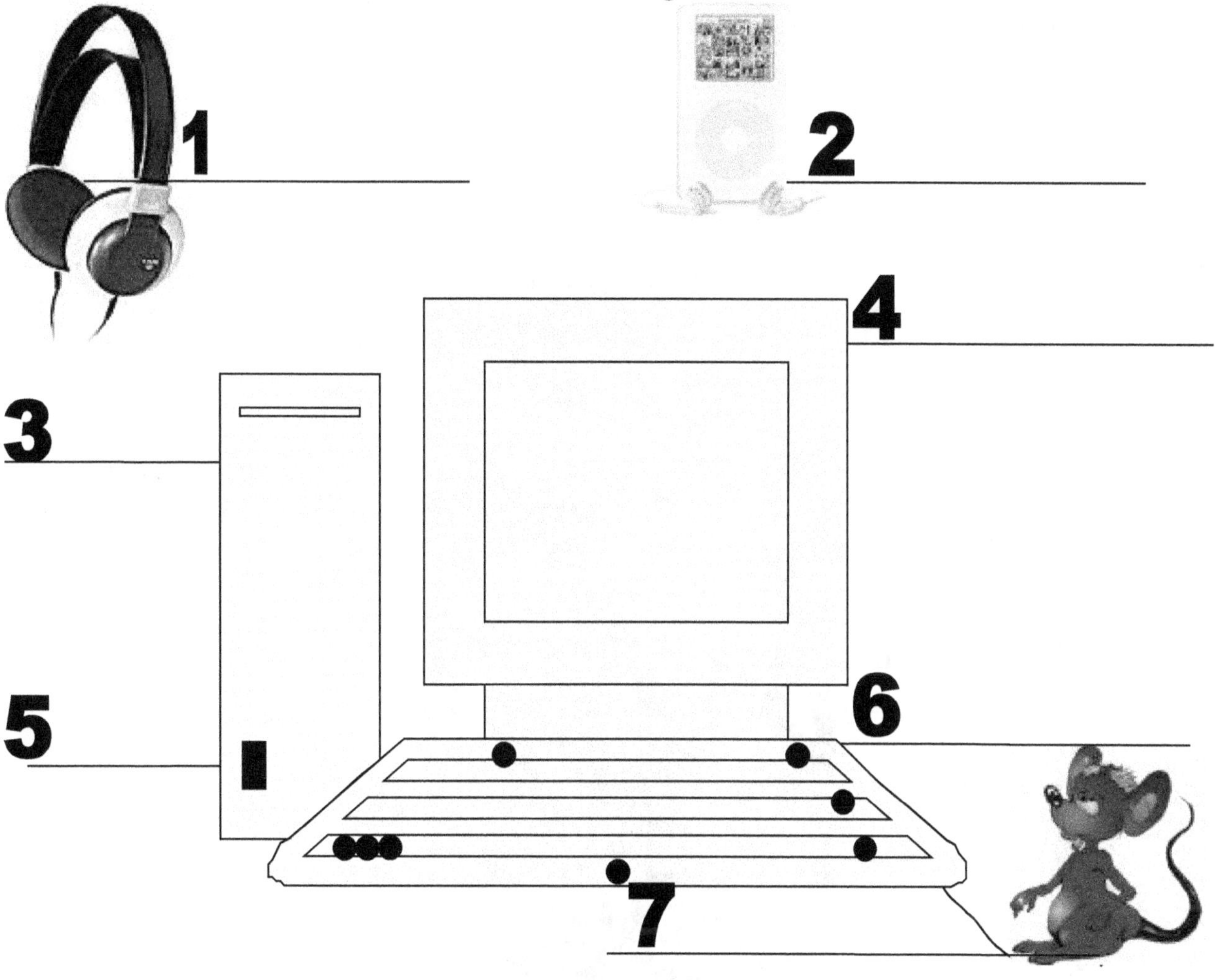

1. _____
2. _____
3. _____
4. _____
5. _____
6. _____
7. _____

Word Bank:

Headphones	*Mouse*	*USB Port*
Keyboard	*Peripheral*	
Monitor	*Tower/CPU*	

Label the keys with a circle ● over them. Use this word bank:

Ctrl	*Spacebar*	*Shift*
Alt	*Flying Windows*	*Enter*
Backspace	*F4*	

Assessment 2—Parts of the smartphone

HARDWARE—PARTS OF THE SMARTPHONE

Adapt this to your needs

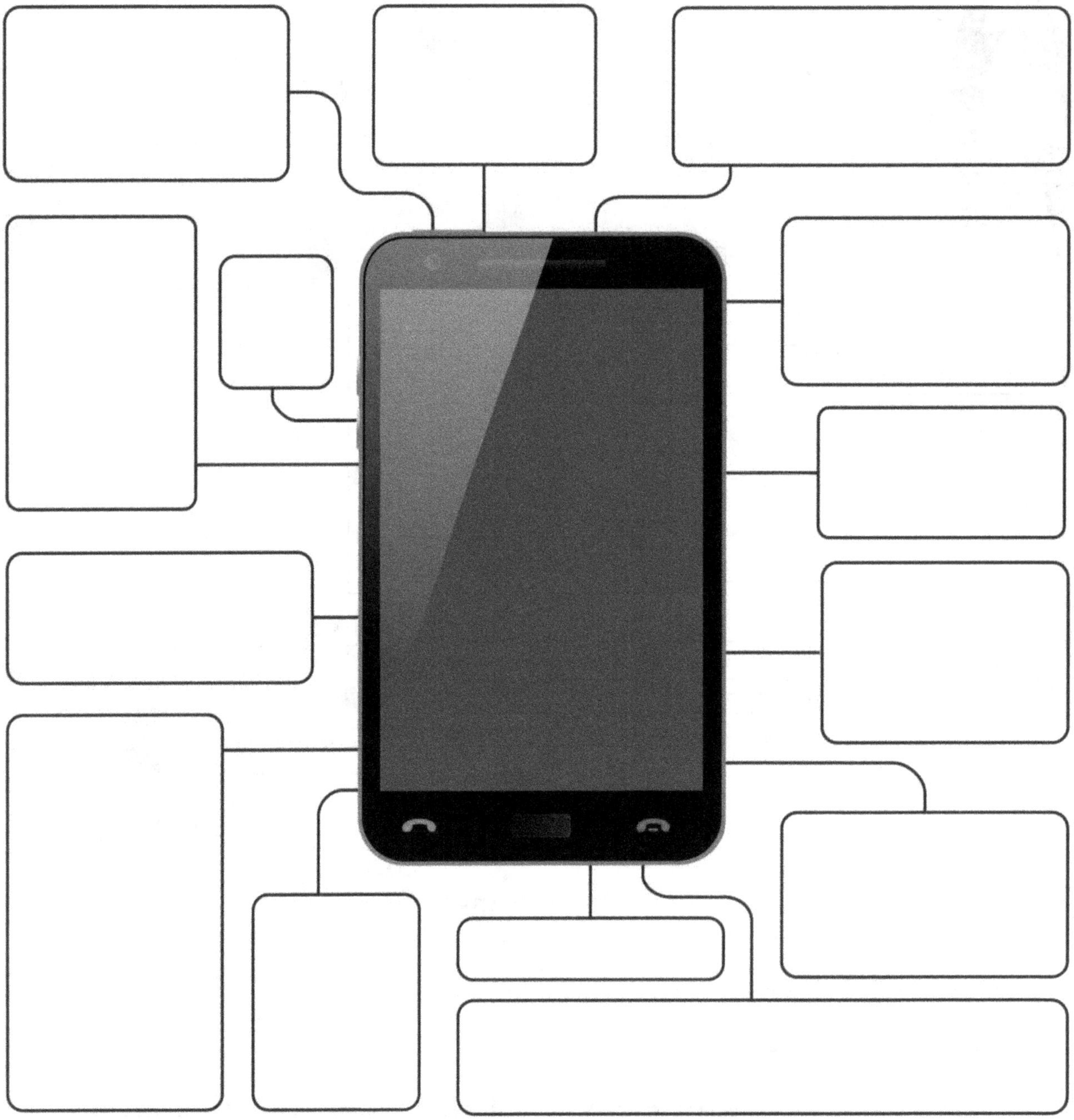

Assessment 3—Parts of an iPad

Parts of an iPad

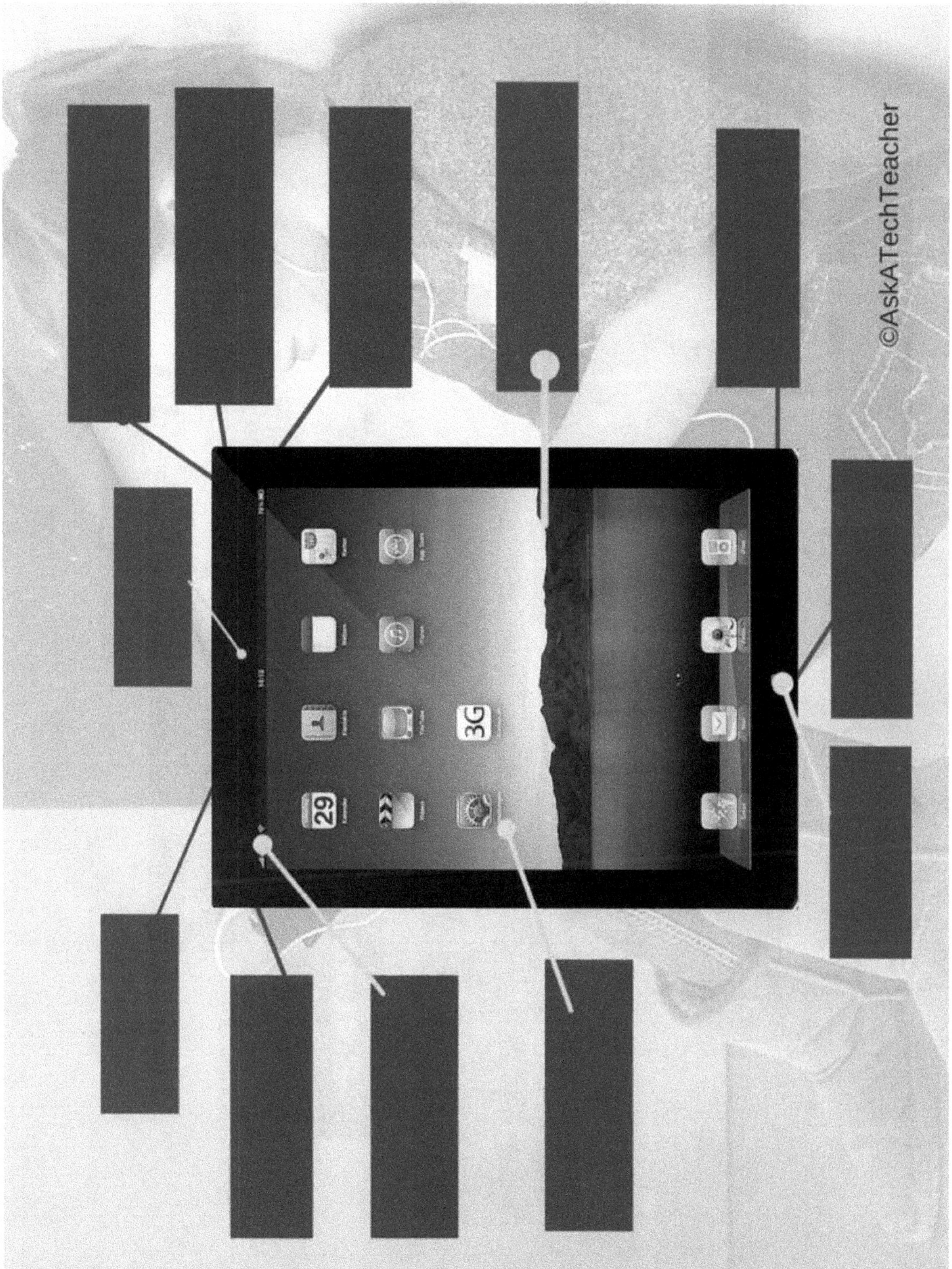

Assessment 4—Chromebook parts

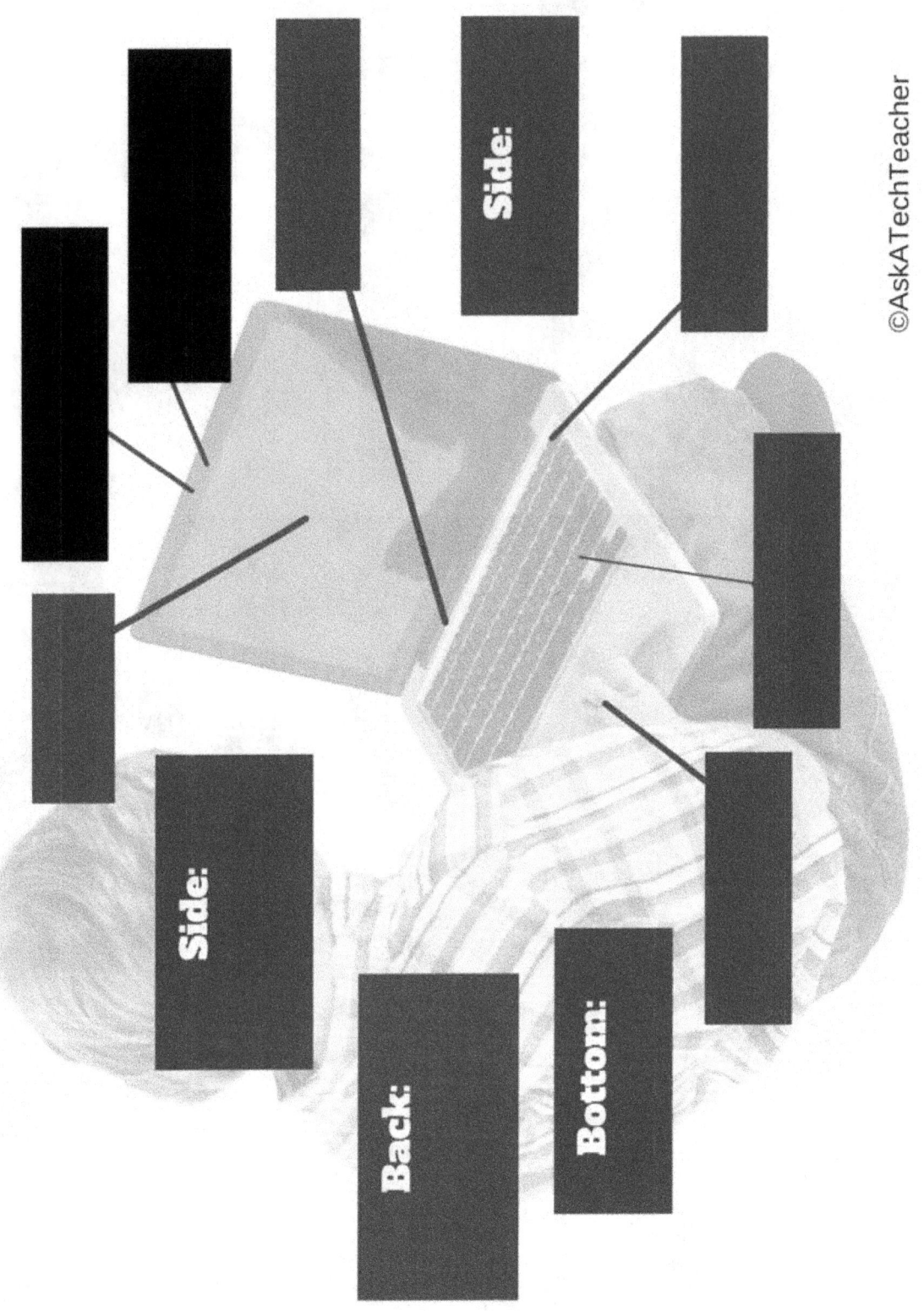

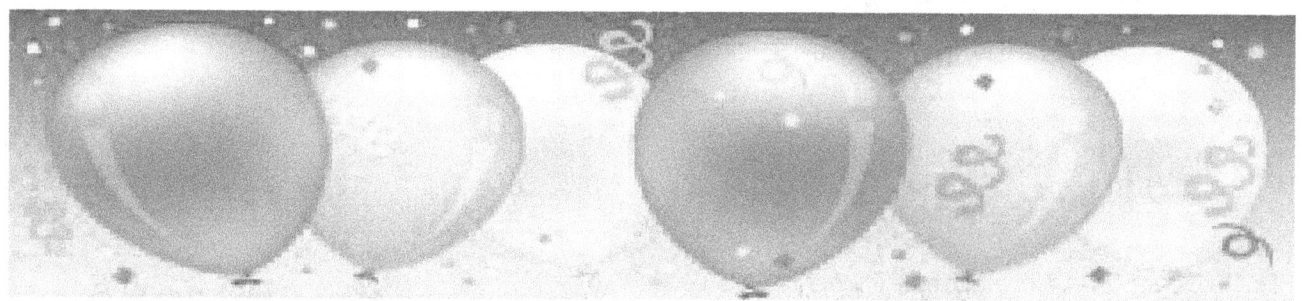

Take Tech into the Classroom

When classroom teacher feels students are settled into the class routine enough to get started on the class pod of computers, if you are the tech teacher, make time to join them and transfer tech class knowledge to the class.

Before going:
- Make sure the class computers work
- Make sure class computers have required links. What are the teacher's favorites?
    - *school website*
    - *tech lab class Internet start page*
    - *typing practice program*
    - *math program*
    - *other links teacher would like included*
- Make sure they are set up the same as the tech lab (or know where the differences are so you can explain to students

During your visit, go over these with students:
- Same rules that apply in the tech class apply in the classroom (add your rules)
    - *No food or drink by computers*
    - *No fooling around*
    - *No grabbing neighbor's equipment*
    - *No Internet except on approved sites*
    - *Try to solve problems before asking for help (especially important because you as tech teacher won't be there to help)*
    - *Read the screen before asking for help*
    - *Leave the station the way you found it*
    - *Print only with permission*
- Practice good habits every time you sit at computer
- Explain the difference between 'save' and 'save-as'—that when students open a document created in the lab, don't 'save as'. Often, they end up saving to 'My Documents' on the class computer
- Take questions

Article 5—Which Class Internet Start Page is Best

Which Class Internet Start Page is Best?

The Internet is unavoidable in education. Students go there to research, access homework, check grades, and a whole lot more. As a teacher, you do your best to make it a friendly, intuitive, and safe place to visit, but it's challenging. Students arrive there by iPads, smartphones, links from classroom teachers, suggestions from friends—the routes are endless. The best way to keep the Internet experience safe is to catch users right at the front door, on that first click.

How do you do that? By creating a **class Internet start page**. Clicking the Internet icon opens the world wide web to a default page. Never take your device's default because there's no guarantee it's G-rated enough for a typical classroom environment. Through the 'settings' function on your browser, enter the address of a page you've designed as a portal to all school Internet activity, called an 'Internet start page'. Sure, this takes some time to set-up and maintain, but it saves more than that in student frustration, lesson prep time, and the angst parents feel about their children entering the virtual world by themselves. They aren't. You're there, through this page. Parents can save the link to their home computer and let students access any resources on it, with the confidence of knowing you've curated everything.

In searching for the perfect Internet start page, I wanted one that:

- *quickly differentiates for different grades*
- *is intuitive for even the youngest to find their page*
- *is customizable across tabbed pages to satisfy changing needs*
- *presents a visual and playful interface to make students want to go there rather than find work-arounds (a favorite hobby of older students)*
- *includes an immediately visible calendar of events*
- *hosts videos of class events*
- *provides collaborative walls like Padlet*
- *includes other interactive widgets to excite students about technology*

Here are some I looked at:

Symbaloo

A logo-based website curation tool with surprising flexibility in how links are collected and displayed. It's hugely popular with educators because collections are highly-visual and easy to access and use. Plus, Symbaloo collections made by one teacher can be shared with the community, making link collections that much easier to curate.

The downside: Links are about all you can collect on Symbaloo.

Protopage

Protopage did everything on my list. It's flexible, customizable, intuitive, and quick to use with a scalable interface that can be adjusted to my needs (2-5 columns, resize boxes, drag widgets between tabs—that sort). I set up a separate tab for each grade (or you can set up tabs for subjects). The amount of tabs is limited only by space on the top toolbar. Resources included on each tab can be curated exactly as you need. Mine includes:

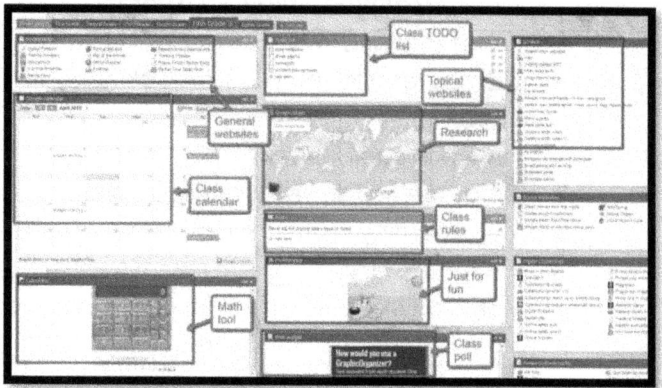

- *oft-used websites*
- *themed collections of websites*
- *a To Do list*
- *an interactive map*
- *a calculator*
- *a calendar of events*

- *edit-in-place sticky notes*
- *pictures of interest*
- *rss feeds of interest*
- *weather*
- *news*
- *widget for polling the class (Padlet)*

In addition, the Protopage folks are helpful. Whenever I have a problem (which is rare), they fix it quickly.

Lesson #3 Keyboarding

Vocabulary	Problem solving	Skills
• Ctrl+P • Digital • Digital portfolios • Keyboarding stages • Log-on • Shortkeys • Systray • Toolbar • Typing • Wpm	• DanceMat won't play flash version (does digital device allow Flash?) • Computer doesn't work (check hardware) • How do I spell-check? • What are red/green/blue squiggles? • Why shortkeys (they're faster and easier for some) • Why do I have to type with all fingers? I do fine on iPads with thumbs.	**New** **Scaffolded** Keyboarding Posture at computer Computer hardware Problem solving Speaking-listening
Academic Applications Academic classes, many parts of life	**Materials Required** speed quiz, keyboard program, keyboard quiz, hardware study guides, student workbooks (if using)	**Standards** CCSS. W.5.6 NETS: 1d, 6a

Essential Question

How do I use a keyboard to share ideas?

Big Idea

Keyboarding is a tool for more rigorous learning

Teacher Preparation

- Be prepared to use domain-specific tech vocabulary.
- Keyboarding speed and accuracy quiz is available.
- Know which tasks weren't completed last week.
- Collect words for Speak Like a Geek Board.
- Know if you need extra time to complete this lesson.
- Include grade-level team, school admin, and parents in building age-appropriate keyboarding skills that enable speed and accuracy by fourth/fifth grade.
- Ask grade-level team and parents if there are any tech problems you can help students with.

Assessment Strategies

- Took keyboarding quiz
- Showed good keyboard habits
- Understood importance of keyboarding
- Signed up for Board
- Worked independently
- Completed warm-up, exit ticket
- Joined classroom conversations
- [tried to] solve own problems
- Decisions followed class rules
- Left room as s/he found it
- Higher order thinking: analysis, evaluation, synthesis
- Habits of mind observed

Steps

Time required: 45 minutes in one sitting or spread throughout the week with a block of 15 minutes set aside for speed/accuracy quiz

Class warm-up: Keyboarding, to prepare for today's speed and accuracy quiz

_____This lesson builds on the keyboarding skills started in kindergarten, preparing students for the rigorous speed and accuracy required in Middle School (*Figure 21a*—full size poster in Appendix). All relevant keyboarding information is collected into this one place so you know where to look when you need it.

Figure 21a—keyboarding curriculum map; 21b—keyboarding hints

K-5 Keyboarding Stages

- **K-1st:** Introduce mouse skills, keyboarding, key placement, posture
- **2nd:** Work on keyboarding, key placement, posture, two-hand position
- **3rd:** Reinforce basics, work on accuracy and technique
- **4th-5th:** Continue accuracy, technique. Begin work on speed

©AskATechTeacher

These keyboarding hints came directly from the classroom, tested on 400 students a year. These are the most common fixes that help students excel at keyboarding:

1. Tuck elbows against sides of body. This keeps hands in the right spot—home row
2. Use thumb for space bar. That leaves hands on home row
3. Curl fingers over home row—they're cat claws, not dog paws
4. Use inside fingers for inside keys, outside fingers for outside keys
5. Use finger closest to the key required. Sounds simple, but this isn't what usually happens with beginners
6. Keep pointers anchored to f and j
7. Play keyboard like a piano (or violin, or guitar, or recorder). You'd never use pointer for all keys
8. Fingers move, not hands. Hands stay anchored to f and j keys
9. Don't use caps lock for capitals! Use shift
10. Add a barrier between sides of the keyboards. I fashioned one from cover stock. That reminds students to stay on the correct side of keyboard

_____Review the keyboarding hints in *Figure 21b* from K-2. These are the most common fixes that help students excel at keyboarding.

_____Review posture and computer positioning (*Figures 22a-b*). As with the mouse, check the posture of a neighbor. If correct posture isn't already a habit, make sure students sit this way everywhere they use a computer—home, school, the library, everywhere:

Figure 22a—Keyboarding posture; 22b—position

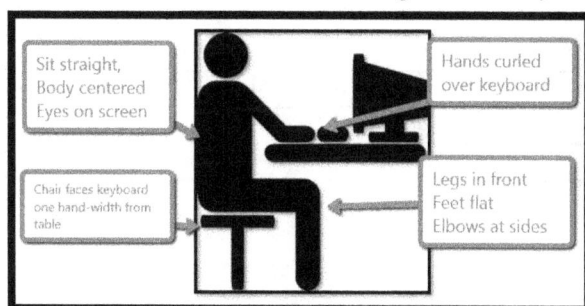

_____Review how student hands should look (*Figure 23*):

_____Keyboarding goal this year:

- *sufficient command of keyboarding to type one-two pages in a single sitting*

- *speed of 30 wpm—about as fast as students handwrite*

Figure 23—Keyboarding hand position

_____Today is the first speed and accuracy quiz of the year. Remind students of quizzes in 4th grade. They will take one per grading period.

_____*Figure 24* will help you evaluate student keyboarding technique (full-size at end of lesson):

Figure 24—Keyboarding technique checklist

Student					
Keyboarding Technique Checklist (3rd – Middle School Grades)					
Technique	Date	Date	Date	Date	Date
Feet placed for balance and sits up straight.					
Body centered to the middle of keyboard.					
Eyes on the screen.					
Types with correct fingering.					
Types with a steady, even rhythm.					
Keeps fingers on home row keys.					
Has a good attitude and strives for improvement.					
WPM (words per minute)					
Accuracy percent					

4 pts = Mastery level   2 pts = Partial Mastery level
3 pts = Near Mastery level   1 pt = Minimal Mastery level

_____Load a digital copy of *Figure 24* (*Assessment* at end of lesson) for each student onto your iPad and then use an annotation tool like Notability or Adobe Reader to assess.

_____If your students have just started to practice keyboarding, pick only a few of these criteria to assess. As the K-4th graders get more practice, they'll come to 5th grade with a greater facility and you can expect more out of them. If you use iPads for keyboarding, adapt this list to that digital device. There is a small amount of research that shows iPad keyboarding is as fast as traditional—especially for users who have grown up with that keyboard. It will take years before we know how fast and efficient iPad keyboards are compared to traditional. Consider doing your own research in the lesson on *Keyboarding and Science*.

_____Review parts of computer (or digital device) for quiz next week (study guides in prior lesson). Sound out, roots, prefixes and suffixes. Spelling counts.

_____Review how parts connect—behind CPU, under table, in front ports.

_____The speed quiz can be delivered in several ways:

- *Place a page from a book being read in class or a sample document on the class screen. Students will copy it for the quiz. This method forces their heads up rather than on their hands.*
- *Print a page from a book being read in class or a sample document for each student. They place it to the side of their keyboard and type from it.*
- *Use an online typing test like TypingTest.*

_____Students type for three-five minutes, then save/share/print.

_____This first quiz is a benchmark—to evaluate skills. The rest of the quizzes will be based on improvement. If students do their homework and tenaciously use good keyboarding habits whenever they sit at the computer, they'll do fine.

_____Here's the scale for the rest of the year (*Figure 25*):

Figure 25—Grading scale for keyboarding

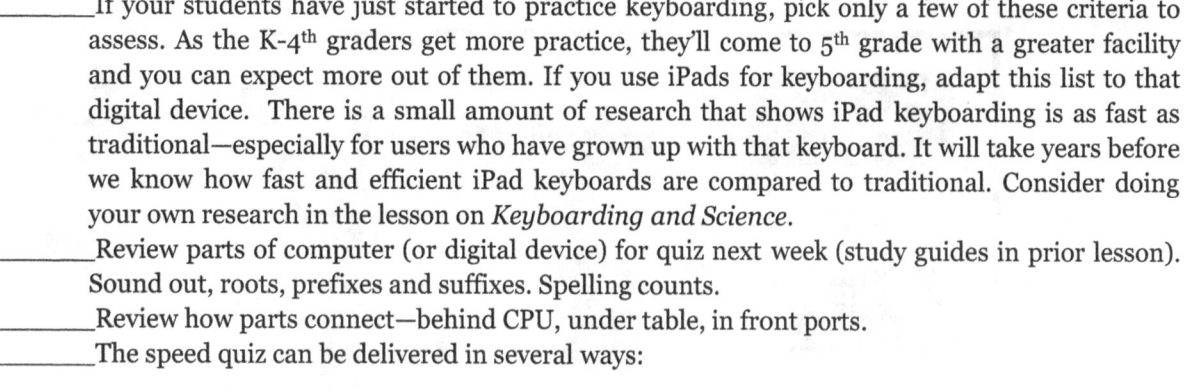

_____Using *Figure 26*, discuss why students should care about keyboarding:

Figure 26—Why learn to keyboard

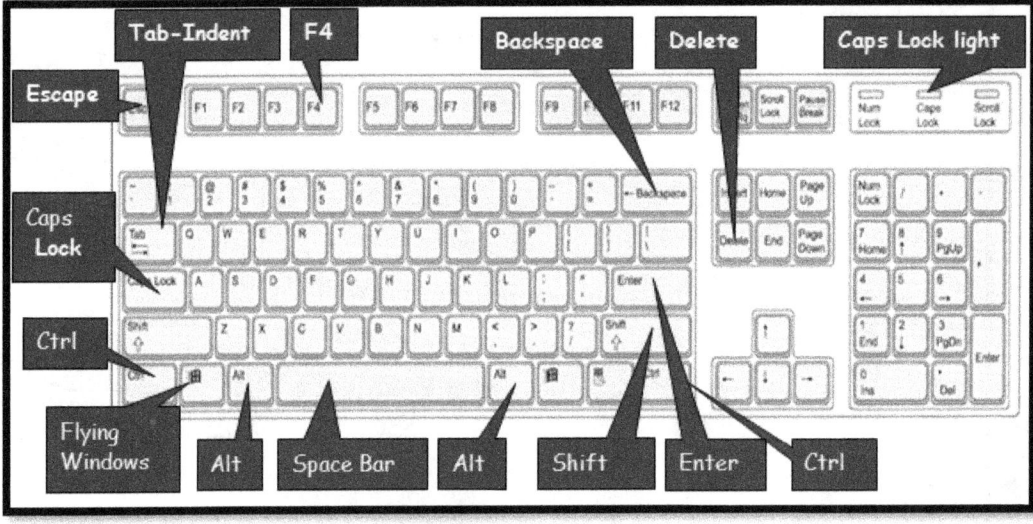

____Review important keys for quiz (see *Assessment 6*) students will take in a few weeks (*Figure 27*):

Figure 27—Important keys

____*Assessment 7* is a blank keyboard—use to evaluate student keyboarding knowledge in a later week.
____Throughout class, check for understanding.
____One more note: Keyboarding skills include more than typing. 'Good keyboarding' includes many of the basics required to excel at summative year-end testing. This includes drag-and-drop,

highlighting, copy-paste, and stamina. See *"How to Prepare Students for PARCC/SBA Testing"* at the end of this Lesson.

_____To insure students achieve speed and accuracy requires much more than drill. Read *"5 Ways to Make Classroom Keyboarding Fun"* at end of this lesson.

Class exit ticket: *Create a poll using Google Forms (or another tool) and ask students which of the reasons listed on Figure 26 resonate with them? Put it on the class screen so students can vote as they leave.*

Differentiation

- Consider turning music on to establish a typing rhythm for students.
- Discuss what's inside computer—motherboard, etc.
- Add Hardware, blank keyboard, and important keys quizzes to class calendar.
- Use mental math to figure out keyboard quiz words per minute from word count.
- Early finishers: visit class internet start page for keyboard practice sites.
- If this lesson doesn't work for your students, use one from How to Jumpstart the Inquiry-based Classroom available from Structured Learning. It has 5 projects aligned with SL curriculum.

Assessment 5—Keyboarding quiz

Student _____

Keyboarding Technique Checklist
Duplicate for each student

Technique	Date	Date	Date	Date	Date
Feet placed for balance and sits up straight					
Body centered to the middle of keyboard					
Eyes on the screen					
Types with correct fingering					
Types with a steady, even rhythm					
Keeps fingers on home row keys					
Has a good attitude and strives for improvement					
WPM (words per minute)					
Accuracy percent					

4 pts = Mastery level   2 pts = Partial Mastery level
3 pts = Near Mastery level   1 pt = Minimal Mastery level

Credit: 'Bernadette Roche, Director of Technology for a Midwest independent school

5th Grade Technology Curriculum: Teacher Manual

Assessment 6—Important Keys

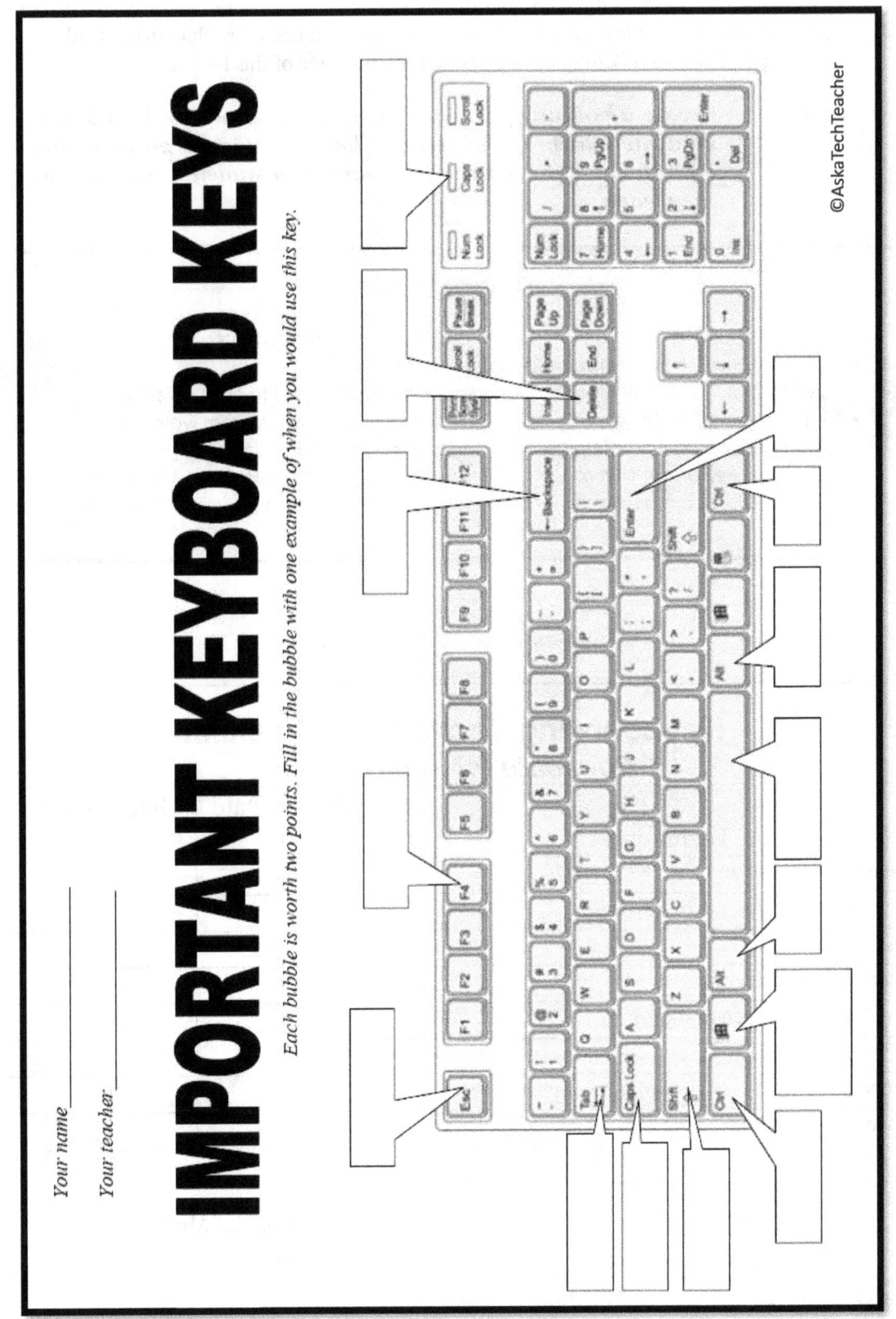

65

Assessment 7—Blank keyboard quiz

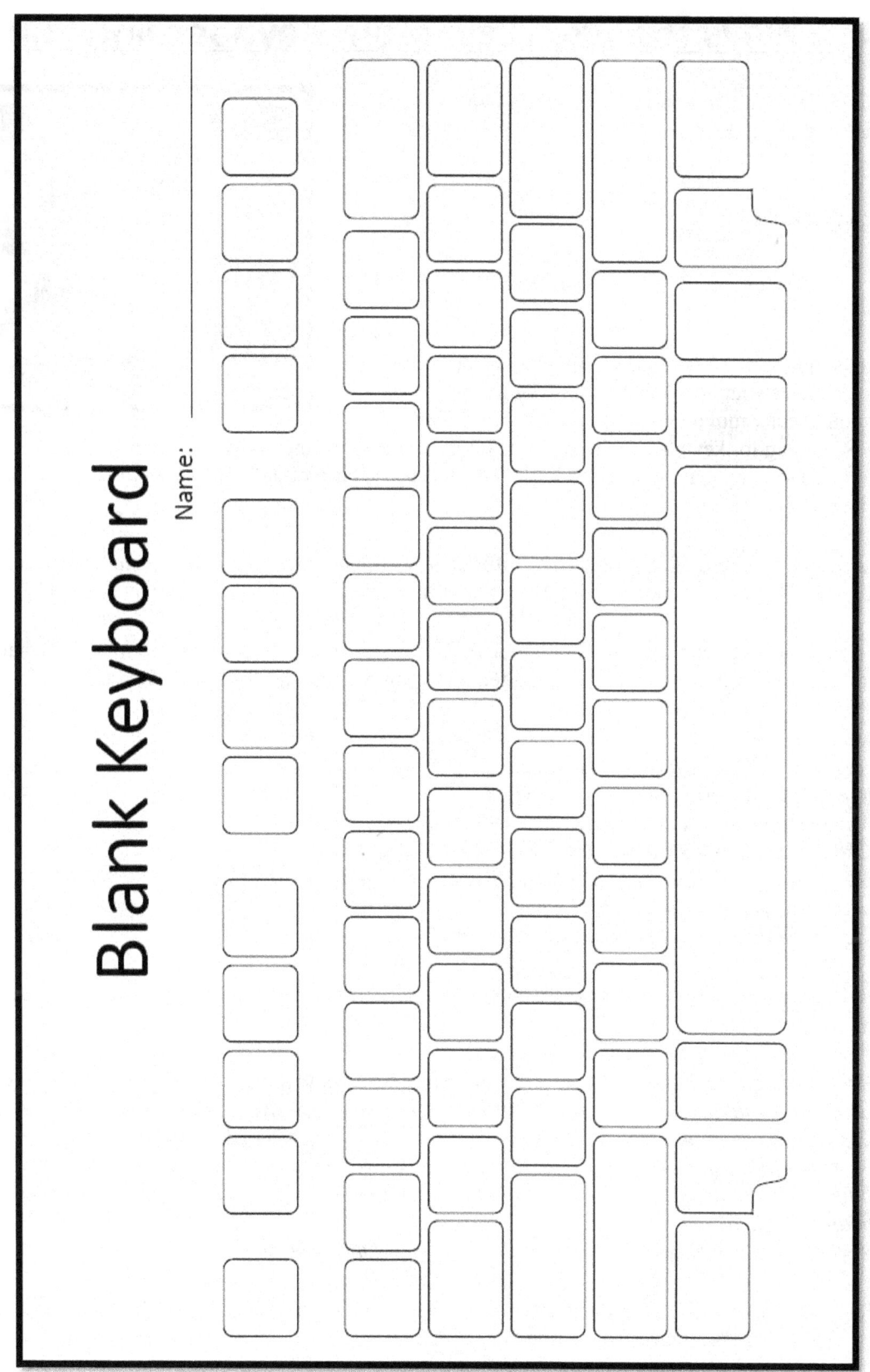

66

Article 6—5 Ways to make classroom keyboarding fun

5 Ways to Make Classroom Keyboarding Fun

When you teach typing, the goal isn't **speed and accuracy**. The goal is that students type well enough that it doesn't disrupt their thinking.

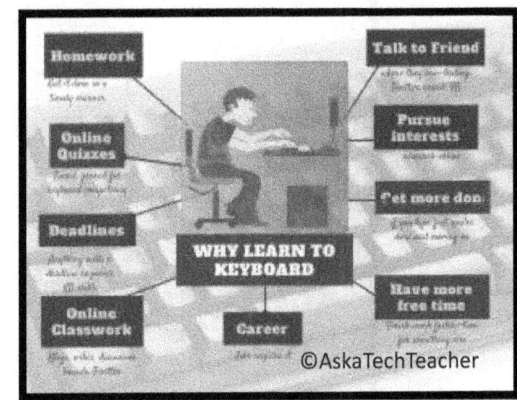

Let me say that again:

The goal of keyboarding is students type well enough that it doesn't disrupt their thinking.

Much like breathing takes no thought and playing a piano is automatic, students want to be able to think while they type, fingers automatically moving to the keys that record their thoughts. Searching for key placement shouldn't interfere with how they develop a sentence. Sure, it does when students are just starting, but by third grade students should be comfortable enough with key placement to be working on speed.

To type as fast at the speed of thought isn't as difficult as it sounds. When referring to students in school, 'speed of thought' refers to how fast they develop ideas that will be recorded. 30 wpm is the low end. 45 wpm is good.

Students used to learn typing in high school, as a skill. Now, it's a tool for learning. So much of what we ask students to do on the way to authentic learning requires typing. Consider the academic need to:

- *write reports*
- *comment on Discussion Boards and blogs*
- *journal in blogs and online tools like Penzu*
- *research online (type addresses into a search bar)*
- *take digital notes (using Evernote, OneNote and similar)*
- *collaborate on Google Apps like Docs, Sheets, Presentations*
- *take online quizzes (like PARCC, SB)*
- *use online tools for core classes (Wordle, Animoto, Story Creators)*

If you're a Common Core state, keyboarding shows up often in the Standards, but can be summarized in these three ways:

- *Keyboarding is addressed tangentially–students must be able to type *** pages in a single sitting (see CCSS.ELA-Literacy.W.4.6 for example. The 'pages in a single sitting' starts in 4th grade with one page and continues through 6th where it's increased to three–see CCSS.ELA-Literacy.W.6.6)*
- *By 3rd grade, Common Core discusses the use of keyboarding to produce work, i.e., CCSS.ELA-Literacy.W.3.6 which specifically mentions 'use technology to produce and publish writing (using keyboarding skills)'*
- *Keyboarding is required to take Common Core Standards **assessments** in the spring.*

The myth is that students will teach themselves when they need it. That's half right. They will teach themselves, but it won't necessarily be in time for their needs. If you're in a tech-infused school, it's your obligation to teach them the right way to type so they can organically develop the tools to support learning.

Most teachers roll out typing with a graduated program like Type to Learn or Typing Club. In September of the new school year, students start Lesson 1. Sometime around May, they are through all the lessons and considered trained. Everything is on auto-pilot with little intervention from the teacher. That works for about ten percent of students. Those are the ones who are intrinsically motivated to learn and nothing gets in their way.

The other 90% need a little more help. Here are six ideas to make your typing lessons fun and effective:

Drill

Drill is part of every granular typing program. Students must learn key placement, finger usage, posture, and all those other details.

There are a lot of options for this—both free like Typing Web and fee-based like QwertyTown. Students usually start enthusiastically, which wanes within a few months as it becomes more of the same rote practice.

Games

When your organic typing program shows signs of wearing on students, throw in a sprinkling of games that teach key placement, speed and accuracy. Big Brown Bear is great for youngers; NitroType for olders, and Popcorn Typer for the in-between grades of 2nd-5th.

Offer games sporadically, not on a schedule. Make it a reward for keyboarding benchmarks.

Team Challenge

Students work in teams to answer keyboard-related questions in a game show format. You can use a Jeopardy template that includes not only keyboard questions, but shortkeys that students use often.

Integrate into Class Inquiry

Within a month of starting a keyboarding program, have students use their growing skills authentically in class projects. This can be book reports, research, a brochure for history class, or a collaborative document through Google Apps. The keyboarding is a tool to communicate knowledge in a subject, much like a pencil, an artist brush or a violin. The better their keyboarding skills, the easier it is to complete the meat of the project, like a blog response, trading cards on characters in a book, or a family tree.

Remind students to use the keyboarding skills they've learned to make this real-life experience easier—hands on their own side of the keyboard, use all fingers, good posture, elbows at their sides. Let their team of grade level teachers know what traits to look for as students research in class or the library. Get parents to reinforce it at home.

ASCII Art

ASCII Art uses keyboarding skills to create artistic representations of class learning. This is a fun way to use keyboarding in other classes. All students do is find a picture that represents the class inquiry topic being addressed, put it as a watermark into the word processing program, type over the washed out image with a variety of keys, then delete the watermark. This takes about thirty minutes usually and always excites students with the uniqueness of their work.

Article 7—How to Prepare Students for PARCC/SBA Tests

How to Prepare Students for PARCC/SBA Tests

As part of my online tech teacher persona, I get lots of questions from readers about how to make technology work in an educational environment. This one from Terry is probably on the minds of thousands of teachers:

Any help for identifying and re-enforcing tech skills needed to take the online PARCC tests (coming in 2014-15)? Even a list of computer terms would help; copy, cut, paste, highlight, select; use of keys like tab, delete, insert; alt, ctrl and shift. There does not seem to be any guidelines as to prepping students on the "how to's" of taking an online test and reading and understanding the directions. It would be great to take advantage of the time we have before the PARCC's become a reality. Thanks!

Every spring, more than 4 million students in 36 states and the District of Columbia will take near-final versions of the PARCC and Smarter Balanced efforts to test Common Core State Standards learning in the areas of mathematics and English/language arts. Tests will be administered via digital devices (though there are options for paper-and-pencil). The tests won't produce detailed scores of student performance (that starts next year), but this field-testing is crucial to finding out what works and doesn't in this comprehensive assessment tool, including the human factors like techphobia and sweaty palms (from both students and teachers).

After I got Terry's email, I polled my PLN to find specific tech areas students needed help with in preparing for the Assessments. It boils down to five tech areas:

Keyboarding

Students need to have enough familiarity with the keyboard that they know where keys are, where the number pad is, where the F row is, how keys are laid out. They don't need to be touch typists or even facilely use all fingers. Just have them comfortable enough they have a good understanding of where all the pieces are. Starting next school year, have them type fifteen minutes a week in a class setting and 45 minutes a week using keyboarding for class activities (homework, projects—that sort). That'll do it.

Basic computer skills

These skills—drag-and-drop, keyboarding with speed and accuracy, highlighting, playing videos—are not easy for a student if they haven't had an instructive course in using computers. It won't surprise any adult when I say using and iPad isn't the same as using a computer. The former has a bunch more buttons and tools and the latter more intuitive. And typing on an iPad virtual keyboard is not the same as the reassuring clackity-clack of a traditional set-up. Will students get used to that? Yes, but not this month.

Make sure students are technologically proficient in their use of a variety of digital devices, including computers and iPads. This means students have an understanding of what defines a digital device, how it operates, what type of programs are used on various types (for example, apps are for iPads and software for laptops) and how do they operate, and what's the best way to scaffold them for learning? Being comfortable with technology takes time and practice. Make digital devices and tech solutions available at every opportunity—for note-taking, backchannel communications, quick assessments, online collaboration, even timing an activity. Make it part of a student's educational landscape.

One area Terry asks about is vocabulary. The words she mentioned—*copy, paste, cut, highlight*—these are domain-specific. Use the correct terminology as you teaching, but observe students. If they don't understand what you're saying, help them decode it with context, affixes, or an online dictionary for geek words. Keep a list of those words. Soon, you'll have a vocabulary list for technology that's authentic and specific to your needs.

Stamina

Expect students to type for extended periods without complaint. Common Core requires this. That's what 'one page in a sitting in 4th grade, 2 pages in a sitting in 5th grade, 3 pages in a sitting in 6th grade' means. The Assessments expect students have that sort of stamina. They're long tests with lots of keyboarding and other tech skills. Make sure your students have practiced working at computers for extended periods.

A good idea is to have students take some online assessments prior to this summative one. These can be created by the teacher using any number of online tools like Google Forms or use already-created tests like those that follow BrainPop videos.

Problem Solving

Make sure students know what to do when a tech problem arises. They should be able to handle simple problems like 'headphones don't work' or 'caps lock won't turn on' or 'my document froze'. This is easily accomplished by having students take responsibility for solving tech problems, with the teacher acting as a resource. They will soon be able to differentiate between what they have the ability to handle and what requires assistance.

A great starting point when teaching problem solving are Common Core Standards for Mathematical Practice. These are aligned with the Math Standards, but apply to all facets of learning.

Teacher Training

Make sure teachers administering the online tests are familiar with them and comfortable in that world. They should know how to solve basic tech issues that arise without calling for outside help. This is effectively accomplished by having teachers use technology in their classroom on a regular basis for class activities, as a useful tool in their educational goals. Helps teachers make this happen.

5th Grade Technology Curriculum: Teacher Manual

Lesson #4 Student Blogs

Vocabulary	Problem solving	Skills
• Avatars • Blog • Comments • Keyboard shortcut • Mulligan Rule • Netiquette • Post • Shortkeys • Web log	• I don't see my post (teacher approve it) • Why can't I use my picture in blog? (discuss digital privacy) • Someone made a mean comment (teacher is moderating; it won't show) • Can't figure it out (breathe deeply, check screen, you can do it) • Log-in didn't work (verify UN and PW before asking teacher for help)	**New** Blogging **Scaffolded** Speaking and listening Problem solving Keyboarding Digital citizenship
Academic Applications Writing, research, collaboration, sharing, publishing, use of evidence, online safety	**Materials Required** hardware quiz, keyboard program, blog log-ins, blog posts for student response, Problem Solving Board sign-ups, Evidence Board badges, student workbooks (if using)	**Standards** CCSS: W.5.1 NETS: 2b, 3c-d, 6d, 7a-b

Essential Question

How do I share with classmates?

Big Idea

Students become aware of how tech enhances educational

Teacher Preparation

- Have Problem-solving Board sign-up sheets.
- Have copies of Blogging Agreement (if necessary).
- Collect words for Speak Like a Geek Board presentations.
- Know which tasks weren't completed last week.
- Set up accounts in a blogging program.
- Remind students to bring science book next week.
- Know if you need extra time to complete this lesson.
- Talk with grade-level team so you tie into conversations.
- Ensure that all required links are on student computers.
- Ask about tech problems students are having difficulty with. Cover them during tech lessons.
- Be prepared to integrate domain-specific tech vocabulary into lesson.

Assessment Strategies

- Completed hardware quiz
- Annotated workbook (if using)
- Signed up for Board
- Completed blog assignments
- Worked independently
- Used good keyboarding habits
- Completed warm-up, exit ticket
- Joined classroom conversations
- [tried to] solve own problems
- Decisions followed class rules
- Left room as s/he found it
- Higher order thinking: analysis, evaluation, synthesis
- Habits of mind observed

Steps

Time required: 45 minutes in one sitting or spread throughout the week with a block of 30 minutes for blogging

Class warm-up: Keyboarding homerow on class typing program

_____Start Hardware Assessment. Give students 5-10 minutes. Spelling counts. If they are unhappy with their score, retake for full credit (called the Mulligan Rule, from golf).

_____When students finish the hardware assessment, return to keyboarding using Dance Mat Typing, Popcorn Typer, or another online site that **focuses on one row at a time** while the rest of the class finishes. Students used these last year so should be able to begin independently (Google for website addresses or visit Ask a Tech Teacher's resources pages for *Keyboarding*).
_____Turn music on to establish a typing rhythm for students. Encourage them to type with the beat.
_____While keyboarding, sign up for Problem-solving Board—starts next week. Remember 3rd and 4th grade? This is the first of three Presentation Boards this year:

- *Post sign-up sheets by the class door where they're easily found. Include slips of paper (Figure 28) that students can track important information. If students have workbooks, fill in the form in it with their annotation tool:*

Figure 28—Info for Problem-solving Board

My name: _____

My question: _____

My presentation date: _____

- *Alternatively, have sign-ups online where they can be shared through:*
    - *Google Apps—either the Calendar or Spreadsheets*
    - *Google Forms*
    - *Office 365*
    - *Padlet (using calendar template)*
    - *Appointment Slots in Google Calendar that you shared with students*

- *Each student signs up for a date to present.*
- *Each student selects a unique problem they will teach classmates to solve.*
- *Students get solution from family, friends, or even teacher as a last resort.*
- *Presentation date: Students tell classmates problem, how to solve it, take questions.*
- *Entire presentation takes about three minutes.*
- *Review grading.*

_____Students may sign up in groups, as long as there is one problem per group member.
_____Load a digital copy of the Presentation assessment (*Assessment 8*) for each student onto your iPad and then use an annotation tool like iAnnotate or Adobe Reader to assess.

Assessment 8—Problem-solving Board rubric

PROBLEM SOLVING BOARD
Grading Rubric

Name: _____

Class: _____

- Knew question _____
- Knew answer _____
- Asked audience for help if didn't know answer _____
- No umm's, stutters _____
- Look audience in eye _____
- No nervous movements (giggles, wiggles, etc.) _____
- No nervous noises (giggles,) _____
- Overall _____

_____*Figure 29* is an example of the types of problems you may include:

Figure 29—Common computer problems

Common Computer Problems	
What if the double-click doesn't work	What is protocol for email subject line
What if the monitor doesn't work	What does 'CC' mean in an email
What if the volume doesn't work	How do I exit a screen I'm stuck in
What if the computer doesn't work	How do I double space in Word
What if the mouse doesn't work	How do I add a footer in Word
What's the right-mouse button for?	How do I add a watermark in Word
What keyboard shortcut closes program	How do I make a macro in Word
How do I move between cells/boxes?	How do I add a border in Word
How do I figure out today's date?	How do I add a hyperlink in Word
What if the capital doesn't work	Keyboard shortcuts for B, I, U
What if my toolbar disappears	What if the program disappears
What if the document disappears	What if the program freezes
Keyboard shortcut for 'undo'	What is the protocol for saving a file
How do I search for a file	

_____A little background: Problem-solving Board covers tech issues faced during class, as they happen. As you move through the year, collate a list of problems for next year's Board. Start with the problems students suggested as a class exit ticket after Week #1. Include problems students had with tech in homework, at home as they used tech for a school assignment, or problems they had with classroom computers.

_____Include shortkeys like *Figure 30*:

Figure 30—Common shortkeys

Windows	
Maximize window	Double click title bar
Quick Exit	Alt+F4
Toggle between two windows	Alt+tab
Show start menu	WK (Windows key)
Show desktop	WK+M
Peek at your desktop	WK+spacebar
Walk through the taskbar	WK+T, WK+Tab
Open new browser tab	Click scroll on mouse
Minimize all but 1 open window	Shake win. u want (aero-shake)
Task Manager	Ctrl+Shift+Escape

General			
CTRL+C:	Copy	CTRL+L:	Left align
CTRL+X:	Cut	CTRL+R:	Right align
CTRL+V:	Paste	CTRL+B/U/I:	Bold,Unline/italic
CTRL+Z:	Undo	CTRL+or-:	Zoom in/out www
CTRL+P:	Print	CTRL+2	Double space
CTRL+K:	Add hyperlink	Shift+Alt+D/T:Date/Time	
CTRL+E:	Center align		

_____Problem solving will be addressed in more detail in the ***Problem-solving*** lesson.

_____All Board presentations in this curriculum are independent investigation, risk-taking for cautious students who feel a Right Answer lives out there somewhere. They also provide an authentic method of practicing presentation skills discussed in Common Core under 'Speaking and Listening'.

_____When all students are signed up, review speed quiz results.

_____Any evidence of learning to post on Evidence Board?

_____Introduce the concept of 'blogging'—short articles published online, enhanced with images or videos, with the express purpose of sharing ideas and garnering feedback. In the case of 5th graders, you are particularly interested in their facility to:

- o engage effectively in collaborative discussions with diverse partners
- o build on others' ideas
- o express their own ideas clearly

_____Blogging provides this opportunity.

_____Review the article at lesson end on "*13 Ways Blogs Teach Common Core*".

_____Before beginning, students must sign an agreement similar to *Fifth Grade Blogging Rules (Assessment 9)*. Ask them to discuss the agreement with parents and bring it to school before the next class. If you're using workbooks, students can sign the copy in there, take a screenshot, and email that to you.

_____Students can create blogs in Edublogs, Class Blogmeister, Blogger (latter comes with Google Apps)—Google for addresses. Teacher sets up class account. It can be public or private, the latter providing a safe, walled garden for students to share information and comment on each other's work.

_____Students use blogs for reflection, sharing digital tools (like Vokis, Animotos), posting and sharing Google Docs (through embed feature), collaborating on work, commenting on projects of classmates, and more.

_____Before beginning, circle back on discussions about Internet privacy, and digital rights and responsibilities. This is covered in more detail in the lessons on **Internet Search**.

_____Students can create a profile picture with an avatar creator *like Figure 31* (Google for address, use your favorite, or visit Ask a Tech Teacher's resource pages for *Digital Citizenship>Avatars*):

Figure 4--Avatar

- *Voki yourself*
- *With comics (like Storyboard That!)*

_____Follow good digital citizenship habits: Make the avatar look nothing like the student!

_____These can be used in student blogs or other digital platforms that require a profile picture.

_____While blogging, students will:

- *follow agreed-upon blogging rules)*
- *write articles based on evidence from a variety of resources*
- *contribute to discussion and/or elaborate on others' remarks by adding comments to the posts of classmates*

_____Studies show blogs (i.e., *Figure 32*) 1) attract a wider audience than traditional reading venues, 2) improve student writing skills by making it fun and hip, 3) incorporate discovery into education, and 4) draw learners into self-guided discussions. Blogs require critical thinking and give content ownership to students.

_____Here are other skills students learn from blogging:

Figure 5--Student blog

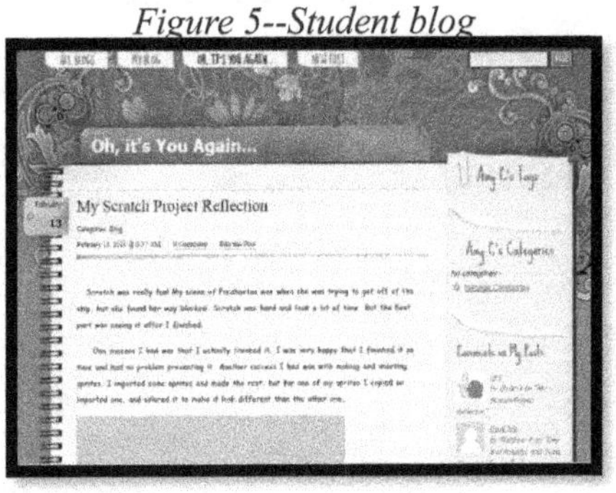

- *how to protect privacy*
- *about their Digital Footprint*
- *how to embed information*

_____Discuss blogging netiquette—like email etiquette:

- *be polite*
- *use good grammar and spelling*
- *don't write anything everyone shouldn't read (school blogs are private, but get students used to the oxymoron of privacy and the Internet)*

_____Students sign onto their blog account.

_____Start by showing students your blog. Have several entries that tie into class inquiry. Ask students to select an entry and post a comment. Continue this over a period of several days. Encourage students to respond to classmates with supportive and positive comments.

_____Next, students post a blog about themselves. Only provide information they are comfortable sharing. Include images, video, or music. Make this self-directed as you encourage students to explore widgets and tools available on blog.

_____Remind students to practice good keyboarding as they type the entry.

_____Once a month, have students post an article that discusses an inquiry topic. Additionally, students should visit and comment on five classmate blogs.

_____Student comments aren't always appropriate? Set account so you approve comments before they go live. And chat with students about how supportive comments contribute to the conversation.

Figure 6--Blogging rubric

_____Occasionally throughout the year, use the Student Blogs Rubric *(Figure 33* and *Assessment 10)* to assess student progress.

_____How students access their blog will be slightly different if they use a computer (PC, Mac, even a Chromebook) or an iPad. IPad's will access the blog via an app, which often has different steps to accomplish a goal and often has different skills available than computers or Chromebooks. Accommodate instructions for which digital device students are using.

_____If you teach in a lab, have a student post a reminder on the class calendar to bring the science book next week for a lesson on outlining.

_____Remind students to transfer knowledge to classroom or home.

Class exit ticket: *Have students email you their Problem-solving Board date and question.*

Differentiation

- Add Important Keys quiz (next week) to calendar.
- Have students label each computer part on assessment as 'input' or 'output'.
- If homework is due, make sure it's added to class calendar.
- Early finishers: visit class internet start page for websites that tie into classwork.
  Add an after-school blogging group to help students get started. Ask Middle School students to help out.
- Consider letting students work in groups as they build their class blog.
- If you don't have student blogs, replace with 4th Grade Lesson #4 Book Reviews by the Characters in curriculum extenders (from Structured Learning).
- If you don't have student blogs, replace this lesson with 4th Grade Lesson #5 IPads 101 in curriculum extenders (from Structured Learning).
- If you don't have student blogs, replace this lesson with 5th Grade Lesson #1 Scratch in curriculum extendors (from Structured Learning).

Assessment 9—Student blogging agreement

Fifth Grade Blogging Rules
(adapted from Academy of Discovery)

1. I will not give out any information more personal than my first name
2. I will not plagiarize; instead I will expand on others' ideas and give credit where it is due.
3. I will use language appropriate for school.
4. I will always respect my fellow students and their writing.
5. I will only post pieces that I am comfortable with everyone seeing.
6. I will use constructive/productive/purposeful criticism, supporting any idea, comment, or critique I have with evidence.
7. I will take blogging seriously, posting only comments and ideas that are meaningful and that contribute to the overall conversation.
8. I will take my time when I write, using formal language (not text lingo), and I will try to spell everything correctly.
9. I will not bully others in my blog posts or in my comments.
10. I will only post comments on posts that I have fully read, rather than just skimmed.
11. I will not reveal anyone else's identity in my comments or posts.

Any infraction of the Fifth Grade Blogging Rules may result in loss of blogging privileges and an alternative assignment will be required.

Student Signature _____ Date _____

Assessment 10—Blog grading rubric

Student Blog Rubric

Adapted from University of Wisconsin-Stout

Evaluation scale:

Exemplary:	32-36 points
Proficient:	28-31 points
Partially Proficient or Incomplete:	< 28 points (resubmit)

CRITERIA	Exemplary	Proficient	Partially	Incomplete	POINTS
Relevance of Content to Students and Parents	**9 points** • Content has useful information • Content is clear, concise; points readers to up to date resources. • Blog is updated frequently	**6 points** • Content points readers to quality resources, is informative • Resources are clearly described so readers can navigate easily	**3 points** • Content points to unrelated information. • Resources are not clearly described so readers cannot navigate easily.	**0 points** • Resources pointed to are inaccurate, misleading or inappropriate • Annotations are missing, do not describe what is found	
Use of Media	**6 points** • Media enhance content and interest. • Creativity enhances content	**4 points** • Most media enhance content. • Most files show creativity	**2 points** • Some media don't enhance content. • Some use of creativity is evident to enhance content.	**0 points** • Media are inappropriate or detract from content.	
Fair Use Guidelines	**6 points** Fair use guidelines are followed with proper citations.	**4 points** Fair use guidelines are frequently followed; most material is cited.	**2 points** Sometimes fair use guidelines are followed with some citations.	**0 points** Fair use guidelines are not followed. Material is improperly cited.	
Links	**3 points** All links are active and functioning.	**2 points** Most links are active	**1 point** Some links are not active.	**0 points** Many links are not active.	
Layout and Text Elements	**3 points** • Fonts are easy-to-read • Use of bullets, italics, bold, enhances readability. • Consistent format throughout	**2 points** • Sometimes fonts, size, bullets, italics, bold, detract from readability. • Minor formatting inconsistencies exist	**1 point** • Text is difficult to read due to formatting	**0 points** • Text is difficult to read with misuse of fonts, size, bullets, italics, bold • Many formatting tools are misused	
Writing Mechanics	**3 points** No grammar, capitalization, punctuation, spelling errors	**2 points** Few grammar, capitalization, punctuation, and spelling errors	**1 point** 4+ errors in grammar, capitalization, punctuation, and spelling	**0 points** More than 6 grammar/ spelling/ punctuation errors.	
				TOTAL POINTS	/36

Article 8—13 Ways Blogs Teach Common Core

13 Ways Blogs Teach Common Core

If you aren't blogging with your students, you're missing one of the most effective tools available for improving student literacy and math. Blogs are easy to use, fun for students, encourage creativity and problem-solving, allow for reflection and feedback, enable publishing and sharing of work, and fulfill many of the Common Core Standards you might be struggling to complete. Aside from math and literacy, Common Core wants students to become accomplished in a variety of intangible skills that promote learning and college and career readiness. Look at these 13 benefits of blogging and how they align with Common Core:

1. **provide and get feedback**—building a community via comments is an integral part of blogging. If you didn't want feedback, you'd publish a white paper or submit work the old fashioned hard copy way. When students publish their ideas in blogs, other students, teachers, parents can provide feedback, join the conversation, and learn from the student.
2. **write-edit-review-rewrite**—teachers don't expect students to get it right the first time. Part of the writing process is revising, editing, rewriting. This is easy with blogs. Students publish a topic, collect comments, incorporate these ideas into their own thinking, and then edit their post.
3. **publish**—the idea that student work is created for a grade then stuffed away in a corner of their closet is disappearing. Current educators want students to publish their work in a way that allows everyone to benefit from the student's knowledge and work. There are many ways to do that—blogs are one of the easiest.
4. **share**—just like publishing, students no longer create for a grade; they share with others. Blogs allow for sharing of not only writing, but artwork, photography, music, multimedia projects, pretty much anything the student can create.
5. **collaborate**—blogs can easily be collaborative. Student groups can publish articles, comment on others, edit and rewrite. They can work together on one blog to cover a wider variety of topics and/or make its design attractive, appealing and enticing to readers.
6. **keyboarding**—blogs are small doses of typing—300-500 words, a few dozen for comments. This is an authentic opportunity to practice the keyboarding skills students will need for Common Core Standards in 4th grade and up.
7. **demonstrate independence**—blogs are about creativity. No two are alike. They offer lots of options for design and formatting so students can tweak it to their preference. Because they are open 24/7, students can do blog work when it suits them, not in the confines of a 50-minute class.
8. **build strong content knowledge**—blog posts can be drafted as the student collects information, posted when the student is ready. Links can be included to provide evidence of student statements, as well as linkbacks for reference and deeper reading for interested students.
9. **respond to the varying demands of audience, task, purpose, and discipline**—Students can create their work in whatever digital tool fits the audience, task, purpose they are focused on, and then embed it into their blog post. This is possible even in a simplified blogging platform like Kidblog. Most online tools (such as Voki, Wordle, and Tagxedo) provide the html codes that can be easily placed in the blog

post. Then, the student at their option can focus on presenting their ideas as music, art, photos, text, an infographic, a word cloud—whatever works for their purposes.

10. **comprehend as well as critique**—student bloggers are expected to critique the posts of others by thoroughly reading the post and commenting based on evidence. If the reader doesn't understand, they ask questions in the comments. This insures that when they evaluate the post, they have all the information required to reach a conclusion.
11. **value evidence**—blogs make it easy to provide all the necessary evidence to support a point of view. Students can link back to sources to provide credit and link to experts to provide credibility for statements. In fact, in the blogosphere, good bloggers are expected to do this as a means of building credibility for opinions they write
12. **use technology and digital media strategically and capably**—certainly, blogs are great for writing, but they're also excellent as digital portfolios to display student work developed in a variety of places. Students pick the technology that fits what they're expected to accomplish in a class, then publish it to the blog. Have you seen the movies students put together on a topic? Some are amazing.
13. **understand other perspectives and cultures**—blogs are published to the Internet. Even private blogs are accessed by many more people than possible with a hand-written paper. Students write knowing that people of all cultures and perspectives will read their material, knowing they can add comments that share their beliefs. This encourages students to develop the habit of thinking about *perspective* as they write.

Don't try all of this at once. Spiral into it, starting in second or third grade. Let their blogging grow with their intellectual skills.

Basics of Posts

Blogs used to be too cutting edge for pedestrian rules like grammar and spelling. That's not true anymore. Before students write their first post, remind them:

- *make content pithy*
- *use correct spelling and grammar*
- *avoid slang*
- *appeal to readers with content and design*
- *interact with readers via questions in the blog and answering comments*
- *avoid mistakes, redundancies, jerky flow by proof reading*

Blogs are everything you want in a school activity—student-centered, independent, supportive of problem solving and creative thinking, transferable to many classes and home activities. If you have questions, add them to the comments. I'll see if I can help.

5th Grade Technology Curriculum: Teacher Manual

Lesson #5 Organizing Ideas

Vocabulary	Problem solving	Skills
• Alignment • Bullets • Citations • Heading • Icons • Indent/exdent • Monitor • Mulligan • Outline • Shift+tab • Title	• What is today's date (check clock in lower right corner or use shortkey) • I can't find my word processing program (if it's software, use Search field) • I got out of outline (backspace to the last bullet and push enter) • What's the difference between a heading and a title? • Can't get outline to work (try shortkeys) • Computer crashed (save early save often)	**New** Brainstorming Mindmapping **Scaffolded** Outlining Keyboarding Speaking/listening Digital citizenship
Academic Applications Writing, research, history, literacy, math, any class to organize thoughts, ideas, research	**Materials Required** textbook and notes, word processing program, graded hardware quizzes, Important Keys quiz, Problem Solving Board sign-up, Evidence Board badges, student workbooks (if using)	**Standards:** CCSS: W.5.5 NETS: 3c, 4b, 5c

Essential Question

How do I organize information more efficiently?

Big Idea

Organizing information precedes analysis and reflection

Teacher Preparation

- Know which tasks weren't completed last week.
- Graded hardware tests.
- Have Important Keys quiz (or link to file).
- Talk with grade-level team so you tie into inquiry.
- Collect words to include in Speak Like a Geek Board.
- Know if you need extra time to complete this lesson.
- Verify all required links are available.
- Integrate tech vocabulary into lesson.
- Ask grade-level team and parents if there are any tech problems students need help with.
- Remind students to bring a science/history/etc. book and notes for today's lesson.

Assessment Strategies

- Anecdotal
- Completed project
- Followed directions
- Signed up for Board
- Completed warm-up, exit ticket
- Joined class conversations
- Used good keyboarding habits
- [tried to] solve own problems
- Decisions followed class rules
- Left room as s/he found it
- Higher order thinking: analysis, evaluation, synthesis
- Habits of mind observed

Steps

Time required: 45 minutes in one sitting or spread throughout the week, allowing a block of 30 minutes to complete the mindmap, brainstorm, or outline

Class warm-up: Keyboard homerow--DanceMat Typing or Popcorn Typer (Google sites)

_____Turn music on to establish a typing rhythm for students. Encourage them to type to

the beat.

_______Review Hardware Quiz. Remind students of Mulligan Rule.

_______Give students the important keys quiz, using sample in keyboarding lesson. If students have workbooks, they can fill out the template from there using the class annotation tool. Allow 5-10 minutes for this quiz. They should know these keys.

_______If you are going to give this multiple times during the year, treat this first quiz as a benchmark and grade subsequent quizzes based on individual improvement (as you do with the speed/accuracy quiz).

_______Review homework (see end of text for complete list)—homerow practice only this month! Use correct posture, hand position.

_______Start Problem-solving Board. Students stand in front of class, share their problem and solutions, and take questions from classmates. You may model this if necessary. Students follow speaking and listening expectations discussed in class. As they present, fill out assessment rubric (*Figure 35*):

Figure 7--Keyboard keys quiz

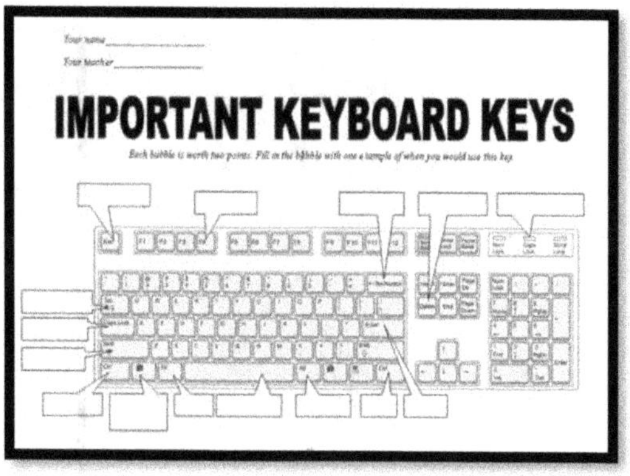

Figure 35—Problem-solving board rubric

PROBLEM SOLVING BOARD

Grading Rubric

Name: ____________________

Class: ____________________

Knew question ____________
Knew answer ____________
Asked audience for help if didn't know answer ____________
No umm's, stutters ____________
Look audience in eye ____________
No nervous movements (giggles, wiggles, etc.) ____________
No nervous noises (giggles,) ____________
Overall ____________

_______Any evidence of learning to post on Evidence Board?

_______Discuss the importance of organizing thinking. How have students done this in the past?

_______Common Core asks that students learn ways to scaffold and support a deeper level of understanding to provide an engine for future learning. This lesson discusses two:

- *brainstorming and mindmapping*
- *outlining*

_______Pick one or both based on the unique needs of your learners and the digital devices you use.

Brainstorming and mindmapping

_____Remind students that they created a mindmap as a large group in first grade (*Figure 36*):

Figure 36—1st grade mindmap

_____This year, students create a mindmap—or brainstorm a topic—in small groups.
_____Introduce concept of 'brainstorming', also called 'mindmapping'—a collaborative visual approach to thinking through and presenting ideas. Brainstorming is a great way to tackle prewriting. It helps students come up with many ideas about a topic.
_____Here are basic classroom brainstorming rules:

- *There are no wrong answers.*
- *Get as many ideas as possible.*
- *Record all ideas.*
- *Do not evaluate ideas presented.*
- *Build new ideas on those of others.*
- *Stress quantity over quality.*

_____General steps for brainstorming:

- *Sit in a comfortable group.*
- *Add central idea to middle of page. Include image if possible.*
- *Add big ideas that support theme. Don't worry if contributions don't seem 'big'—they'll find a home later as a sub-idea, connected to another.*
- *Add ideas as they come.*
- *All ideas down? Now drag ideas around to connect topics that relate.*
- *Evaluate placement of ideas to determine if like ideas are grouped appropriately.*
- *If possible, edit connectors to be fatter for main ideas and thinner for sub ideas. This enables the mind to subconsciously visually categorize ideas.*
- *Add emphasis where needed with color, images, fonts, size (if available).*

_____There are a lot of tools online to create mindmaps. If you don't have a favorite, visit Ask a Tech Teacher's resource pages for *Brainstorming/Mindmaps* and select one that works for you. Some work better depending upon your digital device. You can also use Google Draw or Word.

_____Open selected program on class screen to demonstrate.
_____Map a book being read, a historic event, or a mathematical concept. Examples include *Figure 37a* in SpiderScribe; *Figure 37b* in MindMaple; *Figure 37c* in Bubbl.us:

Figure 37a—SpiderScribe; 37b—MindMaple; 37c—Bubbl.us

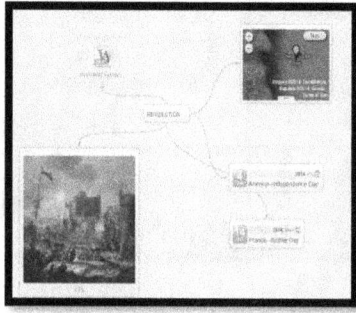 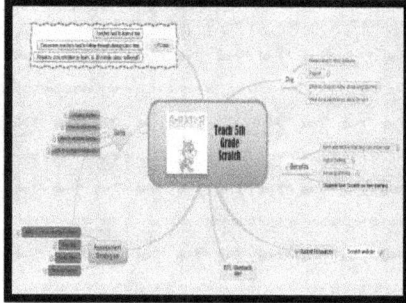 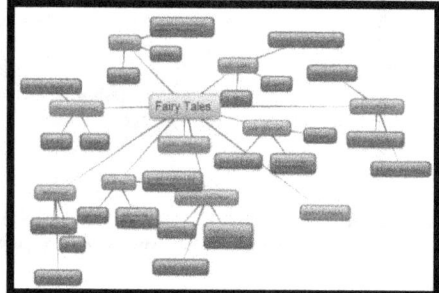

_____Once you've demonstrated, have small groups map their ideas.
_____For a complete lesson plan on *Brainstorming and Mindmapping*, visit Structured Learning Lesson Plans.

Outlining

_____How students access an outline tool will differ if they use a computer (PC, Mac, and Chromebook) or an iPad. Be familiar with the app you plan to use so you can adapt instructions as needed.
_____Discuss outlining with students. Help them understand that outlines:

- *encourage a better understanding of a topic*
- *promote reflection on a topic*
- *assist analysis of a topic*

_____Open a word processing program. Put heading at top (name, teacher, date). What's the purpose of the heading? Add date with shortkey.
_____If you don't use MS Word or Google Docs on your digital device, try:

- *OneNote—software, a web app, or an iPad app*

_____If you're an iPad school, try one of these:

- *The Google Docs or MS Word app*
- *Quicklyst – quick notes and list on iPads*
- *OmniOutliner –for iPads and online*

_____Any time students go online, remind them how to do so safely.
_____Center title beneath heading. What's the purpose of a 'title'?
_____Adapt for the toolbar in the word processing program you use. In MS Word and Google Docs, use: 1) bullet or numbered list, 2) indent—push text to right (subpoint), and 3) exdent—push text

to left (more important point). See *Figure 38* (in MS Word—similar in Google Docs):

Figure 38a—How to outline in MS Word; 38b—Google Docs

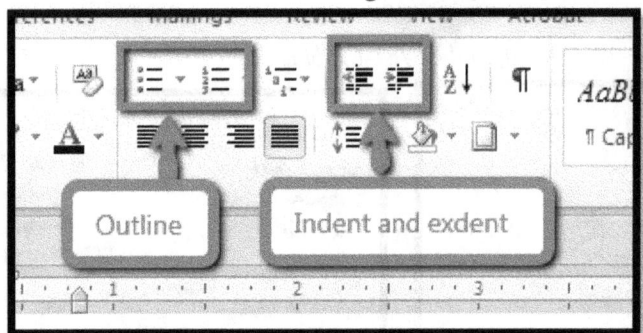 

_____Or use tab to indent and Shift+tab to exdent (for Word and Docs)—I like this better.
_____Outline chapter headings, subheadings. Summarize and/or paraphrase relevant points in text.
_____Once completed (*Figures 39a-c*), work with a neighbor to add information by editing the outline. Use data from print/digital sources, class discussion, and personal experience. Note source where relevant.
_____Work individually or in small groups.

Figure 39a—Outline in Word; 39b—Google Docs; 39c--Workflowy

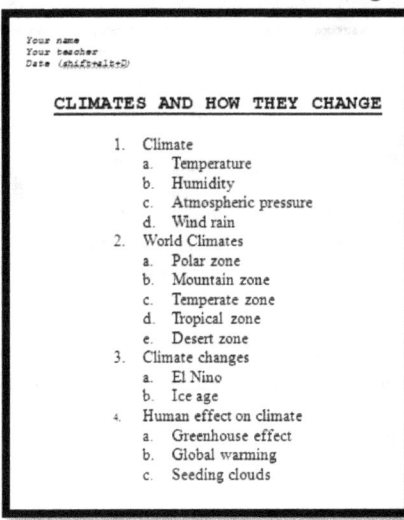 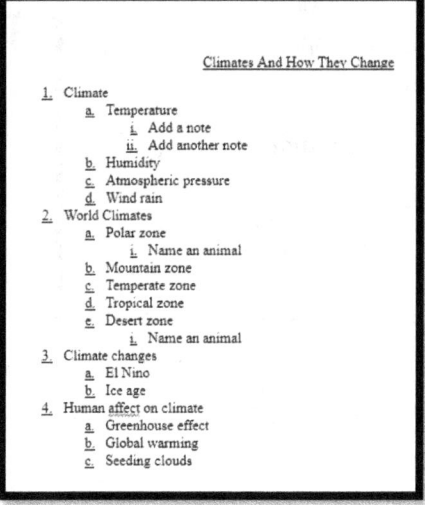 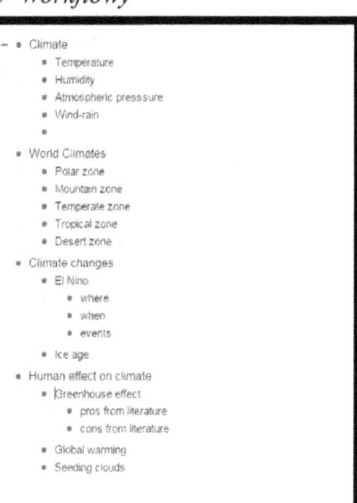

_____Remind students: Every time they use computers, practice keyboarding skills.
_____Remind students: Save early save often. Why? How often?
_____Throughout class, check for understanding.
_____If printing, preview to be sure outline takes only one page. Save (or save-as? Which is right for this situation) with student last name in the file name. Close with Alt+F4.
_____Why include student name in file name when saving? Demonstrate a search for a student document. See how their files show up even if they didn't save it to their digital portfolio. Putting last name in file name makes it harder to lose work.
_____Remind students to transfer knowledge to classroom or home.
_____Review how students save (*Figure 40* is a thumbnail of poster in Appendix):

Figure 40—How to save your file

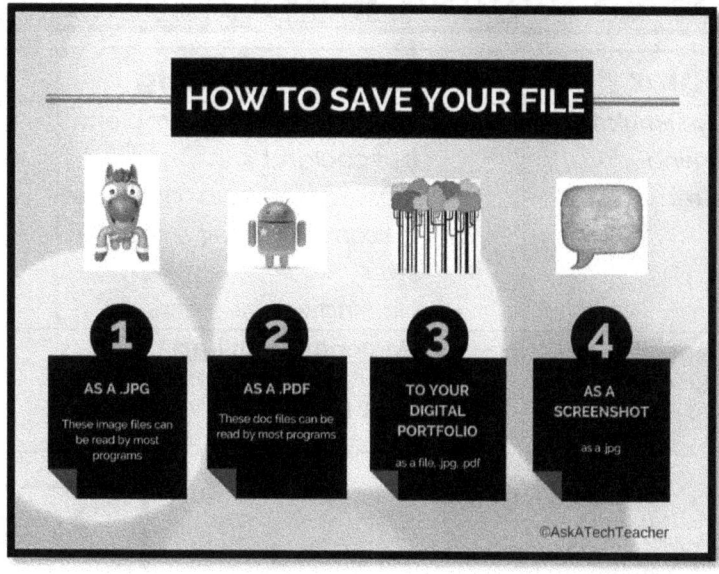

Class exit ticket: *Share or email outline to teacher.*

Differentiation

- Add Board presenters to class calendar.
- Add Blank Keyboard quiz to class calendar.
- Set up a 'Discussion Board' on class website or blog where students post the problem solving question they answered in their presentation. This can be a resource in student daily work and during the upcoming (optional) assessment.
- Early finishers: visit class internet start page for websites that tie into classwork.
- Show how to give credit for sources with an online site like EasyBib (Google for address)

Lesson #6 Problem Solving

Vocabulary	Problem solving	Skills
• Cerebrally-stimulating • Habits of mind • Inductive reasoning • Irrelevant • Life skill • Relevant	• I tried to solve the problem, but couldn't • I asked for help and the person didn't know the answer • Nothing works!	**New** Using a poll **Scaffolded** Problem solving Keyboarding
Academic Applications Any class, school and life, college and career	**Materials Required** keyboard program, Problem Solving Board rubrics, Evidence Board badges, student workbooks (if using)	**Standards** CCSS Standards for Math. Practice NETS: 4a, 5c

Essential Question

How do I solve a problem I've never seen before?

Big Idea

Problem solving is 'cerebrally-stimulating'—and fun!

Teacher Preparation

- Know which tasks weren't completed last week.
- Have Important Keys quizzes ready to review.
- Be prepared to use domain-specific tech vocabulary.
- Know whether you need extra time to complete lesson.
- Ask grade-level team and parents if there are any tech problems students need help with.
- Collect words students don't understand for Speak Like a Geek. Use a physical Vocabulary Wall (i.e., a bulletin board) or a virtual wall like Padlet. Let students add words independently.

Assessment Strategies

- Anecdotal
- Committed to solving own problems
- Decisions followed class rules
- Left room as student found it
- Completed warm-up, exit ticket
- Joined classroom conversations
- Higher order thinking: analysis, evaluation, synthesis
- Habits of mind observed

Steps

Time required: 45 minutes in one sitting or spread throughout week with 30 minutes set aside for Problem Solving discussion and activities

Class warm-up: Ask students to solve a class-specific problem (say, how to get to Thursday's field trip) using a strategy in Figure 42

_____Practice home row using DanceMat Typing or Popcorn Typer (Google for website). Observe student posture, elbows at side, hand position.

_____Turn music on to establish a typing rhythm for students. Encourage them to type at the speed of the beat.

_____Continue Problem-solving Board presentations. Review expectations and grading.

_____Any students have tech problems they'd like to share?

_____Any evidence of learning to post on Evidence Board?

_____Review results of Important Keys quiz with students. Discuss grading.

_____Give students blank keyboard quiz (*Figure 41* is a thumbnail—full size in Keyboarding Lesson). They can work in groups. Flip all keyboards over so no one is tempted.

Figure 41—Blank keyboard quiz

_____If students are using workbooks, they can fill in the template found there.
_____Since students will take this multiple times this year, treat it as you do the speed/accuracy quiz: This first quiz is a benchmark. Next will be graded on improvement.
_____Discuss Problem Solving. This is a life skill that transcends a subject.
_____Discuss what it means to be a 'problem solver'. Who do students go to when they need a problem solved? Parents? Do students believe that person gets it right more often than others? Would they believe most people are wrong half the time?
_____Review the two articles at the end of the lesson:

- *"How to Teach Students to Problem Solve"*
- *"How Minecraft Teaches Problem Solving"*

_____Problem solving is closely aligned with logical thinking, critical thinking, reasoning, and habits of mind. Discuss why students should become problem solvers.
_____Discuss characteristics of a 'problem solver' (from Common Core):

- *Use appropriate tools strategically.*
- *Attend to precision.*
- *Make sense of problems and persevere in solving them.*
- *Value evidence.*
- *Comprehend as well as critique.*
- *Understand other perspectives.*
- *Demonstrate independence.*

_____Discuss student responsibility to make up missed classes. How is this 'problem solving'?
_____Discuss why you ask students to solve hardware problems independently.
_____Discuss common problems students will be expected to solve by the end of 5th grade by referring to those included in the Problem-solving Board.
_____Problems at the beginning of weekly lessons relate to the activities they will complete during the week. They may or may not be different/the same as those on the Problem-solving Board. By the

end of each lesson, expect students to solve these independent of assistance.
_____See *Figure 42* for list of **How to Solve a Problem** (full size in appendix):

Figure 42—How to solve a problem

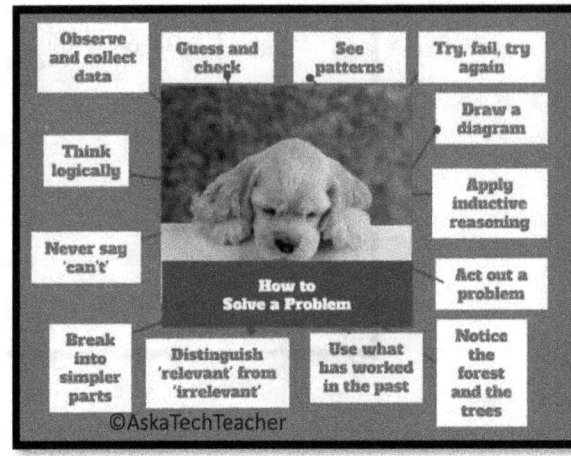

_____When students face a problem, use *Figure 42* strategies to solve it before asking for assistance.
_____Discuss 'Big Idea': Is problem solving 'cerebrally-stimulating? Is it fun? Why or why not? Discuss great quotes in *Figure 43*.

Figure 43—Problem-solving quotes

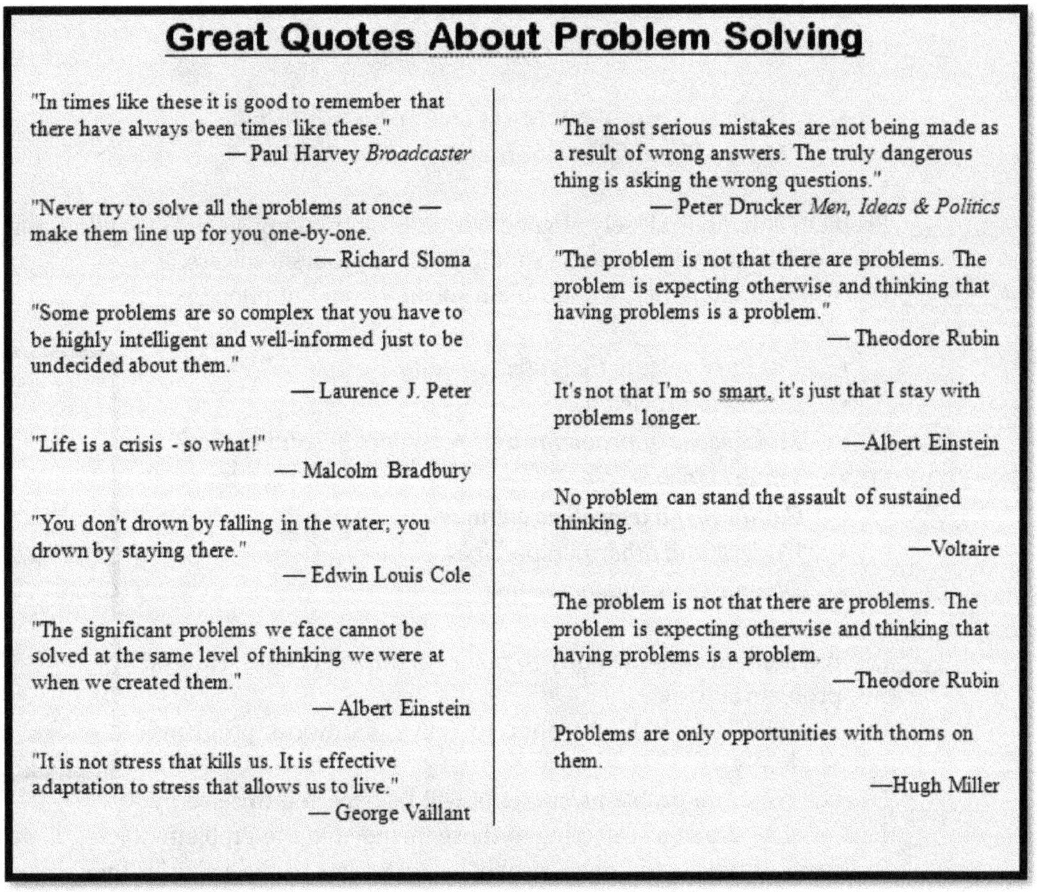

Great Quotes About Problem Solving

"In times like these it is good to remember that there have always been times like these."
— Paul Harvey *Broadcaster*

"Never try to solve all the problems at once — make them line up for you one-by-one.
— Richard Sloma

"Some problems are so complex that you have to be highly intelligent and well-informed just to be undecided about them."
— Laurence J. Peter

"Life is a crisis - so what!"
— Malcolm Bradbury

"You don't drown by falling in the water; you drown by staying there."
— Edwin Louis Cole

"The significant problems we face cannot be solved at the same level of thinking we were at when we created them."
— Albert Einstein

"It is not stress that kills us. It is effective adaptation to stress that allows us to live."
— George Vaillant

"The most serious mistakes are not being made as a result of wrong answers. The truly dangerous thing is asking the wrong questions."
— Peter Drucker *Men, Ideas & Politics*

"The problem is not that there are problems. The problem is expecting otherwise and thinking that having problems is a problem."
— Theodore Rubin

It's not that I'm so smart, it's just that I stay with problems longer.
—Albert Einstein

No problem can stand the assault of sustained thinking.
—Voltaire

The problem is not that there are problems. The problem is expecting otherwise and thinking that having problems is a problem.
—Theodore Rubin

Problems are only opportunities with thorns on them.
—Hugh Miller

_____Discuss shortkeys. How are these problem solving? Demonstrate this by asking students to tell you how to perform a skill. Is it easier to share the shortkey? See *Figures 44a* and *44b* for examples of platform-specific shortkeys (full-size posters in Appendix):

Figure 44a—iPad shortkeys; 44b—Chromebook shortkeys

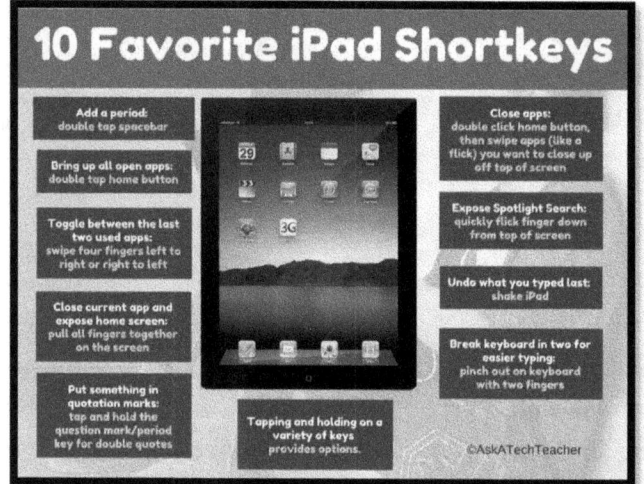 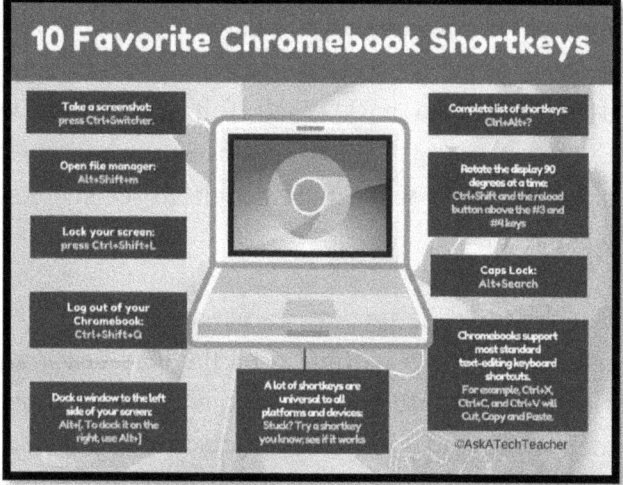

_____Throughout class, check for understanding.
_____Remind students to transfer knowledge to other classes and home.
_____Occasionally when students have difficulty doing what you are teaching, ask why. And listen. You may be surprised by the answer.

Class exit ticket: ***Take a poll that asks students to choose problem-solving strategies they are most likely to use in the future.***

Differentiation

- *Remind students to post their Problem-solving Board problem to the Discussion Board on class website or blog where it can be a resource for other students and during the upcoming assessment.*
- *Early finishers: visit class internet start page for websites that tie into classwork.*

Article 9—How to Teach Students to Solve Problems

How to Teach Students to Solve Problems

Of all the skills students learn in school, **problem solving** arguably is the most valuable and the hardest to learn. It's fraught with uncertainty—what if the student looks stupid as he tries? What if everyone's watching and he can't do it—isn't it better not to try? What if it works, but not the way Everyone wants it to? When you're a student, it's understandable when they decide to let someone tell them what to do.

But this isn't the type of learner we want to build. We want risk-takers, those willing to be the load-bearing pillar of the class. And truthfully, by a certain age, kids want to make up their own mind. Our job as teachers is to provide the skills necessary for them to make wise, effective decisions.

It's not a stand-alone subject. It starts with a habit of inquiry in all classes—math, LA, history, science, any of them. I constantly ask students questions, get them to think and evaluate, provide evidence that supports process as well as product. Whether they're writing, reading, or creating an art project, I want them thinking what they're doing and why.

Common Core puts problem solving front and center. It comes up in ELA ("*Students will be challenged and asked questions that push them to refer back to what they've read. This stresses critical-thinking, problem-solving, and analytical skills that are required for success in college, career, and life.*"), but is inescapable in Math. In fact, students cannot fully meet the Math Standards without understanding how to effectively approach the unknown. Consider the Standards for Mathematical Practice that overlay all grade levels K-12:

- *Make sense of problems and persevere in solving them*
- *Reason abstractly and quantitatively*
- *Construct viable arguments and critique the reasoning of others*
- *Model*
- *Use appropriate tools strategically*
- *Attend to precision*
- *Look for and make use of structure*
- *Look for and express regularity in repeated reasoning*

Do these sound like great strategies for more than math? How about deciding what classes to take? Or whether to make a soccer or basketball game on the weekend? Or which college to attend? Using these eight tools strategically, with precision, and tenaciously is a great first step.

The question becomes: How do students **learn to use them**? Certainly, as they accomplish their grade-level math curriculum, you as teacher remind them they aren't doing a multiplication problem (or an Algebra one); rather they're reasoning abstractly or using appropriate tools strategically, or expressing regularity in repeated reasoning. But for deep learning, hands-on authentic experience is required. Let's say, for example, the class is investigating the purchase of an MP3 player. Should they purchase an IPod, a smartphone, a dedicated use MP3 player, or a different option? How do students arrive at a decision—solve that problem? Ask students to work through the steps below as they address a decision. Ask them to note where they accomplish one or more of the Standards for Mathematical Practice above:

1. What do you want in an MP3 player? Should it play music, show videos, pictures, communicate with others, be a phone also? Make that list so you know how to evaluate information as you collect it (**compare/contrast**).
2. What do you know about the topic (**evidence**)? Have you seen some you liked or didn't like? What have you heard about those on your list? You are a good resource to yourself. Don't discount that. You'll be surprised how much you know on a variety of topics. This step is important to college and career. Future employers and schools want you to think, to use your intelligence and your knowledge to evaluate and solve problems.
3. What advice do knowledgeable friends have (**perspective taking, collaboration**)? You want the input of MP3 users. Your friends will think whatever they own is the best, because they're vested in that choice, but listen to their evidence and the conclusions they draw based on that. This is important to a team-oriented environment. Listen to all sides, even if you don't agree.
4. **Dig deeper (close reading)**. Check other resources (**uncover knowledge**). This includes:
   o *people who don't like the product*
   o *online sources. Yep, you might as well get used to online research if you aren't yet. Statistics show more people get their news from blogs than traditional media (newspapers, TV) and you know where blogs are.*
   o *your parents who will bring up topics friends didn't, like cost, longevity, reliability*
5. **Evaluate your resources (integration of knowledge)**. How much money do you have? Eliminate the choices that don't fit your constraints (money, time, use, etc.) If there are several choices that seem to work, this will help you make the decision. You might have to save money or get a job so you can afford the one you've chosen. Or, you might decide to settle for a

cheaper version. Just make sure you are aware of how you made the choice and are satisfied with it.
6. What are the **risks involved** in making the decision (**reflection**)? Maybe buying an MP3 player means you can't do something else you wanted. Are you comfortable with that choice?
7. **Make a decision (transfer learning)**. That's right. Make a decision and live with it knowing you've considered all available information and evaluated it logically and objectively.

Optionally, you might have students evaluate problem solving in their favorite game, say, Minecraft. All it requires is that as they play, think about what they're doing:

- *What is the goal of Minecraft? How is it best achieved*
- *What does the student know about playing the game that can be used in achieving the goal?*
- *Does working with friends and gaining feedback make life easier in Minecraft?*
- *How does experience in the game affect progress?*
- *And so on...*

This is how students become the problem solvers required of their Future. When the day comes that how they solve a problem affects the direction their life takes (college, career, marriage, children, a tattoo), they'll be happy to have strategies that make it easier.

Article 10—How Minecraft Teaches Problem Solving

How Minecraft Teaches Problem Solving

Recently, *Scientific American* declared "..."*not only is Minecraft immersive and creative, but it is an excellent platform for making almost any subject area more engaging.*" A nod from a top science magazine to the game many parents wish their kids had never heard of. This follows Common Sense Media's seal of approval. On the surface, it's not so surprising. Something like 80% of five-to-eight year-olds play games and 97% of teens. Early simulations like Reader Rabbit are still used in classrooms to drill reading and math skills.

But Minecraft, a blocky retro role-playing simulation that's more Lego than svelte hi-tech wizardry, isn't just the game *du jour*. Kids would skip dinner to play it if parents allowed. Minecraft is role playing and so much more.

Let me back up a moment. Most simulation games—where players role-play life in a pretend world—aren't so much Make Your Own Adventure as See If You Survive Ours. Players are a passenger in a hero's journey, solving riddles, advancing through levels and unlocking prizes. That's not Minecraft. Here, they create the world. Nothing happens without their decision—not surroundings or characters or buildings rising or holes being dug. There isn't a right or wrong answer. There's merely what You decide and where those decisions land You. Players have one goal: To survive. Prevail. They solve problems or cease to exist. If the teacher wants to use games to learn history, Minecraft won't throw students into a fully fleshed simulation of the American Revolution. It'll start with a plot of land and students will write the story, cast the characters, and create the entire 1776 world. Again, think Legos.

And still, my students hang my picture in the Teacher Hall of Fame every time I let them play Minecraft—which I do regularly. Of course, I provide guidelines. Which they love. It's fascinating that today's game playing youth want a set of rules they must beat, parameters they must meet, levels (read: standards) they must achieve, and a Big Goal (think: graduation) they can only reach after a lot of hard work, intense thinking, and mountains of problems. Look into the eyes of a fifth grader who just solved the unsolvable—something most adults s/he knows can't do. You'll remember why you're a teacher.

A note: Any time students use the Internet, start with a discussion on how to use it safely. This is especially important with multi-player games like Minecraft (you will close the system at school, but that may not be the case in the student's home). It is fairly easy for students to create their own servers (requires no hardware, just a bit of coding) and invite friends into their Minecraft world. Encourage this rather than entering an unknown server-world.

In case you must 'sell' this idea to your administration, here are three great reasons why students should use Minecraft in school: Reading, Writing, and Problem Solving.

Problem Solving

Because Minecraft is not story-based, everything that happens requires a decision on the player's part. How well-thought out those decisions are affects what happens next. This is great motivation for critical thinking and problem solving.

Of all Minecraft's educational strengths, this may be the greatest. Players start with nothing and must build their way to security, safety, food, shelter, companionship. What a primer in problem solving. I've found throughout my teaching career that the most effective lessons are those with real-world applications. Theory makes sense to only a few and scares the rest. Here, in a world students eagerly enter, are real problems they must solve that will make a difference in their life. When a settler's wagon floods in Oregon Trail, players get another one. When they are attacked in Minecraft and have nowhere to hide because they haven't built shelter, it ruins the player's day.

That's reality.

In case you're not a Minecraft aficionado, I'll let you in on a secret: There are no manuals. Players learn by doing, failing, trying again. Suddenly, Common Core Standards for Mathematical Practice take on a whole new importance:

What Math Standard Expects	What Game Delivers
Make sense of problems and persevere in solving them	Students work to understand and solve problems within game constructs
Reason abstractly and quantitatively	To play effectively requires student understand what is occurring and visualize solutions.
Construct viable arguments and critique the reasoning of others	The game's nature requires students interact with others to discern who can assist in achieving goals.
Model	Game models reality students likely will never experience, but wish they could.
Use appropriate tools strategically	As with real life, players must determine what tools are available (both physical and psychological) and how to use them to achieve goals
Look for and make use of structure	Life in the game works better with a plan

If you're using Minecraft as a class activity, consider these best practices:

- *Expect a learning curve and plan time for one. Some students won't need it; others will.*
- *Have students work in groups. This helps non-gamers with mechanics.*
- *Be involved. Don't let gamers intimidate you from observing and directing*
- *Set behavioral expectations. Your goals are different from typical game-play. Let students know what they are.*
- *Align goals with learning. Make this clear to students.*
- *Scaffold non-gamers with groups.*
- *Update parents consistently. They will question using a game to learn reading and writing.*
- *Make failure fun. Game purpose isn't to win; it's to learn.*
- *Expect students to play in many locations. In fact, encourage that.*

There you have it—how I use Minecraft to scaffold reading, writing, and problem solving. From this beginning, you'll find unlimited applications. I have online efriends whose students use Minecraft to build molecules for a chemistry class, designs for 3D printing, and bridges for an 8th grade science project. Students quickly move beyond my list of questions to creating their own. We use Twitter as a shared resource, and students become Minecraft Tweeple, tweeting questions and answers using #hashtags. When they solve a prickly game problem, they type #problem with their name into our class Twitter stream. That appears on the class screen for everyone's benefit.

One last point: I'm not going to kid you. Using Minecraft takes a commitment on the teacher's part. It's new. You're breaking ground. You'll have to talk yourself blue explaining to stakeholders why this is a good decision. You'll put long hours in researching, studying, managing, and few will thank you.

But the kids will. And when they move on, they'll remember that season with you, and how you taught them to think—I mean, let them play their favorite game.

5th Grade Technology Curriculum: Teacher Manual

Lesson #7 Graphic Organizers

Vocabulary	Problem solving	Skills
• Background • Copyright laws • Diagram • Fair use • Graphic organizer • Public domain • Scholarly research • Table • Visual learners	• What if log-on doesn't work? • My computer crashed (did you save early save often?) • My screen froze (is a dialogue box open, asking a question?) • I forgot my Presentation (if there's room, move to later week) • Image has a word written in background (find a different one)	**New** Padlet **Scaffolded** Graphic organizers Digital citizenship Keyboarding skills Speaking/listening
Academic Applications Science, history, literature, more	**Materials Required** Board rubrics and badges, word processing program or online widget that organizes ideas	**Standards:** CCSS.W.5.4 NETS: 4b, 5b-d, 6a-d

Essential Question

How do I use the computer to communicate visually?

Big Idea

Students use visual communications to share ideas in a clearer, more succinct fashion

Teacher Preparation

- Talk with grade-level team so you tie into their inquiry.
- Be prepared to use domain-specific tech vocabulary.
- Verify all required links are available.
- Know whether you need extra time to complete lesson.
- Ask grade-level team and parents if there are tech problems students need help with.
- Is class shorter than 45 minutes? Highlight items most important to class studies and leave the rest for 'later'.
- Know which tasks weren't completed last week and whether they are necessary to move forward.
- Collect words students don't understand to include in Lesson 20 Speak Like a Geek Board presentations.
- If you offer afterschool tech help manned by students, verify they will be there during their class.

Assessment Strategies

- *[tried to] solve own problems*
- *Left room as student found it*
- *Completed warm-up, exit ticket*
- *Joined class conversations*
- *Worked well in a group*
- *Used good keyboarding habits*
- *Completed project*
- *Saved to digital portfolio*
- *Used data from various sources*
- *Understood how graphic organizers aid understanding*
- *Higher order thinking: analysis, evaluation, synthesis*
- *Habits of mind observed*

Steps

Time required: 45 minutes in one sitting or broken up throughout the week with 30 minutes set aside for the graphic organizer

Class warm-up: Students post five words describing a 'visual organizer' on a Padlet wall. Embed this into class start page, blog, or another place that allows it.

_____Continue Problem-solving Board presentations.

_____Any evidence of learning to post on Evidence Board? Have students used problems discussed last week or have they had tech problems they'd like to get solutions to?

_____Today, students create a graphic organizer. Share examples from past years (*Figures 45a-c*):

Figure 45a-c—Graphic organizers in K-4

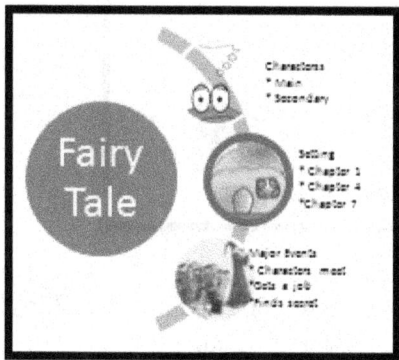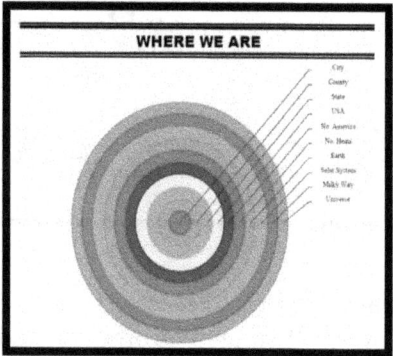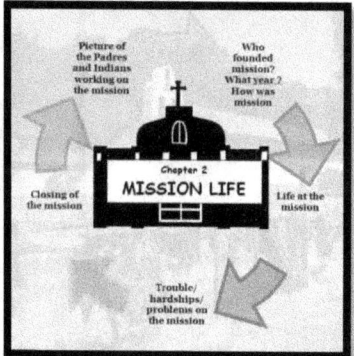

_____Discuss visual learning. How do graphics organize the topic? What task might they be particularly appropriate to? How about what audience?

_____Open the program you use to create graphic organizers. It might be MS Word, Office 365, Google Draw, or an online tool. *Figures 45a -c* are in MS Word. *Figure 46a* uses Google Draw. *Figure 46b* uses an online tool:

Figure 46a—Graphic organizer in Google Draw; 46b—in online tool

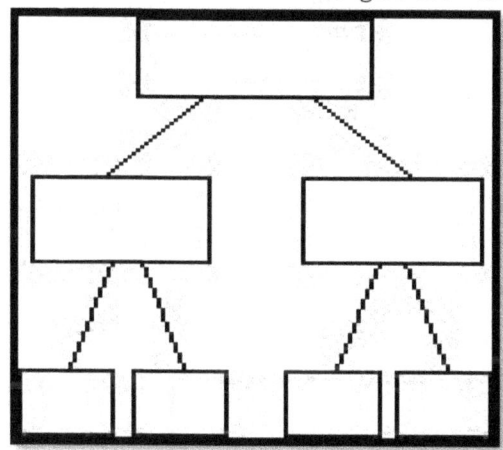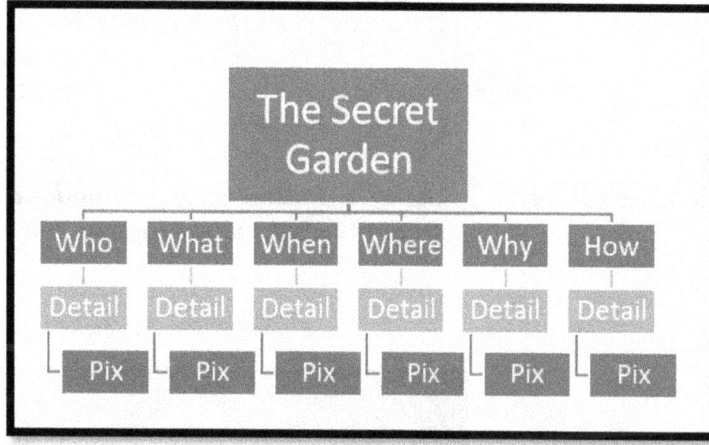

_____For more options of mostly free online graphic organizers, visit Ask a Tech Teacher's resources pages, *Visual Organizers*.

_____Discuss how to find the template that matches the topic.

_____After selecting a graphic organizer, students add heading (name, teacher, and date), then watch as you demo the graphic organizer on the class screen.

_____If necessary, show students how to turn the page from 'portrait' to 'landscape'.

_____Have students suggest categories and subcategories that fit the topic (for example, in *Figure 47*, what adaptations helped animals survive?) and record their input. Show how to add shapes.

_____This can be a formative assessment of what they remember about graphic organizers from K-4.

_____If you're going to add pictures (as shown in *Figure 47*), review how to search for them on the Internet, and copy-paste to the organizer.

Figure 47—5th grade graphic organizer

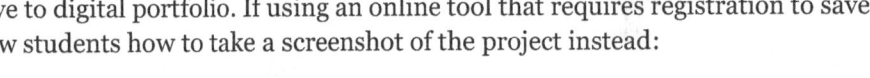

____Discuss using Internet images (discussed in detail in the Lesson on Digital Citizenship).
____Now students complete their graphic organizer individually or in small groups.
____Remind students: Every time they use the computer, practice keyboarding skills.
____If necessary, add citations to page.
____Save to digital portfolio. If using an online tool that requires registration to save, show students how to take a screenshot of the project instead:

- **Windows**: *the Snipping Tool*
- **Chromebook**: *hold down the control key and press the window switcher key*
- **Mac**: *Command Shift 3 to do a full screenshot and Command Shift 4 to take a partial*
- **Surface tablet**: *hold down volume and Windows button at the same time*
- **iPad**: *hold Home button and power button at same time*

____If printing, print preview first to be sure everything fits on one page.
____Throughout class, check for understanding.

Class exit ticket: **Using a Padlet wall (embedded into class start page as in Figure 48), students share what type of project would suit a graphic organizer.**

Figure 48—Padlet embedded into class start page

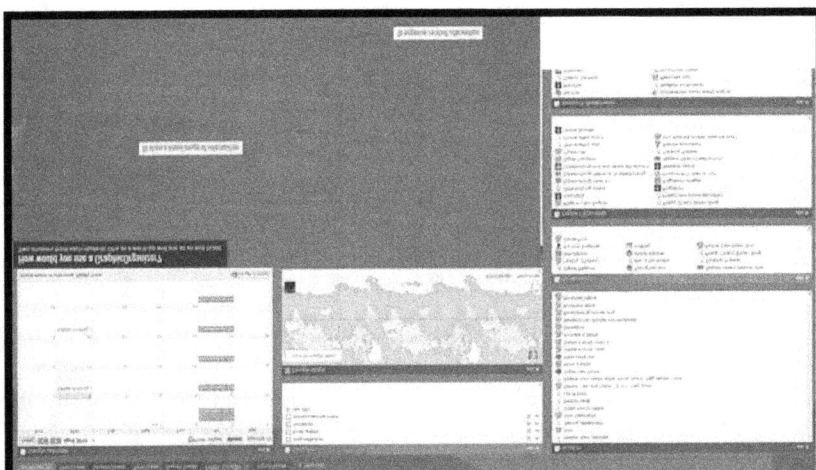

Differentiation

- Create a table to convey the same information a different way.
- Use another visual organizer. What's the difference in communication of ideas?
- Remind students to post their Problem-solving Board problem to the Discussion Board on class website or blog where it can be a resource for other students.
- Early finishers: visit class internet start page for websites that tie into classwork.
- Replace this with 5th Grade Lesson #3 Classify Animals Like a Pro in curriculum extenders (from Structured Learning).

Problem solving: If your screen freezes:

- *"Smash forehead on keyboard to continue..."*
- *"Enter any 11-digit prime number to continue..."*

5th Grade Technology Curriculum: Teacher Manual

Lesson #8 Word Processing

Vocabulary	Problem solving	Skills
• Align • Assessment • Autoshape • Dialogue • Squiggly lines • Synonym • Text box • Word processing • Wrap	• Can I use F7 for spell check? (Yes) • Can't find a word on a page (Ctrl+F) • Can't move image (check wrap) • Didn't finish (That's OK. Assessment tells which skills were difficult). • I deleted my story (push Ctrl+Z) • My screen is too small (click + in lower right corner or Ctrl+) • Where are synonyms (right click)	**New** **Scaffolded** Word processing tools Keyboarding habits Speaking and listening
Academic Applications All writing-intensive classes—lit, history, more	**Materials Required** word processing, Problem Solving Board rubrics, Evidence Board badges, project guidelines, student workbooks (if using)	**Standards** CCSS.W.5.3 NETS: 1d, 3d

Essential Question

What are essential skills required to create scholarly documents?

Big Idea

Students understand the basics of word processing

Teacher Preparation

- Each student brings a story they've written.
- Be prepared to integrate domain-specific vocabulary.
- Talk with grade level team--tie into writing conventions.
- Collect words to include in Speak Like a Geek Board.
- Know if you need extra time to complete this lesson.
- Know which tasks weren't completed last week and whether they are necessary to move forward.
- Ask grade-level team and parents for tech problems students need help with.
- If you offer afterschool tech help manned by students, verify students will be there.

Assessment Strategies

- Completed word processing assessment
- Followed directions
- Transferred knowledge from prior lessons
- Completed presentation
- Completed warm-up
- Used good keyboarding habits
- [tried to] solve own problems
- Left room as student found it
- Higher order thinking: analysis, evaluation, synthesis
- Habits of mind observed

Steps

Time required: 45 minutes in a single sitting or 35 minutes in one sitting with other activities (Problem Solving Board, discussions, Evidence Board) spread throughout the week

Class warm-up: Keyboarding QWERTY row (or whichever row you've reached)

_____Continue Problem-solving Board presentations.

_____Homework due last day of month. Add that it's due 'by midnight' to remind students the Internet is open 24/7.

_____ Any tech problems students need help with? Any evidence of learning for Evidence Board?
_____ Open the word processing program you use at your school—MS Word, Office 365, Open Office, Google Docs, Notes. Review layout with students if necessary.
_____ If you have iPads, you can use the free Microsoft and Mac apps, but be familiar with these as they will have differences from the fully-functioning software or online tools.
_____ Remind students of their many 2nd-4th word processing projects (*Figures 49a-d*)—if you've been using the SL technology curriculum:

Figure 49a-d—Projects in word processing

  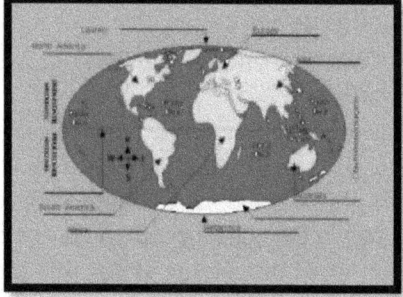

Once there was a ghost, a   and a pumpkin. They lived in a haunted house. **Guess** what their favorite holiday was?

_____ Review tips in articles at the end of the lesson on MS Word and Google Docs.
_____ Students take the next half hour to type and format a story they've written. It will:

- *orient reader by establishing a situation and introducing a character*
- *organize an event sequence that unfolds naturally*
- *use narrative techniques, such as dialogue, description, and pacing, to develop experiences and events or show the responses of characters to situations*
- *use a variety of transitional words, phrases to manage the sequence of events*
- *use concrete words and phrases and sensory details to convey events precisely*
- *provide a conclusion that follows from the narrated experiences or events*

_____ Additionally, provide evidence of student tech skills using word processing:

- *heading right-aligned at top of page*
- *title centered underneath in Comic Sans, 14 font size, bold*
- *story written in 12 font size, Times New Roman*
- *2nd paragraph written in 16 font size, Papyrus*
- *bulleted list (maybe items your main character took with them)*
- *'The End' in Word Art or another title font and appearance*
- *footer with student name*

_____ It should take less than fifteen minutes to type. Do the math with students:

300 words per page
WPM rate of 25 WPM
300 /25 = 12 minutes

_____ Remind students: Every time they use computer, practice good keyboarding.

_____Discuss how to come up with a title. It must:

- *be concise and pithy*
- *draw the reader in*
- *be exciting*

_____When finished, add:

- *border*
- *picture with citation*
- *text is wrapped around the picture*
- *colored call out*
- *shaded text box with a quote from the story or the theme*

_____Here are two sample instructions to share with students: *Figure 50a* in MS Word (or Office 365) and *Figure 50b* in Google Docs. If you'd like to use this lesson as a summative assessment (*Assessment 11*) on word processing skills, this template makes that easy. Otherwise, use it to allow students to be more independent and self-directed in their work:

Figure 50a—MS Word; 50b—Google Docs

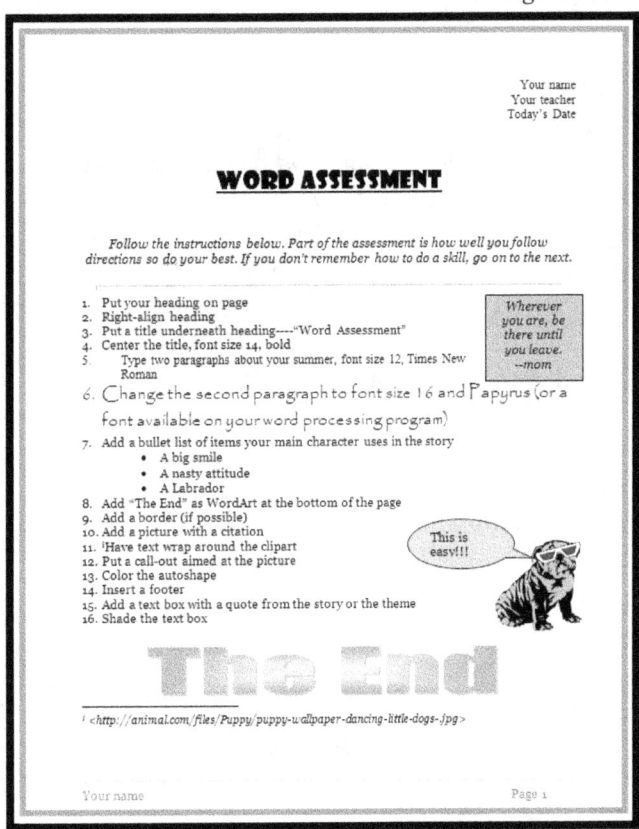 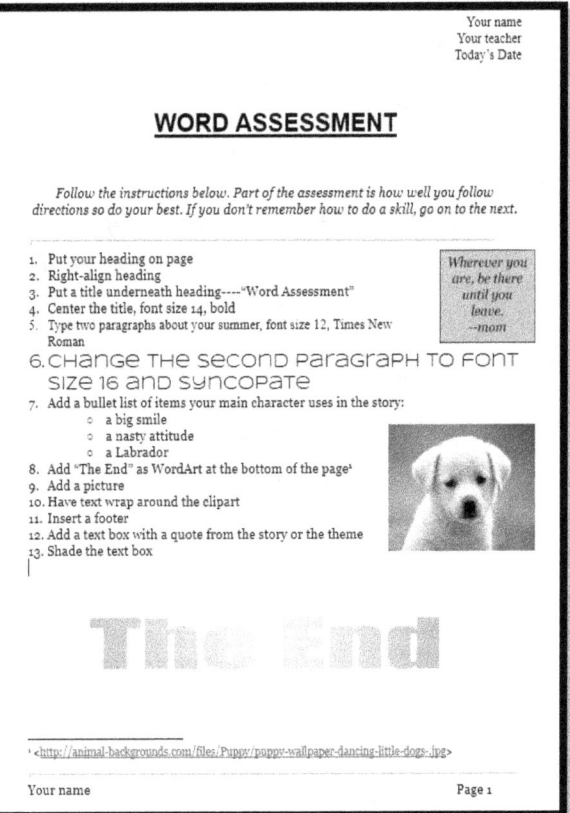

_____If students are using workbooks, they can access this assessment there.
_____Adapt as needed for Chromebooks or iPads.
_____Remind students: Every time they keyboard, practice good habits.

5th Grade Technology Curriculum: Teacher Manual

_____Use technology to spell- and grammar-check (red and green squiggly lines). Explain grammar-check is often wrong so students must decide themselves whether to accept corrections.

_____Use synonym finder (right click) to add descriptive detail and find interesting non-repetitive words to communicate story ideas.

_____Save to digital portfolio. Why 'save' once and 'save-as' the second time? What's the difference?

_____Make sure story fits on one page. Resize images as needed. Print/share/publish as is the custom in your classroom.

_____After submitting assessment, students work with a partner to highlight (use word processing highlighter tool) story parts that include:

- *effective technique*
- *descriptive details*
- *clear event sequences*

_____Throughout class, check for understanding.

_____Remind students to transfer knowledge to classroom or home.

Class exit ticket: None

Differentiation

- *Insert watermark.*
- *Change font, font color and font size for 5 words.*
- *Share stories on blogs (if they have one). Comment on stories of classmates.*
- *Save stories as PDFs, then import into reader and share during Silent Reading time.*
- *Remind students to post their Problem-solving Board problem to the Discussion Board on class website or blog where it can be a resource for other students.*
- *If homework is due, add to class calendar.*
- *Early finishers: visit class internet start page for websites that tie into classwork.*
- *Remind students to blog about their Fascinating Fact—at least one sentence. These will be used for Google Earth Tour in Lesson 21.*
- *Replace with 3rd Grade Lesson #1 Compare with Venn Diagrams in curriculum extenders (from Structured Learning).*

"I have traveled the length and breadth of this country and talked with the best people, and I can assure you that data processing is a fad that won't last out the year."

– *The editor in charge of business books for Prentice Hall, 1957*

Assessment 11—Word processing summative (optional)

Your name
Your teacher
Today's Date

WORD ASSESSMENT

Follow the instructions below. Part of the assessment is how well you read and complete directions. Do your best. If you don't remember how to do a skill, go on to the next.

- Put your heading on page
- Right-align heading
- Put a title underneath heading——"Word Assessment"
- Center the title, font Comic Sans, font size 14, bold
    - Type two paragraphs about your summer, font size 12, Times New Roman
- Change the second paragraph to font size 16 and Papyrus
- Add bullets with
    1. Your daily activities
    2. What you ate
    3. Who you played with
- Add "The End" as WordArt at the bottom of the page
- Add a border

> Wherever you are, be there until you leave.
> —mom

- Add a picture
- Have text wrap around the clipart
- Put a call-out aimed at the picture
- Add an autoshape
- Color the autoshape pink or red
- Insert a footer

- Add a text box with what your mom said the most this summer
- Shade the text box
- Add a table with seven columns and three times during the day
- Add information for each day and each time of day

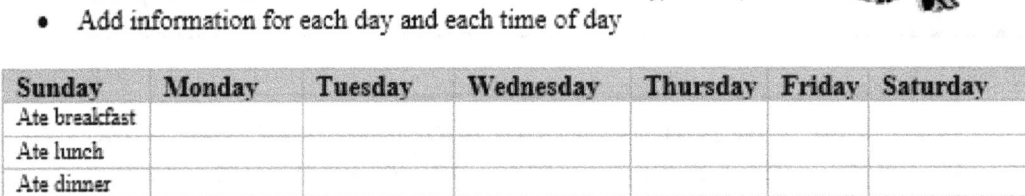

Sunday	Monday	Tuesday	Wednesday	Thursday	Friday	Saturday
Ate breakfast						
Ate lunch						
Ate dinner						

Assessment 12—Word processing assessment

WORD PROCESSING ASSESSMENT

Question		1	2	3	4	5	6	7	8	9	10	11	12	13	14	15	16
1	heading																
	all parts																
2	right align																
3	title																
	underneath																
4	center																
	Comic sans																
	size 14																
	bold																
5	2 paragraphs																
	size 12																
	TNR																
6	Para. 2																
	size 16																
	Papyrus/other																
7	bullets																
	*1																
	#2																
	#3																
8	The End																
	Wordart																
	page bottom																
9	Border (or not)																
10	picture																
	citation																
11	text wrap																
12	call-out (or note)																
	colored																
13	footer																
14	text box																
	shade text box																
	Total																

7 MS Word Tricks Every Teacher Should Know

Computers are a foreign language. Even with small class sizes, the more students can do for themselves, the more fun they have learning the intricacies of technology.

The good news is students love independence. It's cool to know how to do something no one else can. In my class, students love showing off their problem solving skills by helping neighbors. Here are 7 tricks that cover common problems students face with MS Word:

1. **Ctrl+Z–undo**
   This will be your favorite. There are too many times I've had a frantic student, almost in tears because s/he thought s/he'd lost his/her document, and I retrieved it in two seconds. I was a hero for a period.

2. **Macro for a heading**
   This is great for students who have to remember MLA rules. What goes in a heading? How big are margins? Where's a page number go? No worries. Create a macro and save as a template.

3. **How to find lost documents**
   It takes a while to get accustomed to saving files on a network. Often, documents end up lost. My students learn early to use 'search' on the start menu.

4. **How to insert data**
   The 'insert' key is so confusing it's disappearing from newer keyboards. If students complain they lose data as they type, this is probably why. Show them how to push 'insert' and all will be fixed.

5. **Show-hide tool.**
   Kids try to strong-arm Word into doing their will–often the wrong way. My favorite is 'enter enter' to double space. It seems to work until they have to edit, and then everything gets messed up. Have students push **show-hide** to see if they're using the double space tool.

6. **Tables—they work so much better than columns and tabs.**
   Teach it to kids **early and use it often**. It will save you miles of distress.

7. **How to insert the date**
   It takes until Middle School for students to remember the date. Until then, show them **Shift+Alt+D** to insert current date.

Article 12—9 Google Docs Tricks Every Teacher Should Know

9 Google Docs Tricks Every Teacher Should Know

The list below highlights tools that are available only in Google Docs and in my estimation make a big difference in an academic setting. See if you agree:

1. **Revision History**
   Use revision history to track student involvement and go back in time to a version that worked better

2. **Share/Collaborate**
   Multiple students can use the same document and it is automatically saved to their Google account. Take advantage of that for note-taking, projects, wherever it's suited. The document is automatically shared with all stakeholders (rather than 'save as' to multiple accounts).

3. **Research**
   Use the 'Research function to insert graphics so citations are seamless

4. **Don't worry about saving**
   Google does that for you—constantly. Once a document is created it is automatically saved to the cloud

5. **Spell-check on only the red line**
   There's no 'spell check tool' or F7. Find the red squiggle, right click, pick the correct spelling (or use Research to assist)

6. **Download As**
   Create the document in Google Docs, but download it in any format—Office, Open Office, whatever works for stakeholders. Some users may not be comfortable with Google Docs—help them out by sending the doc as an MS Word

7. **Embed**
   Once a document is created in Google Apps, it can be embedded into a student blog, class website, a wiki, or any number of online locations. Called 'publishing', this is simple, requires an html code that is automatically generated by the program.

8. **Copyright-free images**
   Available through Google, Life, and stock images. This is similar to MS Office's clipart gallery, but a different selection of images

9. **Easily insert comments**
   Add notes to a collaborative document so stakeholders can see ideas from other members. These are automatically created and shared with involved parties. This is possible in MS Word, but not as smoothly.

5th Grade Technology Curriculum: Teacher Manual

Lesson #9 Coding: Hour of Code

Vocabulary	Problem solving	Skills
• Coding • Debug • Hotkey • If-then • Macro • Programming • Sequence • Shortkey • Symbolism	• I don't know how to use the programming tool (experiment; be a risk-taker) • I don't like coding (why?) • My partner does lots of the work (that's OK if you do your part also) • I tried to debug my program, but it didn't work (start over)	**New** coding/programming macros hotkeys programming shortkeys **Scaffolded** problem solving coding
Academic Applications Math, critical thinking, habits of the mind	**Materials Required** Coding links and memberships in onsite program (i.e., Code.org)	**Standards** CCSS: Standards for Math. Practice NETS: 4a-b, 5c-d

Essential Question

How do I use a program I've never seen before?

Big Idea

By thinking critically and using information from other parts of my life, I can create something new and useful.

Teacher Preparation

- Talk with grade-level team so you tie into inquiry.
- Be prepared to use domain-specific tech vocabulary.
- If you're the lab teacher, arrange to extend this lesson to 1.25 hours, to accommodate Hour of Code.
- Test Heading Macro to be sure shortkey is not used for another function.
- Know which tasks weren't completed last week and whether they are necessary to move forward.
- Collect words students don't understand to include in Speak Like a Geek Board presentations.
- If you offer afterschool tech help manned by students, verify they will be there.

Assessment Strategies

- Anecdotal
- Completed exit ticket
- Worked well with partner
- Completed one hour of coding
- Joined classroom conversations
- Higher order thinking: analysis, evaluation, synthesis
- Habits of mind observed

Steps

Time required: 15 minutes to discuss problem solving, coding. 60 minutes to pursue the hands-on coding (one hour and fifteen minutes preferred).

Class warm-up: None

_____Because this lesson is devoted to coding, skip presentations and conversations about the Evidence Board. Return to those next week.

_____Discuss critical thinking, problem solving. Does this apply to, say, games students like playing?

_____The reason educators embrace coding is simple: **It teaches children to think.** Discuss fundamental programming concepts:

- *abstraction and symbolism*–variables are common in math, but also in a student's education. Tools, toolbars, images–these all represent something bigger.

- *creativity—think outside the box; develop solutions no one else has*
- *debugging—write-edit-rewrite; problem-solve; when you make a mistake, you don't throw your hands into the air or call for an expert. You look at what happened step by step and fix where it went wrong.*
- *if-then thinking—actions have consequences*
- *logic—thinking through a problem from A to Z, understanding the predictability of movements*
- *sequencing—knowing what happens when; mentioned in Common Core standards for grades 1 through 5*

_____Most people—students and adults—think programming looks like *Figure 51a* when it actually looks like *Figure 51b*:

Figure 51a-b—What programming feels like vs. what it is

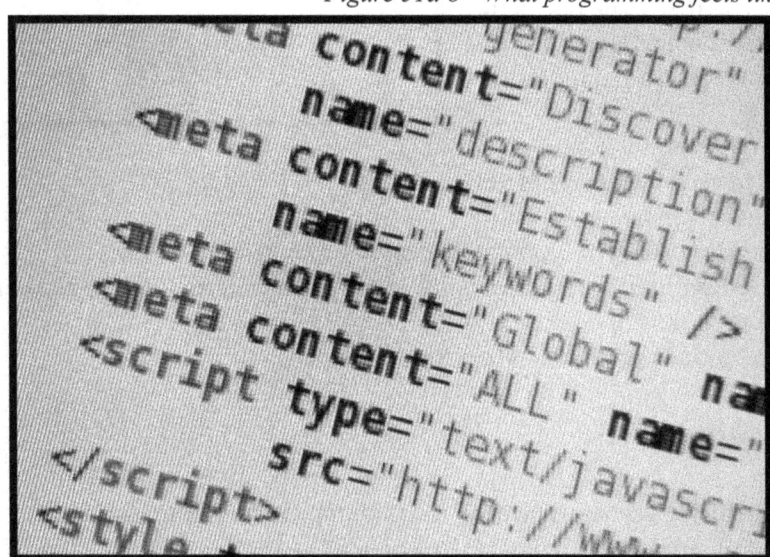
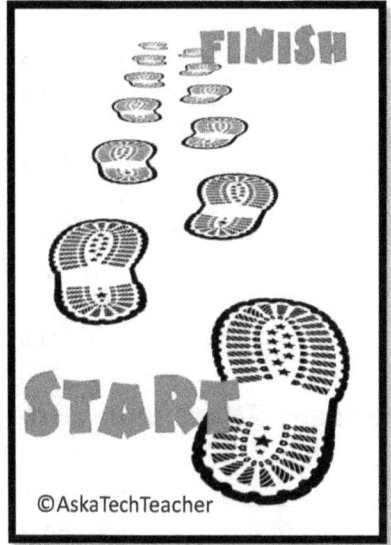

_____Do students remember coding activities from previous years (if you've been using the SL technology curriculum)?

Figure 52a-d—Coding from previous years

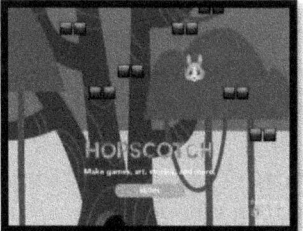

_____December will host the **Hour of Code**, a one hour introduction to students on coding, programming, and why they should love it. It's designed to demystify "code" and show that anyone can learn the basics to be a maker, a creator, and an innovator.

_____This unit may be done individually or in small groups.

_____There are four approaches you can follow:

- *program macros*
- *program shortkeys and hotkeys*
- *follow an online Hour of Code lesson plan*
- *visit miscellaneous websites*

_____ If you did one of these last year, pick a different one this year.

Program Macros

_____By fifth grade, students appreciate technology for how it can speed up class projects. Take advantage of this by introducing pre-programming skills like creating macros. This is popular as an easy way to add MLA headings (or whichever standard your school uses).

_____Here are basic steps for MS Word (adapt for the digital device you use):

1. Click **View - Macros - Record Macros**.
2. Specify a name for the macro.
3. Choose whether it should be a keyboard shortcut or a button.
4. Once you click **OK**, anything you click will be part of the macro. Click all elements you would like to be part of your macro.
5. Stop recording by clicking **View - Stop Recording**.

Program Shortkeys and Hotkeys

_____Creating a shortkey will quickly become a favorite with your students. A popular use is to activate the screenshot program for the digital device you use.

_____Adapt the following directions for the device you use. These are for the windows platform:

- *Go to Start*
- *Right click on the desired program*
- *Select 'properties'*
- *Click in 'shortcut'*
- *Push key combination you want to use, say, Ctrl+Alt+S*
- *Save*

_____Now all I have to do is remember the shortkey!

_____If you are an iPad school, you'll call them 'hotkeys':

- *Go to Settings > General Settings > Keyboard Settings.*
- *Scroll down and click "add new shortcut."*

_____Another great way to add shortkeys is with Auto Hotkey (Google for address). This program must be downloaded to each computer and doesn't yet have education accounts, but may be perfect for you.

Follow one of the free online Hour of Code programs

_____Websites like Code.org (Google for web address) offer full lesson plans for Hour of Code. This is the easiest way to get involved in programming as they do all the planning for you. This may be exactly what you need.

_____Before visiting website, review digital citizenship—especially privacy and safety.

Miscellaneous websites

_____If you don't want to teach a specific skill, here are some great websites. You can Google their websites or visit Ask a Tech Teacher's resources page for Coding:

- Spreadsheets—color code to reveal a secret picture. This is similar to what students did in 1st grade (if they used the SL curriculum)
- Khan Academy Computer Science
- Scratch
- Snap!—runs in your browser
- Tinkercad–3D modeling–fee–perfect for 3D printing
- Wolfram Alpha widgets

_____Here are apps that take coding to an iPad if you're a 1:1 iPad school (find more on the Ask a Tech Teacher resource pages):

- App Inventor–build Android apps on a smartphones; from MIT
- Cargo-Bot—logic iPad game
- Hopscotch (for up to intermediate—more complicated than Kodable)

_____Before going online, review digital citizenship – especially privacy and safety.

_____Coding is a great tie-in to Common Core Math Standards. Any time you can show students how to use their math skills outside of math, it surprises them. They don't expect a discussion on problem solving or modeling to come from math.

_____Review the Common Core Standards for Mathematical Practice. If you are not a Common Core school, review the similar guidelines from your Standards:

- CCSS.Math.Practice.MP2
  Reason abstractly
- CCSS.Math.Practice.MP3
  Construct viable arguments
- CCSS.Math.Practice.MP4
  Model with mathematics
- CCSS.Math.Practice.MP5
  Use appropriate tools strategically
- CCSS.Math.Practice.MP6
  Attend to precision
- CCSS.Math.Practice.MP7
  Look for and make use of structure
- CCSS.Math.Practice.MP8
  Look for and express regularity in repeated reasoning

Class exit ticket: *Have students send you a screenshot of what they programmed. They can use any screenshot option they'd like.*

Differentiation

- *Post Hour of Code on class and school calendar.*
- *Full K-8 digital citizenship curriculum from Structured Learning*

5th Grade Technology Curriculum: Teacher Manual

Lesson #10 Digital Citizenship

Vocabulary	Problem solving	Skills
• Attachment • Bcc/CC • Field • Format • Forums • HTTP/HTTPS • Netiquette • Spam • Texting • Virus	• Home email doesn't match school's (have parents assist in finding parts). • Where's BCC? (click cc) • Why not open attachments? • I don't know teacher email address (post on bulletin board) • Why can't I use 'text' language in email (not appropriate to this method of communication)	**New** Email Digital footprint Digital rights and responsibilities **Scaffolded** Digital citizenship Cyberbullying Plagiarism
Academic Applications Science, history, social studies, any classes that use Internet for resources	**Materials Required** word processing, keyboard program, Problem Solving Board rubric, Evidence Board badges, email program, student workbooks (if using)	**Standards** CCSS.W.5.4 NETS: 2a-d

Essential Question

How do I use technology efficiently to communicate?

Big Idea

Use technology to produce and publish writing as well as interact and collaborate with others

Teacher Preparation

- Talk with grade-level team to tie into conversations.
- Ensure all required links are on student devices.
- Integrate domain-specific tech vocabulary into lesson.
- Know if you need extra time with this lesson.
- Collect words for Speak Like a Geek.
- Ask grade-level team and parents what tech problems students have.

Assessment Strategies

- Completed presentation
- Shared evidence of learning
- Completed blank keyboard quiz
- Used good keyboarding habits
- Emailed appropriate message
- Completed warm-up, exit ticket
- Joined class conversations
- [tried to] solve own problems
- Decisions followed class rules
- Left room as s/he found it
- Higher order thinking: analysis, evaluation, synthesis
- Habits of mind observed

Steps

Time required: 45 minutes in one sitting or spread throughout the week and year
Class warm-up: Keyboard using Popcorn Typer or another tool that focuses on one row. At this point, you are on QWERTY row.

_____ Any evidence of learning to post on Evidence Board?
_____ Remember: Homework due end of each month. Remind students the entire years' worth of assignments is in the back of their student workbook (if you use those).
_____ Continue Problem-solving Board. Review guidelines if necessary. Remind students that they are also graded as an audience—not just a presenter.

Digital Citizenship

_____Discuss **digital citizenship**. You'll cover it in depth throughout the year.
_____Throughout the year, discuss 5th grade topics listed below (*Figure 55*). If you haven't covered K-4 topics, discuss those first. Where possible, students lead the discussion. Spend extra time and adapt to student interests as needed.

For an in-depth digital citizenship curriculum (including projects that reinforce learning, definitions, and scores of websites), refer to the K-8 Digital Citizenship curriculum (from Structured Learning). It's a companion to this tech curriculum (for an additional fee):

Figure 55—Digital Citizenship topics

Digital Citizenship Topics	K	1	2	3	4	5	6
Cyberbullying	x	x	x	x	x	x	x
Digital citizenship	x	x	x	x	x	x	x
Digital commerce						x	x
Digital communications				x		x	x
Digital footprint and Online presence			x	x	x	x	x
Digital law				x			x
Digital privacy				x	x	x	x
Digital rights and responsibilities	x	x	x	x	x	x	x
Digital search and research				x	x	x	x
Fair use, Public domain			x	x	x	x	x
Image copyright			x		x	x	x
Internet safety	x	x	x	x	x	x	x
Netiquette		x	x	x	x	x	x
Online Plagiarism				x	x	x	x
Passwords	x	x	x		x	x	
Social media						x	x
Stranger Danger	x	x	x				©AskaTechTeacher

_____Preview the topics to be sure they're appropriate for your unique student group.

Cyberbullying

- What does 'cyber' mean? What is the same/different about bullying and cyberbullying?
- Use tools employed to deal with neighborhood bullies on cyberbullies.
- Watch these videos (if you can't find them by searching, check the Ask a Tech Teacher resource pages under *Cyberbullying*), like *Common Sense—cyberbullying*

Digital Communications

- This includes email, blog comments, and discussion forums. These are discussed under the lessons about email and blogs. Review here to remind students.

Digital footprint

- Discuss why it is important. How many students are influenced by a digital footprint?
- Watch a digital footprint video such as *Privacy Student Intro Video - The Digital Footprint*

Digital privacy

- Introduce **Digital Privacy**. Discuss how **passwords** protect privacy. Remind students they never share passwords, even with friends.
- Discuss password guidelines and rules.
- Watch a video on passwords.

Digital rights and responsibilities

- What are the **digital rights and responsibilities** of a fifth grader? Watch a video on Digital Rights and Responsibilities from the Ask a Tech Teacher resource page (Digital Citizenship).
- Discuss these concepts:

    - *Act the same online as you'd act in your neighborhood.*
    - *Don't share personal information. Don't ask others for theirs.*
    - *Be aware of your surroundings. Know where you are in cyberspace.*
    - *Always show your best side online.*
    - *Anonymity doesn't protect the individual.*
    - *Share knowledge online.*
    - *If someone is 'flaming', stop it if possible or walk away.*

Fair use, Public domain, Image Copyright

- *Figure 56* (full size poster in Appendix) rephrases the law regarding online media. Discuss with students. Relate it to the conversations about plagiarism in other classes:

Figure 56—Legal use of internet media

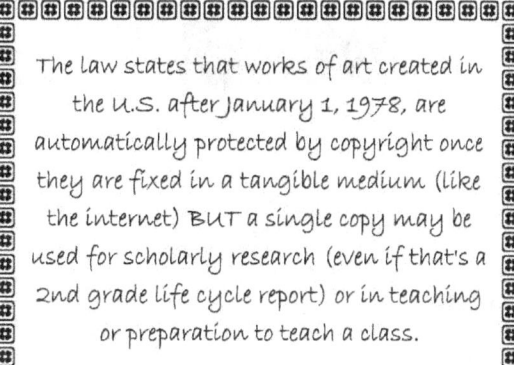

- Take as much time as necessary to answer student questions about copyrights, public domain, and fair use. These are important and authentic topics.

Internet safety

- Ask students how they protect their passwords and online safety when using the Internet.
- What's the difference between 'http' and 'https'? How important is this level of security?

Netiquette

- What is '**netiquette**' to a fifth grader (*Figure 57*—full-size poster in the appendix)?

Figure 57—Netiquette Rules

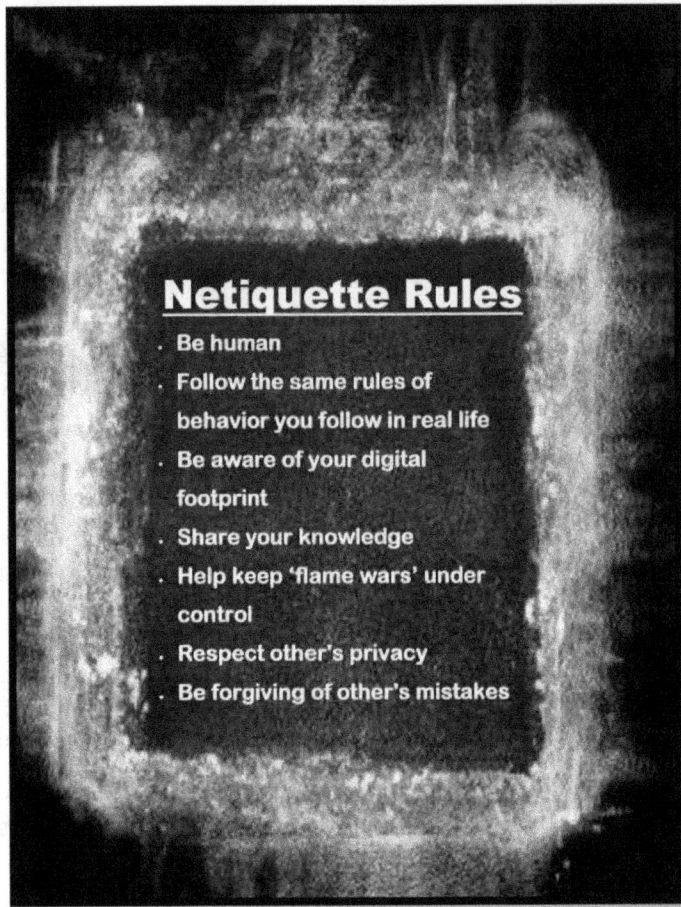

Online search/research

- covered in other lessons

Plagiarism

- What does '**plagiarism**' mean? Why give credit to original authors/artists?
- Watch a Plagiarism video.
- Discuss plagiarism concepts like image copyrights, fair use, and public domain.

Social Media

- Discuss **X/Twitter** (see the article at the end of the lesson) and hashtags.
- Discuss **texting** (see the article at the end of the lesson). Watch a video on Texting.

_____Post the pyramid in *Figure 58* on the wall in your classroom (there's a full-size poster in the appendix). Every time you've discussed a topic, check it off:

5th Grade Technology Curriculum: Teacher Manual

Figure 58—Digcit topic pyramid

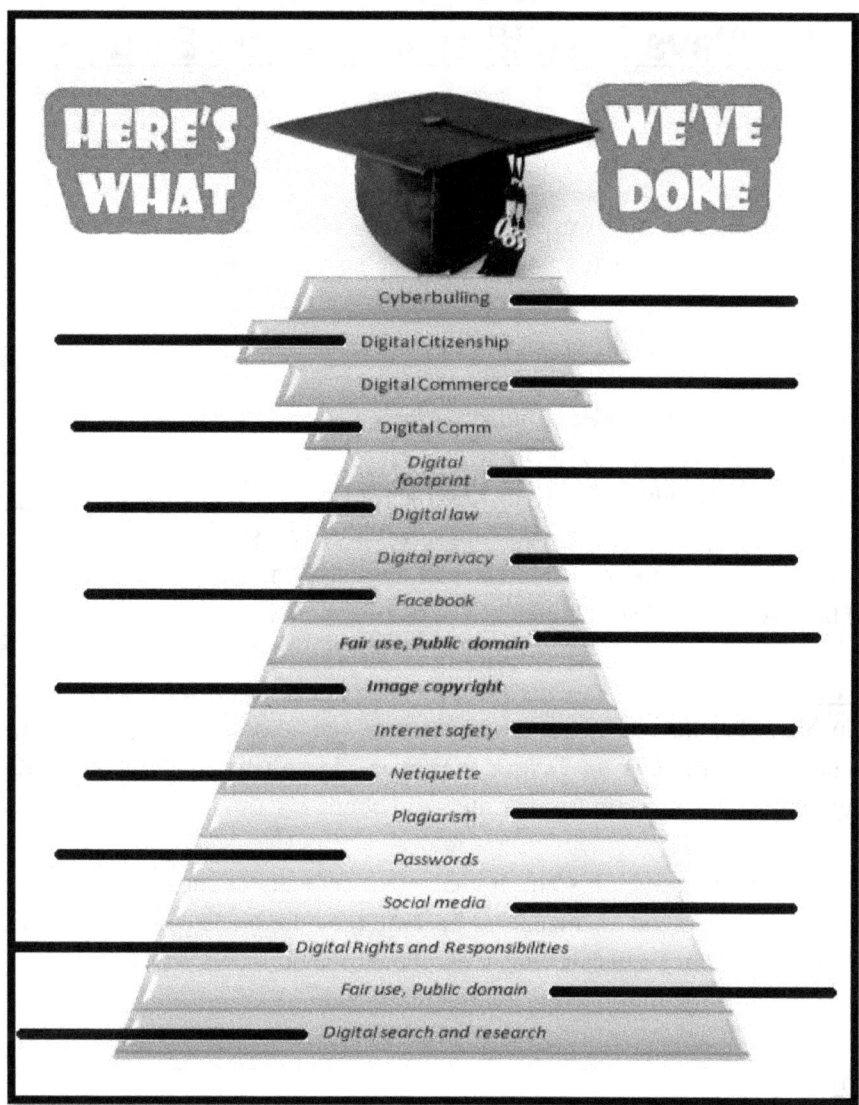

Class exit ticket: *Tweet on the class X/Twitter account (or add a comment to class blog) about how student stays safe online.*

Differentiation

- Review home and QWERTY rows. Repeat keys as a class while waving finger used to type letter.
- Add homework due date to class online calendar for each month.
- Early finishers: visit class internet start page for websites that tie into classwork.

Article 13—11 Ways Twitter improves education

11 Ways X/Twitter Improves Education

A teacher must communicate with students in a way they will hear. Twitter might be perfect for your class.

Twitter can easily be dismissed as a waste of time in the elementary school classroom. Students get distracted. They might see inappropriate tweets. How does a teacher manage a room full of Tweeple?

But, you've read a lot about Twitters usefulness in writing skills and sharing information so you—of the Open Minded Attitude—want to try it. Here's ammunition for what often turns into a pitched, take-sides verbal brawl as well-intended educators try to reach a compromise on using Twitter (in fact, many Web 2.0 tools—blogs, wikis, discussion forums, and websites that require registrations and log-ins—can be added to the list) that works for all stakeholders:

You learn to be concise
Twitter gives you limited characters to get the entire message across. *Letters, numbers, symbols, punctuation and spaces all count as characters on Twitter.* Wordiness doesn't work. Twitter counts every keystroke and won't publish anything with a minus in front of the word count.

At first blush, that seems impossible. It's not. It challenges students to know the right word for every situation. People with a big vocabulary are at an advantage because they don't use collections of little words to say what they mean. All those hints from English teachers about picture nouns and action verbs and getting rid of adverbs and adjectives take on new importance to the Twitter aficionado.

Twitter isn't intimidating
A blank white page holds hundreds of words, demanding you fill in each line margin to margin is intimidating. Twitter's limited characters aren't. Students learn to whittle back, leave out emotional words, adjectives and adverbs, pick better nouns and verbs because they need the room. Instead of worrying what to say on all those empty lines, they feel successful.

Students learn manners
Social networks are all about netiquette. People thank others for their assistance, ask politely for help, and encourage contributions from others. Use this framework to teach students how to engage in a community—be it physical or virtual. It's all about manners.

Students learn to focus
Students can't get off topic or cover tangential ideas. You have to save those for a different tweet. Tweeple like that trait in writers. They like to hear the writer's thoughts on the main topic, not meanderings. When forced to write this way, students will find it doesn't take a paragraph to make a point. Use the right words, people get it. Consider that the average reader gives a story seven seconds before moving on.

Here's an idea: If you must get into those off-topic thoughts, write them in a separate tweet.

Students learn to share
Start a tweet stream where students share research on a topic. Maybe it's Ancient Greece. Have each student share their favorite website (using a #hashtag — maybe #ancientgreece) and you've created a resource others can use. Expand on that wonderful skill learned in kindergarten about sharing personal toys. Encourage students to RT (retweet) posts they found particularly relevant or helpful.

Writing short messages perfects the art of "headlining"
Writers call this the title. Bloggers and journalists call it the headline. Whatever the label, it has to be cogent and pithy enough to pull the audience in and make them read the article. That's a tweet.

Tweets need to be written knowing that tweeple can @reply
This is a world of social networks where people comment on what you say. That's a good thing. It's feedback and builds an online community, be it for socializing or school. Students learn to construct their arguments expecting others to respond, question, and comment. Not only does this develop the skill of persuasive writing, students learn to have a thick skin, take comments with a grain of salt and two grains of aspirin.

#Hashtags develop a community
Create #hashtags that will help students organize their tweets—#help if they have a question, #homework for homework help. Establish class hashtags to deal with subjects you want students to address.

Students learn tolerance for all opinions
Why? Because Tweeple aren't afraid to voice their thoughts. Because the Twitter stream is a public forum (in a classroom, the stream can be private, visible to only class members), students understand what they say is out there forever. That's daunting. Take the opportunity to teach students about their public profile. Represent themselves well with good grammar, good spelling, and well-chosen tolerant ideas. Don't be emotional or spiteful because it can't be taken back. Rather than shying away from exposing students to the world, use Twitter to teach students how to live in it.

Twitter, the Classroom Notepad
I tried this out after I read about it through my PLN. Springboarding off student engagement, Twitter can act as your classroom notepad. Have students enter their thoughts, note, and reactions while you talk. By the time class is done, the entire class has an overview of the conversation with extensions and connections that help everyone get more out of the inquiry.

Twitter is always open
Inspiration doesn't always strike in that 50-minute class period. Sometimes it's after class, after school, after dinner, even 11 at night. Twitter doesn't care. Whatever schedule is best for students to discover the answer, Twitter is there. If you post a tweet question and ask students to join the conversation, they will respond in the time frame that works best for them. That's a new set of rules for classroom participation, and these are student-centered, uninhibited by a subjective time period. Twitter doesn't even care if a student missed class. S/he can catch up via tweets and then join in.

Article 14—Will texting destroy writing skills?

Will Texting Destroy Writing Skills?

Across the education landscape, student text messaging is a bone of contention among teachers. It's not an issue in the lower grades because most K-5 schools successfully ban cell phones during school hours. Where it's a problem are grades 6-12, when teachers realize it's a losing battle to separate students from their phones for eight hours.

The overarching discussion among educators is texting's utility in providing authentic experiences that transfer learning from the class to real life. Today, I'll focus on a piece of that: Does text messaging contribute to 1) shortening student attention span, or 2) destroying their nascent writing ability

Let's start with attention span. TV, music, over-busy daily schedules, and frenetic family life are likely causes of a student's short attention span. To fault text messaging is like blaming the weather for sinking the Titanic. Texting has less to do with the inability to spit out a full sentence than a student's 1) need for quickness of communication, 2) love for secrecy, and 3) joy of knowing a language adults don't.

What about writing? In the thirty years I've been teaching everyone from kindergarteners to college, I can tell you with my hand on a Bible that children are flexible, masters at adjusting actions to circumstances (like the clothes they wear for varying events and the conversations they have with varying groups of people). There is no evidence to support that these elastic, malleable creatures are suddenly rigid in their writing style, unable to toggle between casual texting shorthand with friends and a professional writing structure in class.

In general, I'm a fan of anything that encourages student writing, and there are real benefits to giving students the gift of textual brevity rather than the stomach-churning fear of a five-paragraph structured essay. I've done quite a few articles on the benefits of Twitter's approach to writing and my teacher's gut says the same applies to text messaging. Truth, studies are inconclusive. Some suggest that because young students do not yet have a full grasp of basic writing skills, they have difficulty shifting between texting's abbreviated spelling-doesn't-matter language and Standard English. But a British study suggested students classify 'texting' as 'word play', separate from the serious writing done for class so it results in no deterioration of writing skills. Yet another study found that perception of danger from texting is greater than reality: 70% of the professionals at one college believed texting had harmful effects on student writing skills. However, when analyzed, the opposite was true: Texting was actually beneficial.

It's interesting to note that texting can be a boon to children who struggle with face-to-face situations. These 'special needs' students flourish in an environment where they can write rather than speak, think through an answer before communicating it, and provide pithy conversational gambits in lieu of extended intercourse. In the texting world, socially-challenged children are like every other child, hidden by the anonymity of a faceless piece of metal and circuits. To blame texting for student academic failures is a cop-out by the parents and teachers entrusted with a child's education. Treated as an authentic scaffold to academic goals, teachers will quickly incorporate it into their best-practices pedagogy of essential tools for learning.

Lesson #11 Internet Search

Vocabulary	Problem solving	Skills
• Address • Browser • Cell • Crop • Ctrl+Click • Domain • Extensions • Format picture • Handles • Hits • http and https • Limiters • Lower Row • Search bar • Site Title bar	• Browser toolbar is gone (push F11) • Browser too small (double click title) • Browser text too small (Zoom with Ctrl+) • My website address doesn't link (push spacebar after the address) • Data is in wrong cell (drag-drop) • Ran out of rows in my table (push enter in the last cell) • I forgot my presentation was today (is there time later in the schedule?) • Picture is really big (Resize or grab thumbnail) • Can't find website address (check address bar) Can't find a word on the webpage (Ctrl+F)	**New** Internet search refinements Activate link in Word **Scaffolded** Tables Internet searches Speaking and listening Screenshots Keyboarding Digital citizenship
Academic Applications Research in any topic, quick search on a topic of interest	**Materials Required** Digital Passport log-ins (if using), Evidence Board badges, Problem Solving Board rubrics	**Standards** CCSS.W.5.9 NETS: 1c, 3a-d

Essential Question

How can I use the Internet safely and effectively?

Big Idea

Students safely explore the Internet, understanding their rights and responsibilities.

Teacher Preparation

- Make sure a screenshot program is available.
- Have links available on class Internet start page.
- Talk with grade-level team so you tie into conversations.
- Is class shorter than 45 minutes? Highlight only completed items.
- Know which tasks weren't completed last week and whether they are necessary to move forward
- Be prepared to integrate domain-specific tech vocabulary into lesson
- Collect words students don't understand for Speak Like a Geek presentations beginning Lesson 20.
- Know whether you need extra time to complete this lesson with your student group.
- If you offer afterschool tech help and it's manned by students, verify selected students will be there.

Assessment Strategies

- Anecdotal
- [tried to] solve own problems
- Decisions followed class rules
- Left room as student found it
- Completed warm-up, exit ticket
- Joined classroom conversations
- Higher order thinking: analysis, evaluation, synthesis
- Habits of mind observed

Steps

Time required: 40 minutes in one sitting on effective Internet searches (including project)
Class warm-up: Keyboard Lower Row (or whichever row you've reached at this point)

_____Continue Problem-solving Board presentations.

_____Ask if students used solutions to problems discussed last week. Any they'd like help with?
_____Any evidence of learning to post?
_____Open search engine. Discuss difference between search bar and address bar. Is there a difference? 
_____Watch and discuss BrainPop *Internet Search* (if you don't have a BrainPop subscription, visit the Ask a Tech Teacher resource pages, *Internet Search/Research*) as a class. Answer questions at end as a group.
_____Understand what contributes to successful Internet searches:

- *key words (using a + in front of a word to refine the search)*
- *knowing enough about the topic to pick strong key words*
- *quotes (" ")*

_____See *Figure 59* for more Internet search tips (full size poster in Appendix):

Figure 59—Internet research

STEPS FOR INTERNET RESEARCH

Know Key Words | General understanding of topic | Reliable site extensions | Read sidebars, headings, hyperlinks | Read pictures, insets, maps

GET YOUR DUCKS IN A ROW

©AskaTechTeacher

_____Demonstrate an Internet search on a topic students are studying in class—say, space:

- search 'Saturn rings' with no keywords, no quotes
- search "Saturn rings" with quotes. Notice the decrease in number of hits
- search "Saturn rings" + "discovered by" to focus on a subtopic

_____Now have students try, using a different topic.
_____Remind students to use the vocabulary decoding tools provided on their digital devices (i.e., Dictionary.com or the native right-click in their word processing program).
_____If you use Common Sense's (free) Digital Passport, have students play *Search Shark*.

_____Watch BrainPop *Internet Sources* together. Have students take quiz independently and email to you. If you don't have a subscription, pick any website on the Ask a Tech Teacher Internet Search/Research resource page.

_____Throughout class, check for understanding.

_____Done? Have students practice a search on a topic of their choice for the balance of class. Depending upon your group, you may want to approve these topics.

Class exit ticket: ***Display a Padlet wall (Figure 60a), a Google Form (Figure 60b) or a Google Spreadsheet (Figure 60c) on class screen. As students leave class, they share one important step in searching the Internet effectively.***

Figure 60a—Poll in Padlet; 60b—Google Forms; 60c—Google Spreadsheet

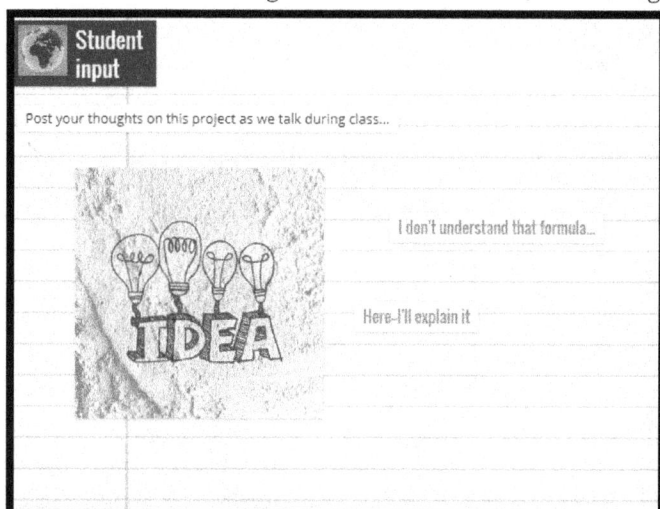
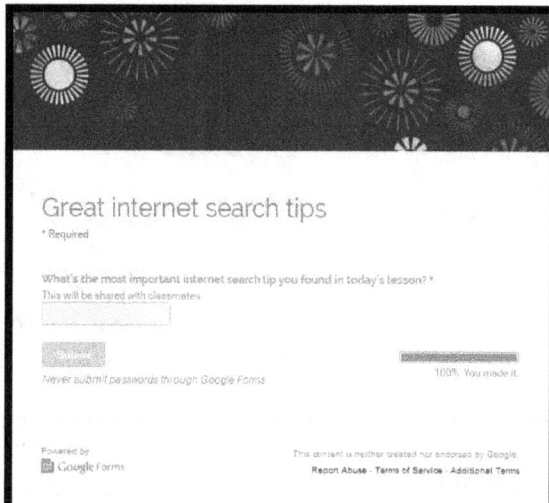
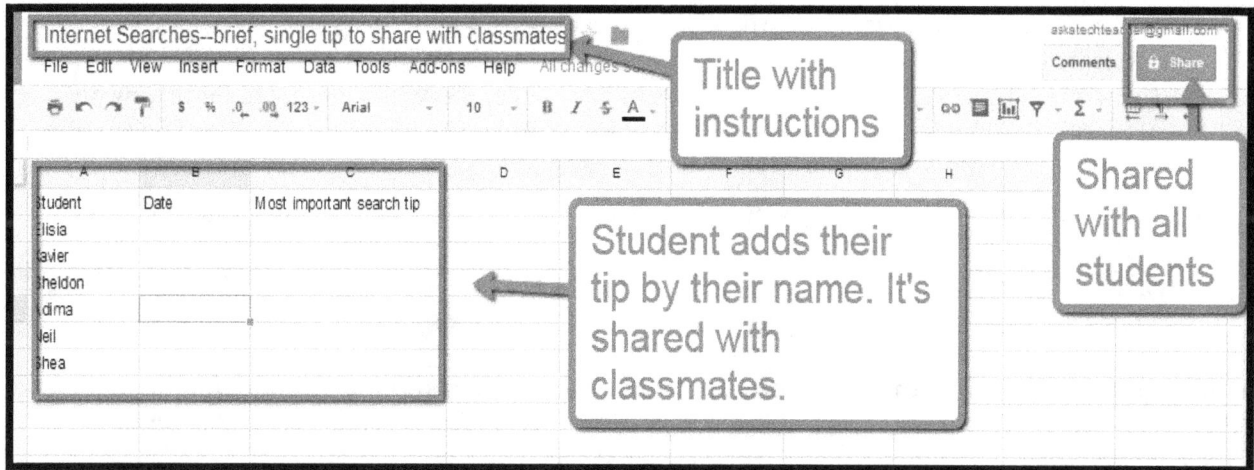

Differentiation

- *For more search tips, visit the Google support page to Improve Your Search Experience.*
- *Remind students to post their Problem-solving Board problem to the Discussion Board on class website or blog where it can be a resource for classmates.*
- *Full digital citizenship curriculum for K-8 available from Structured Learning.*

5th Grade Technology Curriculum: Teacher Manual

Lesson #12 Website Evaluation

Vocabulary	Problem solving	Skills
• Copyright date • Hoax • Keywords • Limiters • Sources • Spoof • Website	• How do I search (type into search bar or address bar) • How do I add keywords (use + or –) • I can't find copyright (try bottom of website—it's not always easy to find) • I can't find author and/or publisher (that tells you something)	**New** **Scaffolded** Internet searches Digital citizenship Speaking and listening Problem solving
Academic Applications Any class that requires online research	**Materials Required** Problem Solving Board rubric, Evidence Board badges, website evaluation forms, Internet sites	**Standards** CCSS.RI.5.6 NETS: 3b

Essential Question

How do I decide which websites are credible for my needs?

Big Idea

Decide which websites are most valuable by evaluating them based on accepted criteria

Teacher Preparation

- Place websites on class Internet start page.
- Know whether you need extra time to complete lesson.
- Be prepared to use domain-specific tech vocabulary.
- Is class shorter than 45 minutes? Highlight critical items and leave the rest for 'later'.
- Know which tasks weren't completed last week and whether they are necessary to move forward.
- Ask grade-level team and parents for tech problems to cover with students.
- Continue collecting words for Speak Like a Geek presentations.
- If you offer afterschool tech help manned by students, verify they will be there during their class.

Assessment Strategies

- Evaluated website(s)
- [tried to] solve own problems
- Worked well in a group
- Decisions followed class rules
- Left room as student found it
- Completed warm-up, exit ticket
- Joined classroom conversations
- Higher order thinking: analysis, evaluation, synthesis
- Habits of mind observed

Steps

Time required: 65 minutes in one sitting or spread throughout the week with 30 minutes for website evaluation project and 25 for Internet websites project.

Class warm-up: Students post how they used tech to the Evidence Board.

_____ Do students need help with a tech problem? Any evidence of learning for Evidence Board?
_____ Remember keyboarding homework due at end of month.
_____ Finish up Problem-solving Board presentations.
_____ This Lesson covers two topics:

- *Internet websites*
- *website evaluations*

Internet Websites

_____Discuss the parts of a website address (see *Figure 61*).

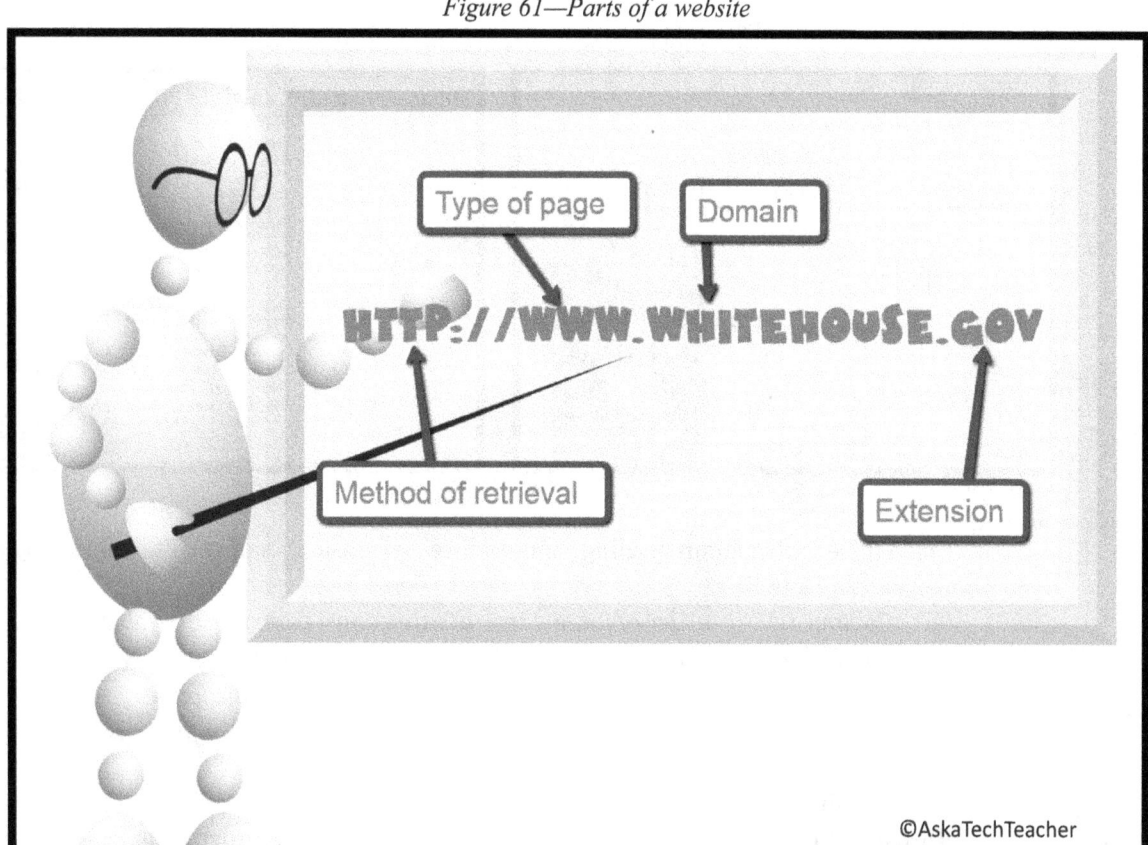

Figure 61—Parts of a website

_____Discuss the types of extensions:

- *gov (government entities)*
- *edu (colleges and universities)*
- *net*
- *org*
- *com*
- *foreign*

_____Discuss foreign extensions (such as .au, .uk).

_____What can extensions tell you about a website? Discuss how they relate to reliability of material on the site. Does it matter if you're looking for a place to buy backpacks? How about if you're writing a research paper? Consider:

- *How can you locate an answer if you don't know whether the website is reliable?*
- *How can you explain how an author uses reasons and evidence to support particular points if you aren't convinced the reasons and points are accurate?*
- *How can you integrate information from several texts to write or speak about the subject knowledgeably if you don't know that the websites are knowledgeable?*

_____For today's project, depending upon your students, they can work in small groups or individually.

5th Grade Technology Curriculum: Teacher Manual

_____Open your word processing program. If you have iPads, you can use the free Microsoft and Mac apps for word processing or spreadsheets. Be familiar with these as creating tables will have differences from the fully-functioning software or online tools.

_____Add heading (name, date, teacher). Why always add a heading?

_____Review table skills learned in 3rd and 4th grade (*Figures 62a and 62b*):

Figure 62a-b—Tables in 3rd and 4th grade

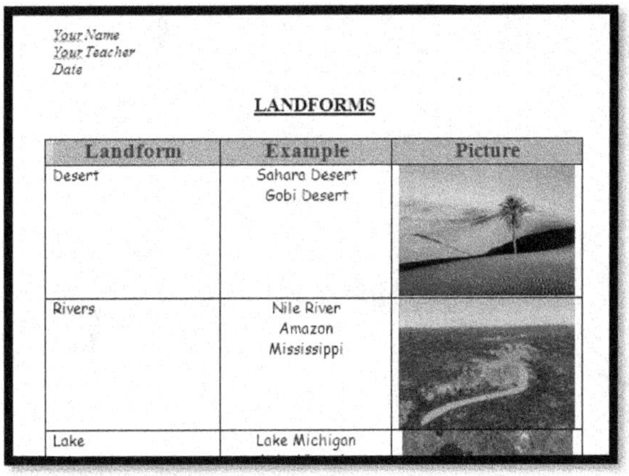

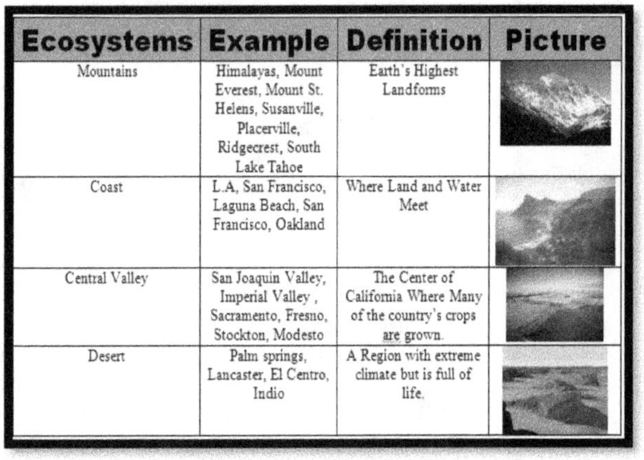

_____Create a table with column headings 'importance', 'extension', 'sample', 'screenshot' (*Fig. 63*).

- *Column 1:* order of importance of extensions, from most reliable to least
- *Column 2:* extension type—.gov, .edu, .org, .net, .com
- *Column 3:* sample website address, copied from its webpage
- *Column 4:* screenshot of website, taken with screenshot program

_____**Column 1**: Fill in from 1-6.
_____**Column 2**: Return to the earlier discussion on extensions and order them from 'most reliable' to 'least reliable'.
_____**Column 3**: Suggest a topic students are studying in class (say, space) and have students run a search on that topic using their search skills.
_____Find a website with each of the mentioned extensions. Go to the site; copy-paste the address into the appropriate cell in the table.
_____**Column 4**: Take a screenshot of the website and paste it into the appropriate cell. Depending upon your digital device, use:

- **Windows**: *the Snipping Tool*
- **Chromebook**: *hold down the control key and press the window switcher key*
- **Mac**: *Command Shift 4 to take a partial screenshot*
- **Surface tablet**: *hold down volume and Windows button at the same time*
- **iPad**: *hold Home button and power button at same time*
- **Online**: *a screenshot tool*

_____Repeat until all extensions have all required information.
_____If you're using Word, show students how to **'activate' link**—by adding a space after words or pushing enter. Show how **Ctrl+Click** will access address. Adapt this to your digital device.
_____Remind students: Every time they use the computer, practice keyboarding skills.
_____Save to digital portfolio with Ctrl+S. What's the difference between 'save' and 'save-as'?

Figure 63—Table of website extensions

Importance	Extension	Sample	Screenshot
1	.gov	http://solarsystem.nasa.gov/kids/index.cfm	
2	.edu	http://tes.asu.edu/	
1	.org	http://www.seds.org/nineplanets/nineplanets/overview.html	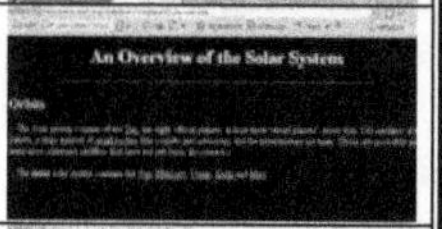
4	.net	http://www.astrobio.net/news/index.php	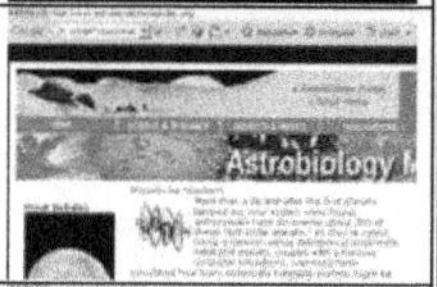
5	.com	http://www.enchantedlearning.com/subjects/astronomy/solarsystem/	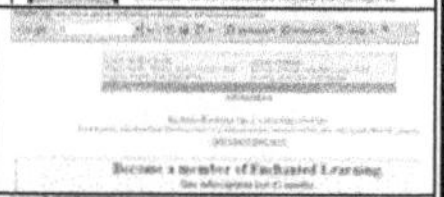
6	.foreign	http://www.bbc.co.uk/science/space/solarsystem/mars/index.shtml	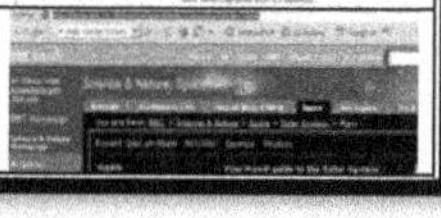

_____If you want students to print, have them first check print preview to be sure table takes only one page. If necessary, resize images before printing.

_____Throughout class, check for understanding.

_____Those who finish can create a holiday card using skills from prior lessons.

Website Evaluation

_____Even knowing which extensions are most reliable, a web search often returns too many hits. How do students tell which to select?

_____Start with this BrainPop video *Online sources.* Take quiz as a group. If you don't have a BrainPop subscription, check Ask a Tech Teacher's resource pages for *Digital Search and Research*.

_____Have a list of websites that tie into classroom discussion on a topic (say, space). Pick one to evaluate as a class. Students can work in groups.

_____Most libraries suggest evaluating websites based on:

- *purpose of the site*
- *trustworthiness of the author*
- *usefulness of the information*
- *up-to-date information*
- *ease of use*

_____There are a variety of checklists available that can be used (Google for website addresses):

- *Common Sense Media*
- *Cornell University*

Figure 64—Sample website eval tool

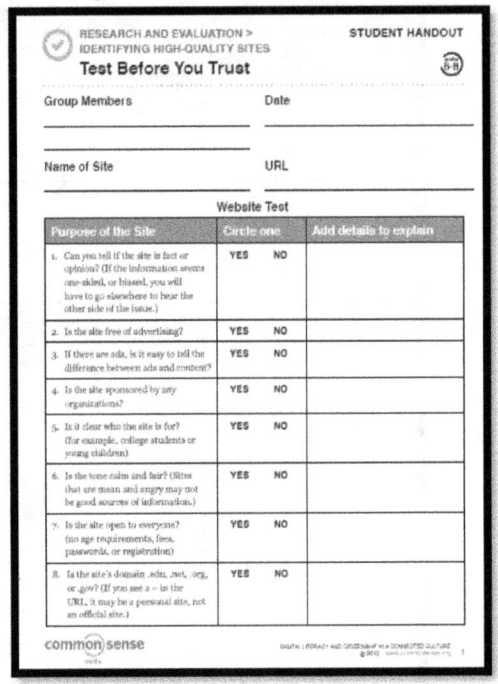

_____Pick one checklist that works for your class and demonstrate on class screen how you make decisions about each question.

_____Now, students work in small groups to evaluate a website from a search they run.

_____Done? Discuss how some websites are hoaxes, how students can identify a 'spoof' website. Show students a fake website such as Save the Tree Octopus or Hoax or Not (Google for addresses or visit the Ask a Tech Teacher resource pages for *Digital Citizenship>Internet Hoaxes*). Do they think it's real? Why? Don't reveal truth until everyone has had their say.

_____Show students 'War of the Worlds'—one of the most famous hoaxes ever. Discuss how easily this story could be confused with reality.

_____Throughout class, check for understanding.

Class exit ticket: *On a topic related to class inquiry, select a website that contributes to the conversation and share with teacher and classmates. Be ready to defend why it's a reliable website.*

Differentiation

- *Remind students to post their Problem-solving Board problem to the Discussion Board on class website or blog as a student resource.*
- *If homework is due, make sure it's added to class calendar.*
- *Early finishers: visit websites from the search students ran on the inquiry topic.*
- *Replace this lesson with 5th Grade Lesson #2 Digital Citizens in the SL curriculum extenders.*
- *Replace this lesson with 6th Grade Lesson #5 Glogster in curriculum extenders.*

Lesson #13 DTP: Newsletter

Vocabulary	Problem solving	Skills
• DTP • Dialogue box • Drop cap • Mulligan Rule • Newsletter • Placeholder • Sidebar • Taskbar • Text box	• My typing disappeared (Ctrl+Z) • How do I undo? (Ctrl+Z) • Can't type on page (add text box) • What's the difference between 'save' and 'save-as'? • When do I backspace or delete? • Screen froze (clear dialogue box) • I didn't do as well as I hoped (Mulligan Rule applies)	**New** A digital DTP tool not previously used **Scaffolded** Research skills Newsletters Screenshots keyboarding
Academic Applications Literacy, writing, history, or any subject requiring collation of information	**Materials Required** DTP, newsletter examples, Evidence Board badges, Problem Solving Board rubrics, Google Earth Board sign-up sheets, student workbooks (if using)	**Standards** CCSS.W.5.2 NETS: 1d, 3a-d, 6a, 6c

Essential Question

How do I use technology to share a mass communication?

Big Idea

Technology is a time-saving tool for group communication

Teacher Preparation

- Students bring two digital stories to class.
- Talk with grade-level team to tie into inquiry.
- Know whether you need extra time to complete lesson.
- Be prepared to use domain-specific tech vocabulary.
- Know which tasks weren't completed last week.
- Collect words for Speak Like a Geek Board.
- If you offer afterschool tech help manned by students, verify they will be there.

Assessment Strategies

- Decisions followed class rules
- Annotated workbooks (if using)
- Left room as student found it
- Used good keyboarding habits
- Completed warm-up, exit ticket
- Joined classroom conversations
- Completed project
- Posted reflection to blog and commented on other articles
- Higher order thinking: analysis, evaluation, synthesis
- Habits of mind observed

Steps

Time required: 45 minutes in one sitting or spread throughout week with a block of about 30 minutes to complete project
Class warm-up: Sign up for Google Earth Board Presentations

_____Tech problems students would like to share? Any evidence of learning?
_____Finish Problem solving presentations. If you're assessing them, do it next week.
_____Sign up for Google Earth Board Presentations using an electronic sign-up:

- *Padlet (the calendar template—Figure 65b)*
- *Office 365*
- *Google Forms*
- *Google Apps Calendar (Figure 65a) or Spreadsheets*

Figure 65a—Presentation board sign ups in Google Calendar; 65b—Padlet

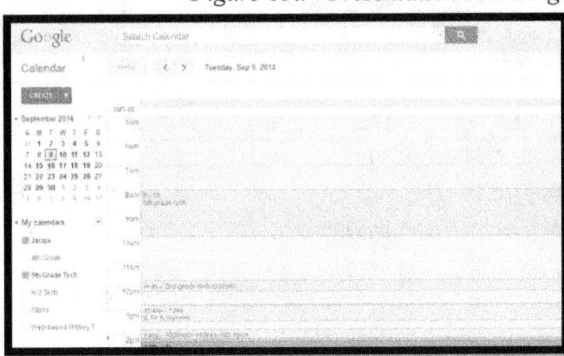 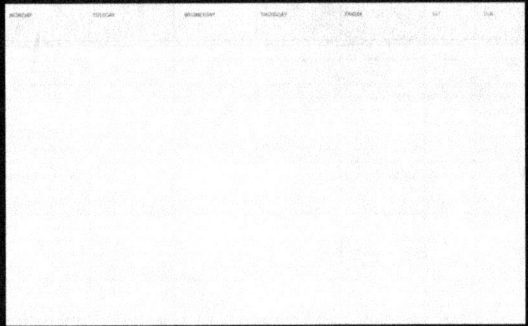

_____Sign up for Google Earth Board, which will start next week. See *Figure 66* for information students should record into their notebooks or digital portfolio:

Figure 66—Google Earth Board notes

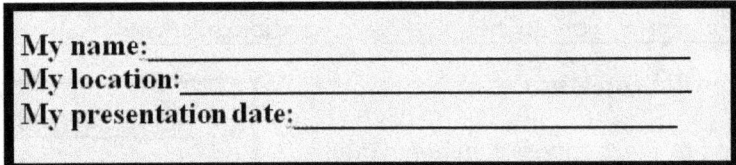

_____If students have workbooks, they can enter this information directly into the PDF.
_____This is the second of three Presentation Boards:

- *Location can be 1) places visited in fifth grade, 2) Wonders of the World, or 3) ??? Figure 67 is an example of what those might be:*

Figure 67—Sample Google Earth locations

Sample Google Earth Locations	
Egyptian Pyramids	Tierra del Fuego
Great Wall of China	Straits of Gibraltar
Stonehenge	The Red Sea
Hagia Sophia, Istanbul	Mt. St. Helens
Leaning Tower of Pisa	San Andreas Fault
The Eiffel Tower	Great African Rift
Panama Canal	Madagascar
Taj Mahal	Istanbul
Victoria Falls	Siberia
Ngorongoro Crater	Death Valley
Mt. Everest	Suez Canal
Ayers Rock	Vatican City
The Ross Ice Shelf	The Chunnel

- *Students use research skills to find a Fascinating Fact about location to share.*
- *Grading is based on criteria listed on rubric (Assessment 13):*

Assessment 13—Google Earth Board rubric

GOOGLE EARTH BOARD GRADING

Name: _____

Class: _____

You were prepared with filled-out project sheet	_____
Your project sheet had a picture of your location	_____
You shared an interested fact with the class	_____
You spoke loudly enough for all to hear	_____
You seemed knowledgeable	_____
You had a calm, confident presence	_____
You didn't use vocal cues that showed nervousness	_____
You didn't use visual cues that showed nervousness	_____
You looked your audience in the eye as you talked	_____
Overall impression	_____

_____ Load a digital copy for each student onto your iPad and then use an annotation tool like iAnnotate or Acrobat to assess.

_____ Today, start a three-project unit using desktop publishing (DTP)—a newsletter, calendar and a trifold—to explore writing in this medium. If you used the SL tech curriculum in past years, you created cards in 2nd grade (*Figure 68a*), a magazine in 3rd grade (*Figure 68b*), and stories/trifolds/newsletter in 4th grade (*Figure 68c-e*):

Figure 68a-e—DTP project from 2nd-4th

_____ What is 'desktop publishing'? Compare/contrast this approach to sharing information with a word processing program, a presentation tool, or a spreadsheet. What are pros and cons, likes and dislikes of each approach? *Figure 69* is a table you can display on the class screen with a few traits filled in:

Figure 69—Compare-contrast digital tools—incomplete

Element	Slide-show	Word processing	Spread-sheets	DTP
Purpose	Share a presentation	Share words		
Basics		Text is essential to design; layout may detract		
Sentences		Full sentences with proper conventions		
Content	Slides cover basics, remind presenter what to say			
Use		As complete resource		
Presentation		Speaker reads from document		
What else				

_____*Figure 70* shows it completely filled in:

Figure 70—Compare-contrast digital tools—complete

Element	Slideshow	Word processing	Spread-sheets	DTP
Purpose	Share a presentation	Share words	Turn numbers into information	Share information using a variety of media
Basics	Graphics-based Design is important to content Layout communicates Few words, lots of images	Text-based Design is secondary to content Layout may detract from words Primarily words communicate	Number-based Focus on tables, graphs Little text; lots of statistics and date Almost no words	Mix of media—equal emphasis on text, images, layout, color
Sentences	Bulleted, phrases	Full sentences with proper conventions	None	Full sentences, bullets,
Content	Slides cover basics, to remind presenter what to say	Thorough discussion of a topic. Meant to be complete document	Statistics, data, charts, graphs	To draw an audience in;
Use	As a back-up to presentation	As complete resource	To support other presentation methods	Good way to group information for easy consumption
Presentation	Speaker presents with their back to the slideshow	Speaker reads from document	Speakers uses it in a presentation or 1:1	Speaker passes out as a handout or take-way
What else				

_____Share this table digitally so students can complete it in their workbooks (if using these) with an annotation tool like Notability or iAnnotate.

_____What is a newsletter? Show some examples to aid discussion. In short, it is *informative/explanatory text that examines a topic and conveys ideas via formatting (e.g., headings), illustrations, design, and multimedia.*

_____Show samples of newsletters, maybe your school's or your class's. Do students see the following critical elements?

- *bold name*
- *short stories with relevant information and concise, pithy titles*
- *attractive, colorful layout*
- *pull-out with info audience will want to read*

5th Grade Technology Curriculum: Teacher Manual

_____Students will work in groups to create a newsletter on a theme that supports class inquiry. Open the two digital stories each student prepared for today's lesson.

_____Now open the desktop publishing tool you use in your school. Depending upon the digital device and platform you use, you may need to adapt the upcoming instructions.

_____This lesson uses MS Publisher (*Figure 71a*)—an easy-to-use, intuitive student-friendly vehicle for all sorts of desktop publishing. Another option: Google Docs (*Figure 71b*):

Figure 71a—Newsletter in Publisher; 71b—in Google Docs

_____*Figure 72a* is a PowerPoint template. *Figure 72b* is a Word template from Microsoft's website:

Figure 72a—Newsletter in PowerPoint; 72b—in Word

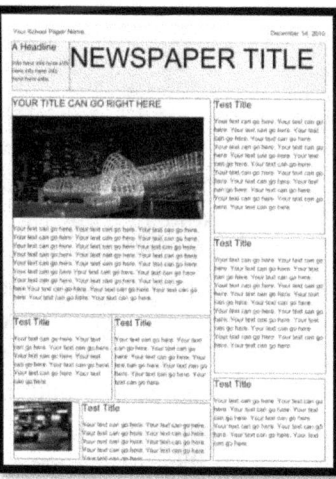

_____You can also use a web-based tool like Learn Alberta (Figure 73):

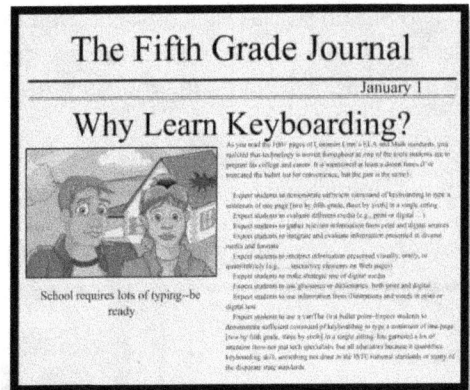

Figure 73—DTP newspaper

_____If you have iPads, you can use the free Microsoft and Mac apps, but be familiar with these as they will have differences from the fully-functioning software or online tools. Other iPad apps (these apps are easily found by searching in a browser):

- *Quark*
- *Pages*
- *Canva*
- *LucidPress*

Figure 74—DTP app

_____Open the desktop publishing tool and demonstrate on the class screen while students follow along on their digital devices. This newsletter will be one page, but you can make it longer if the student groups are larger than two.

_____In Publisher, select 'Newsletters' template. Change font/color schemes if desired.

_____Have students work together to arrange stories so that they explore the topic and share information clearly. Decide where each story fits best and copy-paste from the digital copy into columns. Review them as a group to insure they include facts, definitions, concrete details, quotations, and other information and examples related to the topic. Check for writing conventions, spelling, grammar, sentence flow.

_____When everyone approves, add the title (remember discussions on good titles), slogan, and one picture per story.

_____Fill in 'Inside This Issue' sidebar (if there is one) with a list of article titles.

_____Fill in 'Special Points of Interest' sidebar (if there is one) to highlight what ties articles together.

Assessment 14—Newsletter rubric

Newsletter
Grading Rubric

Your name: _____ Your teacher: _____

---

1. Newspaper title — **4 points**
   a. Title stands out—large font
   b. Spelling

2. Lead story — **2 points**
   a. Headline is creative
   b. Headline summarizes story
   c. Picture applies to story
   d. Grammar/spell check
   e. White space is minimal

3. Secondary story — **2 points**
   a. Headline is creative
   b. Headline summarizes story
   c. Picture applies to story
   d. Grammar/spell check
   e. No white space

4. Quotation (if required) — **2 points**
   a. On topic
   b. Spell/Grammar check

5. Four points of interest — **2 points**
   a. All deal with student's topic
   b. All deal with significant information
   c. Spell/grammar check

6. Additional — **4 points**
   a. Date included
   b. Volume and issue included
   c. Unnecessary template info deleted
   d. Keep info inside print border

7. Overall Professional Look — **4 points**
   a. Fonts/colors consistent
   b. Design pleasing
   c. Attention to detail

_____Students complete *Assessment 14* before submitting, to be sure all details have been addressed. If students have workbooks, they can complete the rubric there with the class annotation tool, take a screenshot and share with teacher.

_____If time is an issue, create a newspaper clipping *(this one from Fodey)*:

Figure 75—Newsletter with webtool

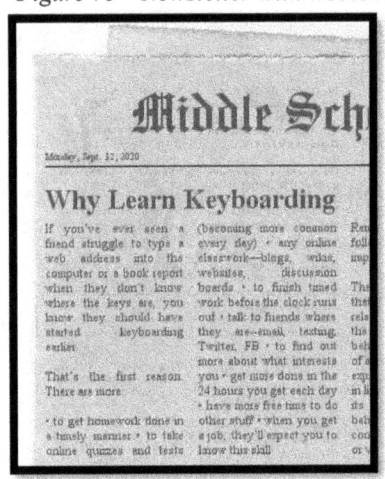

_____Newsletters can be printed and/or saved. Mulligan Rule will apply to this project.

_____Reflect on this project in a blog post with a screen shot of newsletter (use methods listed earlier). What challenges did students face? What was better/worse about working in a group than independently? Comment on three classmate posts to provide feedback on their reflections.

_____Throughout class, check for understanding.

Class exit ticket: *Students add their Google Earth Board presentation date and topic to class calendar.*

Differentiation

- Students handwrote stories? Use this as a keyboarding exercise. At an average fifth grade speed of 30 wpm, this won't take long.
- Add a drop cap at the beginning of each story.
- Instead of a newsletter, collaborate on a blog post on the topic.
- Use student Google Earth Board presentation topic for this DTP project.
- Early finishers: visit class internet start page for websites that tie into classwork.
- Replace with 5th Grade Lesson #3 Tessellations in the SL curriculum extenders.

My computer beat me at checkers, but I sure beat it at kickboxing.
— Emo Philips

The Internet: Where men are men, women are men, and children are FBI agents.
— Anonymous

5th Grade Technology Curriculum: Teacher Manual

Lesson #14 DTP: Calendar

Vocabulary	Problem solving	Skills
• DTP • Embed • Geek • Google Apps • Template	• Text doesn't show—all I see is 'A' (that's overflow. Downsize text) • How do I search Google Calendar (Ctrl+F) • How do I share (embed code)	**New** DTP calendar **Scaffolded** DTP
Academic Applications Classroom management, collaboration, history	**Materials Required** Evidence of Learning badges, Problem Solving Board assessment, calendar tool, student workbooks (if using)	**Standards** CCSS.W.5.4 NETS: 1d, 3d

Essential Question

How do I use technology to get organized?

Big Idea

Technology can organize life!

Teacher Preparation

- Collect list of school/class events.
- Talk with grade-level team so you tie into their inquiry
- Know whether you need extra time to complete lesson.
- Know which tasks weren't completed last week.
- Be prepared to use domain-specific tech vocabulary.
- Collect words for Speak Like a Geek Board presentations.
- If you offer afterschool tech help, verify selected students will be there.

Assessment Strategies

- Annotated workbooks (if using)
- [tried to] solve own problems
- Left room as student found it
- Completed project
- Used good keyboarding habits
- Worked well in groups
- Completed warm-up, exit ticket
- Joined class discussions
- Shared calendar
- Higher order thinking: analysis, evaluation, synthesis
- Habits of mind observed

Steps

Time required: 45 minutes in one sitting or a block of 20 minutes to complete calendar
Class warm-up: If students are taking the Problem Solving Board assessment (sample at end of lesson), they can start as soon as they arrive at class. If not, warm up with keyboarding on class typing tool.

_____Any evidence of learning to post on Evidence Board?
_____Pass out Problem Solving Board assessment. Give students ten minutes to complete—they should know these. Allow them to use Discussion Board as a resource. You can ask them to answer five or ten or all questions. You can grade five or ten, but answer as many as they can for extra credit. Choose what works for your student group.

_____Google Earth Board presentations start today. Students present their research and take audience questions. Grade based on knowledge, confidence, and presentation.
_____*Audience: While listening, decide what locations you'd like to use for upcoming Google Earth Tour.*

_____In preparation for holiday, make a calendar including festive events of the season. Demonstrate on class screen while students work at their stations.

_____Open desktop publishing program you are using at your school.

_____If you don't have a DTP program, MS Word has a template (*Figure 76a*) as does PowerPoint (*Figure 76b*):

Figure 76a—Calendar in Word; 76b—in PowerPoint

_____If your school uses Google, try Google Calendar. It's easily shared on many media.

_____If you have iPads, you can use the free Microsoft and Mac apps, but be familiar with these as they will have differences from the fully-functioning software or online tools.

_____Select calendar template; set date for one month. Change color and font schemes to holiday preference. Change pictures to match holiday (if appropriate). *Figures 77a-b* are examples:

Figure 77a-b—Sample DTP calendars

_____Go over upcoming events as a group. Have students share what they're doing. You add to calendar on class screen while students do the same on their computers. Resize font as needed to fit calendar cell. Add one event per date.

_____Add student name to lower right cell.

_____Before finishing, discuss pros and cons of placing a calendar online:

- *safety*
- *difficult to decorate*
- *easily shared*
- *automatically updates new events*
- *collaboration with others*
- *interaction with others as they read and share*

_____ Students show they're done by turning in the rubric (*Assessment 15*) as a hard copy or digitally-annotated in their workbooks with a tool like iAnnotate or Adobe.

Assessment 15—DTP Calendar rubric

DTP Calendar

Creator: _____

Teacher: _____

1. Layout _____ 8 points _____

    a. Title in large font
    b. Subtitle in smaller font
    c. Student name in small font
    d. Monthly pics relate to theme
    e. One pic in one date cell/Mo.
    f. Text fits in each date cell
    g. Each mo. includes all events
    h. One calendar/month

2. Appearance _____ 8 points _____

    a. Decorative border
    b. Attractive colors
    c. All pieces well-laid out
    d. Spell- and grammar-check
    e. No unusual white space

3. Overall Professional Work _____ 4 points _____

    a. Student worked independently
    b. Students solved own problems
    c. Student worked well in group
    d. Student saved, printed, shared

4. Extra Credit _____

_____ When done, share calendar:

- *Publisher or MS Word: via screen shot on student blogs.*
- *Google Calendars: embed into class website, blog, or Internet start page (Figure 78).*

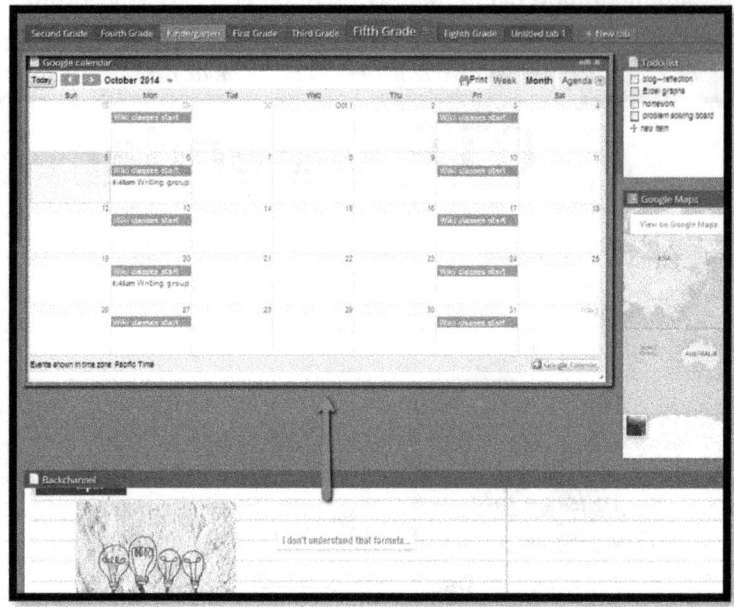

Figure 78—Calendar embedded into start page

_____Throughout class, check for understanding.

_____Done? Practice keyboarding on software or online website. Remember: Keyboard speed goal is 1) 30 wpm by end of year, and 2) ability to type two pages in a single sitting. Use:

- *good posture, hand position*
- *eyes on screen, elbows at sides*

Class exit ticket: **Have students add their birthdays to the class calendar.**

Differentiation

- Use Assessment 15 to determine results of Problem-solving Board.
- Add next week's speed quiz and trifold completion date to class calendar.
- Add picture to date cell to enhance event.
- Have students recreate calendar in Word. Do they prefer Word or the first tool?
- Replace this lesson with QR Me in curriculum extenders (from Structured Learning).

Assessment 16—Problem-solving Board quiz

Problem-solving Assessment

In Column #2 of the table below, type the solution to the problem or answer the question. You must answer at least ten problems. You may use My Falcon as a resource.

Double-click doesn't work	
Monitor doesn't work	
Volume doesn't work	
Computer doesn't work	
Mouse doesn't work	
What's does the right-mouse button do?	
What shortkey closes a program	
How do you move between cells or boxes with the keyboard	
How do you figure out today's date?	
You tried shift and it didn't capitalize the letter. What do you do?	
What's the difference between 'save' 'save-as'	
What's the shortkey for 'undo'	

How do you search for a file	
What is the protocol for saving a file	
How often do I back up?	
The number pad doesn't work. What do you do?	
When editing, what's the difference between *backspace* and *delete*	
How do you double space a Word doc	
How do you add a footer in Word	
How do you add a watermark in Word	
Your taskbar disappeared. How do you use start	
What are shortkeys for B, I, U	
How do you maximize the screen	
How do you zoom in on an Internet page	
How do you print one page of a document	

Lesson #15 DTP: Trifold I

Vocabulary	Problem solving	Skills
• Anecdotal • Brochure • Copyright law • Ctrl • Drill down • Formatting • Grammar • Graphic/Image • Handles • Layering • Line spacing • Page parts • Print border • Text box • Trifold	• Screen froze (Is dialogue box open?) • Page parts are outside print border (drag in) • Can't type on page (add text box) • I lost my work (did you Ctrl+S every ten minutes?) • Design element hid text (use layer tool) • I'm not ready for presentation (is there time later in schedule?) • Text gets behind a print element (use layering tools) • How do I pronounce 'Ctrl'? • I can't type on panel (add text box) • What's the difference between grammar and formatting?	**New** **Scaffolded** Trifold in DTP Speaking/listening Keyboarding Problem solving
Academic Applications Any subject that clumps themed information	**Materials Required** DTP, keyboard program and quiz, Google Earth Board rubrics, Evidence Board badges, trifold template	**Standards** CCSS.W.5.2 NETS: 1d, 3a-d, 6a, 6c

Essential Question

When would I use a trifold to share information?

Big Idea

Trifolds highlight important information quickly.

Teacher Preparation

- Have keyboard quiz (hard copy or link) available.
- Have a trifold template prepared with information students should include on each panel.
- Is class shorter than 45 minutes? Highlight critical items and leave the rest for 'later'.
- Know which tasks weren't completed last week and whether they are necessary to move forward.
- Be prepared to use domain-specific tech vocabulary.
- Continue to collect words students don't understand for Speak Like a Geek Board presentations.
- If you offer afterschool tech help and it's manned by students, verify they will be there.

Assessment Strategies

- *Used good keyboarding habits*
- *Text examines topic and conveys information clearly*
- *[tried to] solve own problems*
- *Presentation*
- *Trifold examines topic and conveys information clearly*
- *Decisions followed class rules*
- *Left room as student found it*
- *Completed warm-up, exit ticket*
- *Joined classroom conversations*
- *Higher order thinking: analysis, evaluation, synthesis*
- *Habits of mind observed*

Steps

Time required: 55 minutes in one sitting or a block of 10 minutes for quiz and 35 minutes for trifold set aside and the rest of class spread throughout the week

Class warm-up: Keyboarding on digital tool used in your school, using all keys

5th Grade Technology Curriculum: Teacher Manual

_____Keyboarding speed/accuracy quiz today. Grade is based on:

- *improvement from first quiz (20%=10/10; 10-19%=9/10; 1-9%=8/10; 0%=7/10; slower=6/10). Remind students they are not competing against the best class typists, only themselves.*
- *observation by you as teacher of good keyboarding habits (elbows at sides, no flying fingers/hands, all fingers used)*

_____Remind students to use good posture, curved hands over home row, elbows at sides, no flying fingers/hands.

_____Review keyboarding hints in *Figure 79*:

Figure 79—Keyboarding hints

Keyboarding Hints

These came directly from the classroom, tested on 400 students a year. These are the most common fixes that help students excel at keyboarding:

1. Tuck elbows against the sides of your body. This keeps hands in the right spot—home row
2. Use your RIGHT thumb for the space bar. That leaves hands on home row
3. Curl fingers over home row—they're cat paws, not dog paws
4. Use inside fingers for inside keys, outside fingers for outside keys
5. Use the finger closest to the key you need. Sounds simple, but this isn't what usually happens with beginners.
6. Keep pointers anchored to *f* and *j*
7. Play keyboard like a piano (or violin, or guitar, or recorder). You'd never use your pointer for all keys
8. Fingers move, not your hands. Hands stay anchored to the *f* and *j* keys
9. Don't use caps lock for capitals! Use shift.
10. Add a barrier between sides of the keyboards. I fashioned one from cover stock. That'll remind you to stay on the correct side of keyboard

_____Type five minutes using a sample or TypingTest.com. I like a hard copy because it provides opportunities to teach more skills (i.e., word count, spell-check, dictionary, save, and print).

_____Give one minute at end of test to spell-check. Type word count at bottom of page.

_____Save (Ctrl+S); print if necessary (Ctrl+P).

_____If students used an online tool like TypingTest.com, have them share a screenshot with you using one of the screenshot tools you've discussed this year.

_____Blank keyboard quiz next week. This will be like the first one taken, but graded.

_____Review results of Problem-solving assessment. What were common errors? What did most students remember?

_____Google Earth Board presentations continue.

_____Any evidence of learning to post on Evidence Board?

_____Continue with DTP Unit. Today, start a trifold brochure. This will be a summative project where students write an informative/explanatory text that examines a topic and conveys student ideas and information clearly. Student will group related information logically, including headings, illustrations, and design elements to aid comprehension.

_____Remind students of 4th grade trifold called 'This Day in History' (*Figures 80a-b*)—if you used the SL tech curriculum last year:

Figure 80a-b—4th grade trifold

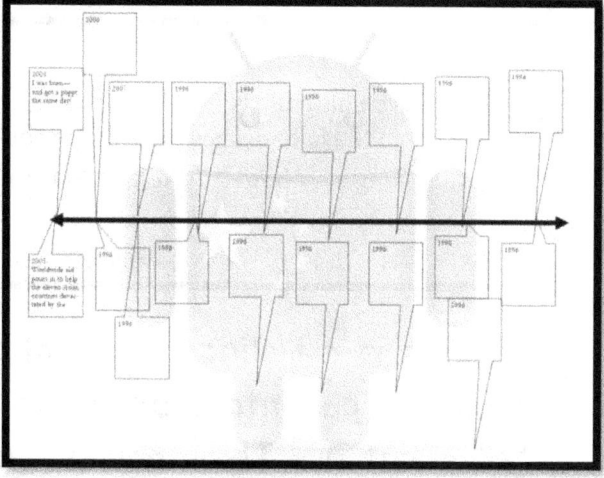

_____Students can use notes unless teacher directs otherwise.

_____*Figure 81a* is an example of a 5th-grade natural disasters trifold and *Figure 81b* on the colonies:

Figure 81a-b: 2 examples of 5th grade trifolds

_____If you don't have a desktop publishing program, you can create a trifold using a free template downloaded from the Microsoft website, like *Figure 82a*. Or, download a template from Google Docs (*Figure 82b*):

Figure 82a—Trifold in Word; 82b—in Google Docs

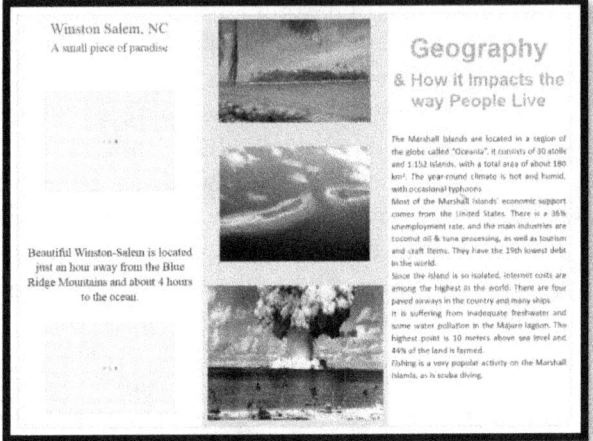

_____If you have iPads, you can use the app versions of MS Office or Mac, but know how they differ from the fully-fleshed program so you can adapt the project to accommodate them.

_____In *Figures 83a-b*, *83a* is grammatically-correct. *83b* makes you eager to read it.

Figure 83a-b: Story as plain text and formatted

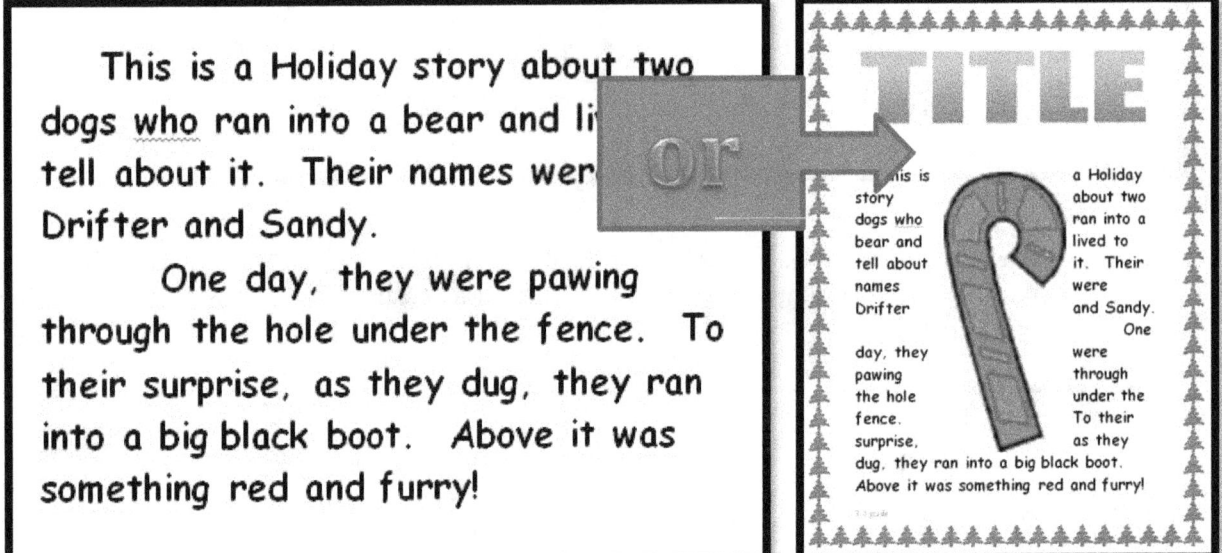

_____This is what you want to accomplish with desktop publishing—make words more consumable.

Trifold Basics

_____General trifold guidelines:

- is an informative text that examines a topic and conveys student ideas and information clearly
- groups related information logically, including headings, illustrations, and design elements to aid comprehension
- discussion of each topic comes from class conversations, books students have used, and other information acquired to understand the topic

_____Each trifold panel has (see *Figures 84a-b*):

- *title*
- *text*
- *image*
- *optional border*
- *optional other page part*

Figure 84a-b—Trifold template

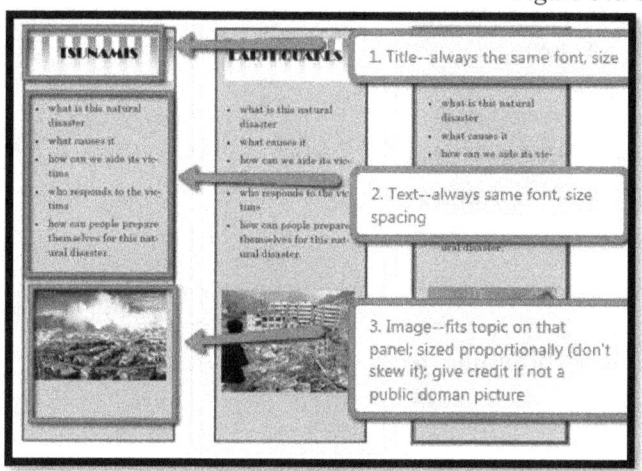 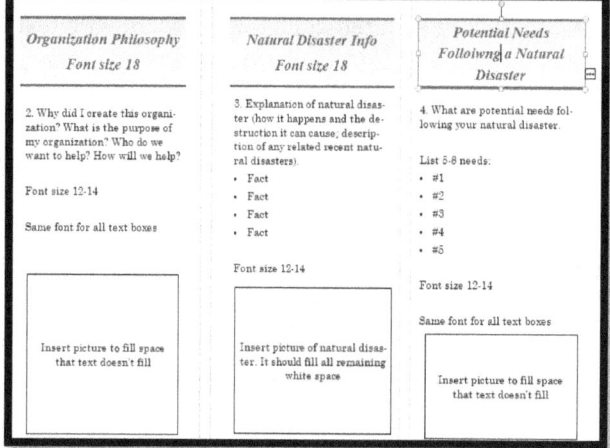

_____Review print border. All page parts must be set back from the margins to print correctly.

_____Before continuing, discuss use of online information (text and images). What are legalities associated with information found on the web? Discuss Internet plagiarism. Explain why common facts are rarely considered plagiarized, but other types of information (i.e., opinions, creative work) are and require credit be given to original author.

_____Open DTP tool. Select preferred layout. Adjust font and color schemes to suit the theme and 'create'.

Page 1

_____Today: Create Page 1, three panels. *Figures 85a-b* are two samples:

Figure 85a-b: Sample trifolds

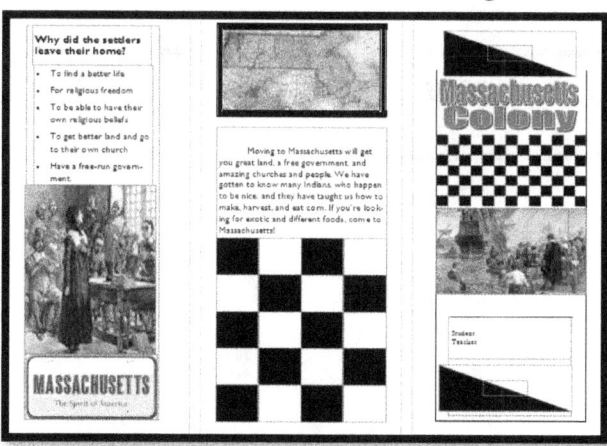 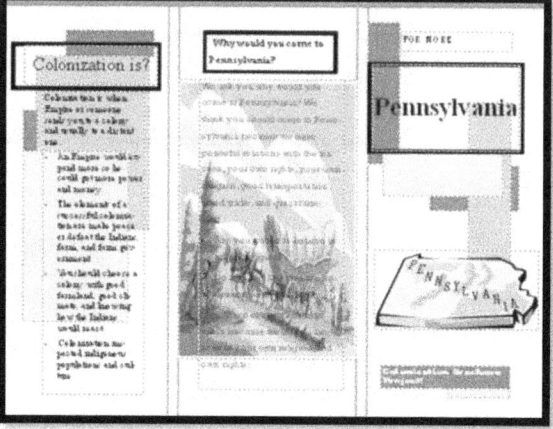

_____Discuss design elements—color, shapes, eye-catchers. Explain the part these play in drawing readers in. See if students can identify the design element pictures in the examples above?

_____Remind students: Discussion of topic comes from class conversations, books they've used, and other information acquired to understand topic. They are expected to provide evidence that they have learned the topic. No research required.

_____**Panel 3** (right side): Delete text boxes. Add title, picture, text box with student profile info (see *Figure 85a* on colonies and *Figure 82b* on natural disasters).

_____**Panel 2** (middle): Second page people look at. It must pull them in: Add text box with title and discussion of topic OR

_____**Panel 1** (left side): Add text box with one of four questions about topic. Bold and center title. Fill remaining white space with text, design elements, picture.

_____As students work, assist where needed.

_____Save every ten minutes.

_____Remind students: Every time they use computer, practice good keyboarding.

_____Throughout class, check for understanding.

_____Save to digital portfolio.

Class exit ticket: Ask students to take three minutes to look at neighbor's work and share thoughts with him/her. Is s/he missing anything? Is it clear? Cogent? Is grammar and spelling accurate? Only take three minutes.

Differentiation

- Add blank keyboard quiz to calendar.
- Have a student post trifold, blank keyboard quiz, and homework due dates on class calendar.
- Students can work in groups.
- Students who finish can add a picture to each panel that relates to discussion.
- If time is limited, add a collage of images on back cover rather than more text.
- Blog about their Fascinating Fact—at least one sentence that sums it up. These will be used for Google Earth Tour that starts Lesson 21. No blogs? Use a Discussion Board.
- Replace this lesson with How to Animoto in curriculum extenders (from Structured Learning).

"Error, no keyboard — press F1 to continue."

Lesson #16 DTP: Trifold II

Vocabulary	Problem solving	Skills
• Assessment • Copyright • Fair use • Formatting • Grammar • Network • Plagiarism • Public domain • Rubric • Text box • Trifold	• Can't print two-sided (print both pages; fold white sides back-to-back; staple corners) • My file isn't there (did you save to your digital portfolio? Or My Documents?) • My typing disappeared (Ctrl+Z) • What's the difference between 'grammar' and 'formatting' (this is trickier than it sounds) • I see 'A...' instead of text (there's too much text for box; enlarge)	**New** **Scaffolded** DTP trifolds Speaking and listening keyboarding
Academic Applications Any subject that clumps themed information	**Materials Required** DTP, graded keyboard quiz, Google Earth Board rubrics, Evidence Board badges, blank keyboards for quiz, student workbooks (if using)	**Standards** CCSS.W.5.2 NETS: 1d, 3a-d, 6a, 6c

Essential Question

When would I use a trifold to share information?

Big Idea

Trifolds are a unique way to share information

Teacher Preparation

- Have copies of blank keyboard (if not using workbooks).
- Have graded speed/accuracy quizzes from last week.
- Have a template with what students include.
- Be prepared to use domain-specific tech vocabulary.
- Is class shorter than 45 minutes? Highlight critical items and leave the rest for 'later'.
- Know whether you need extra time to complete lesson.
- What tech problems do students need help with?
- Know which tasks weren't completed last week and whether they are necessary to move forward.
- Collect words students don't understand to include in Speak Like a Geek Board presentations.
- If you offer afterschool tech help and it's manned by students, verify they will be there.

Assessment Strategies

- Anecdotal
- Annotated workbooks (if using)
- [tried to] solve own problems
- Used good keyboarding habits
- Left room as s/he found it
- Completed project and rubric
- Completed assessment
- Completed warm-up, exit ticket
- Worked well collaboratively
- Joined classroom conversations
- Higher order thinking: analysis, evaluation, synthesis
- Habits of mind observed:

Steps

Time required: 45 minutes in one sitting or 10 minutes throughout week, 10 minutes for assessment, 25 minute block to complete trifold

Class warm-up: Students show neighbors they can open trifold from last week.

_____ Give students blank keyboard quiz (see *Assessments* in Keyboarding lesson for full size). They can work in groups. Students can annotate the sample in the student workbooks if you use these. Flip all keyboards over so no one is tempted. Students get ONLY five-ten minutes for this quiz. They should know key placement by now.

_____Grading for the blank keyboard quiz is the same as the speed/accuracy quiz: based on improvement from the first quiz students took at the beginning of the year.

_____Review speed quiz. What common problems did you notice (flying hands, not using thumb for spacebar)? Who hit grade-level expectation? What was class average? Pass out certificates like *Figure 86a* (if you do this) for Keyboard Speedsters and Best Class. *Figure 86b* is a list you can post on the class bulletin board to honor those who reach 30 wpm:

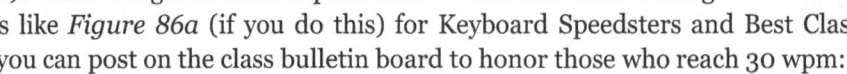

Figure 86a—Keyboarding certificate; 86b—Speedsters

_____Remind students of monthly homework.
_____Continue Google Earth Board presentations.
_____Any evidence of learning?

Page 2, Trifold

_____Today, students finish their trifolds.
_____Put one question as heading on each of the three trifold panels. Headings are font 16, bold, centered. Each answers a question assigned by the teacher.

Figure 87a-b—Trifold templates

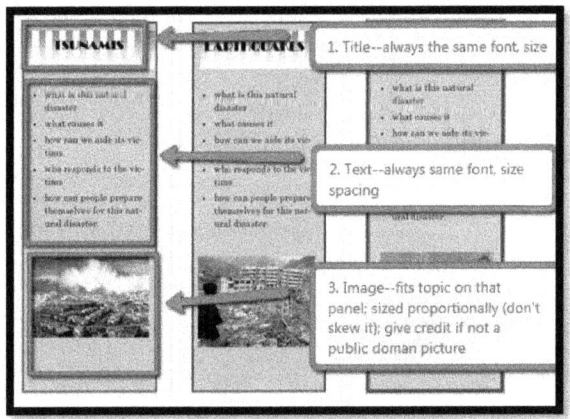
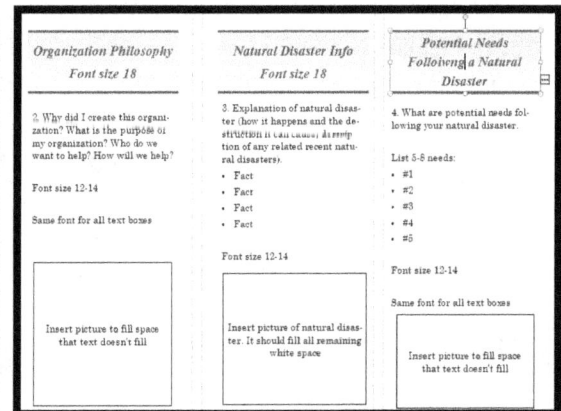

_____Check headings. Do size, font, color, placement match?
_____Add a text box and type in answers to questions. Use good grammar, spelling. Double space (rather than indent) between paragraphs.
_____What's the difference between 'grammar' and 'formatting'? How do you accomplish each? How do they contribute to a well-developed project?

- **Grammar**: *spelling, punctuation, capitalization, red/green squiggly lines*
- **Formatting**: *borders, fancy title, color, layout, images*

Figure 88a-d—Grammar vs. formatting

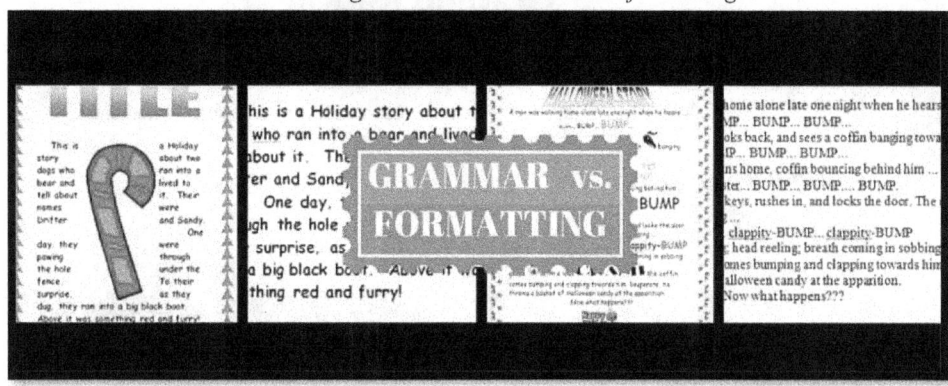

_____In *Figures 88a-d*, which images are formatted (a and c)? Which are simply grammar-checked (b and d)?

_____Add one picture to each trifold panel that expresses main idea. Before students search Internet for images, review Lesson 14 concepts of **plagiarism, copyright, fair use, public domain**. Also circle back on discussions on Internet safety.

_____If trifold has blank white space, fill space with creative design elements that fit topic.

_____Remind students: Every time they use the computer, practice good keyboarding.

_____When done with trifold, work with a partner to complete grading rubric (at end of lesson). Students fill it out for each other, and then make required corrections. If possible, provide digital copies of assessment so students can complete them with an annotation tool.

_____Also, confirm that:

- *trifold is informative, examines a topic, and conveys information clearly*
- *information is grouped logically*
- *discussion of each topic comes from class conversations, books they've used, and other information acquired to understand topic*

_____Print two-sided if possible.
_____Grading: the **Mulligan Rule** is in effect.
_____Save to digital portfolio. Share/publish as is the custom in your classroom.
_____When done, practice keyboarding on software or online websites.

Class exit ticket: ***Grading rubric can be completed in the student workbook and submitted to the teacher as a hard copy or digitally.***

Differentiation

- *Remind students to blog about their Google Earth Fascinating Fact. These will be used for Lesson 21. If you don't have blogs, create a Discussion Board that students can add to.*
- *If this lesson doesn't work for your students, use one from How to Jumpstart the Inquiry-based Classroom (from Structured Learning) with additional projects aligned with SL curricu-*

Assessment 17—Trifold Brochure rubric

DTP TRIFOLD BROCHURE
Grading Rubric

Your name: _____

Your homeroom teacher: _____

1. **Title Page**   **4 points** _____
   - a. *Eye catching and clear* _____
   - b. *All fonts match* _____
   - c. *Brochure title stands out* _____
   - d. *Your name and class in smaller font* _____
   - e. *White space filled* _____
   - f. *Grammar and spelling* _____

2. **Back page**   **4 points** _____
   - a. *Eye catching and clear* _____
   - b. *All fonts match* _____
   - c. *Picture and text fill white space* _____
   - d. *Grammar and spelling* _____
   - e. *Examines topic and conveys ideas clearly* _____
   - f. *Related information is grouped logically* _____

3. **Inside**   **9 points** _____
   - a. *Headings in larger font* _____
   - b. *All fonts match* _____
   - c. *No white spaces* _____
   - d. *Pictures fit events discussed* _____
   - e. *Spell-check* _____
   - f. *Grammar check* _____
   - g. *Examines topic and conveys ideas clearly* _____
   - h. *Related information is grouped logically* _____

4. **Overall Professional Look**   **3 points** _____
   (inside print lines, attractive look, organized, easy to understand, etc.)

   How I grade myself: _____

5th Grade Technology Curriculum: Teacher Manual

Lesson #17 Spreadsheet Formulae

Vocabulary	Problem solving	Skills
• Border • Cell • Decimal place • Formulas • Place value • Right-aligned • Row/Column • Spreadsheet	• I can't find my file (where did you save it?) • Formula doesn't work (click cell and check it) • All I get is ***** (cell isn't large enough; widen column) • I don't see decimal points (check cell formatting)	**New** Arrays Modeling w/ spreadsheets Merge-center **Scaffolded** Formulae for add, subtract multiply, divide
Academic Applications Math, any class that requires data evaluation	**Materials Required** spreadsheet program/rubric, Google Earth rubric, keyboard tool, Evidence Board badges, student workbooks (if using)	**Standards** CCSS: Math.Content.5.NBT.B.7 NETS:1d, 3d, 5a-b

Essential Question

What are the essential skills required to analyze numbers?

Big Idea

Spreadsheets are a unique way to share information

Teacher Preparation

- Talk with grade-level team about essential spreadsheet skills (formulas, formatting, graphs, etc.).
- Know how grade-level team teaches place value.
- Continue to collect words for Speak Like a Geek Board.
- Be prepared to use domain-specific tech vocabulary.
- Know whether you need extra time for this lesson.
- Is class shorter than 45 minutes? Highlight critical items and leave the rest for 'later'.
- Know which tasks weren't completed last week and whether they are necessary to move forward.
- If you offer afterschool tech help and it's manned by students, verify they will be there.

> **Assessment Strategies**
> - Anecdotal
> - [tried to] solve problems
> - Decisions followed class rules
> - Left room as student found it
> - Shared evidence of learning
> - Used prior knowledge
> - Understood decimal places
> - Completed warm-up, exit ticket
> - Completed project
> - Joined classroom conversations
> - Higher order thinking: analysis, evaluation, synthesis
> - Habits of mind observed

Steps

Time required: 45 minutes either in one sitting or spread throughout the week, with a 10 minute block for keyboarding, 10 minutes for start-up tasks, and 25 minutes for spreadsheet lesson

Class warm-up: Keyboard practice. Remind students to pay attention to posture, hand position, elbows, and flying fingers.

_____Want a 'different' keyboard practice? Visit Ask a Tech Teacher *Keyboarding* resource pages.

_____Continue with Google Earth Board presentations.

_____Any evidence of learning for Evidence Board?

_____Remember spreadsheet projects from 2nd (*Figure 89a*-Gingerbread House), 3rd (*Figure 89b*—Auto Math) and 4th (*Figure 89c*—Graphs) grade—if you used the SL tech curriculum in the past:

Figure 89a-c: Spreadsheet projects K-4

 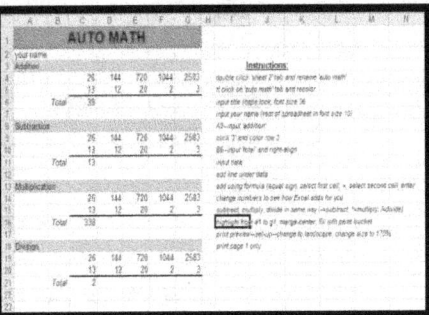 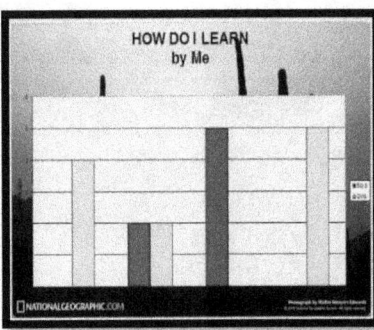

_____For this Lesson, use Numbers, Excel, or Google Spreadsheets. If you have Chromebooks, use the online versions (Office 365 and Google Drive). If you have iPads, use the app versions of MS Office or Mac, but know they will differ from the fully-featured program. Know the differences so you can adapt the project to accommodate them.

_____Today we explore spreadsheet formulas. This lesson ties into pre-programming, logical thinking, and critical thinking (a follow up on coding).

_____What does it mean to 'model' a concept? What are some models you are aware of? Anyone make model airplanes? Lego models? Discuss how important it is that modeling is done carefully, with precision. Each tool used must be exact and structured. In this way, anyone who sees a 'model' gets the message. See *Figures 90a* and *90b* for a math and a science model:

Figure 90a-b: Academic formulae

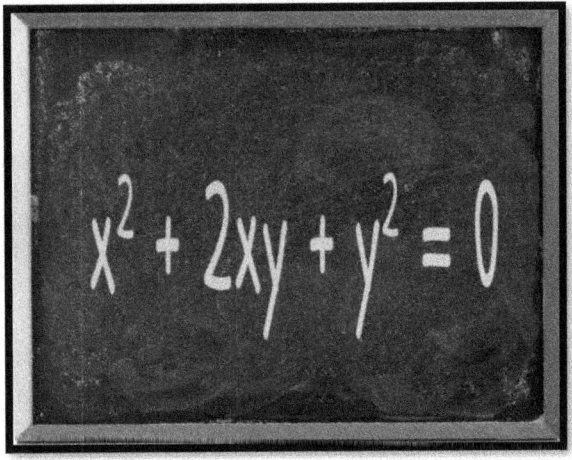 

_____Discuss how spreadsheets support the following Standards for Mathematical Practice:

- *Make sense of problems and persevere in solving them.*
- *Reason abstractly, quantitatively.*
- *Construct viable arguments; critique reasoning of others.*
- *Model with mathematics.*
- *Use appropriate tools strategically.*
- *Attend to precision.*
- *Look for and express regularity in repeated.*

_____Why pick spreadsheets for these goals rather than DTP? Have students revisit the chart you presented when discussing the question (*Figure 91*) earlier this year:

Figure 91—Compare/contrast digital tools

Element	Slideshow	Word processing	Spread—sheets	DTP
Purpose	Share a presentation	Share words	Turn numbers into information	Share information using a variety of media
Basics	Graphics-based Design is important to content Layout communicates Few words, lots of images	Text-based Design is secondary to content Layout may detract from words Primarily words communicate	Number-based Focus on tables, graphs Little text; lots of statistics and date Almost no words	Mix of media—equal emphasis on text, images, layout, color
Sentences	Bulleted, phrases	Full sentences with proper conventions	None	Full sentences, bullets,
Content	Slides cover basics, to remind presenter what to say	Thorough discussion of a topic. Meant to be complete document	Statistics, data, charts, graphs	To draw an audience in;
Use	As a back-up to presentation	As complete resource	To support other presentation methods	Good way to group information for easy consumption
Presentation	Speaker presents with their back to the slideshow	Speaker reads from document	Speakers uses it in a presentation or 1:1	Speaker passes out as a handout or take-way
What else				

_____Why are spreadsheets an appropriate math tool? What insight do they offer (for example, to double check answers)?

_____If students use workbooks, have them fill in the cells in the sample.

_____In this lesson, choose one of these two activities:

- Practice building arrays as an alternative method for answering math problems. This can tie into class discussions on arrays.
- Review spreadsheet formulae for adding, subtracting, multiplying, and dividing discussed in 3rd grade (from Auto Math).

Arrays

_____If you haven't built arrays in a spreadsheet program, you may want to choose this over a review of formulae to widen student numbers literacy. Open spreadsheet program. Double-click 'sheet one' tab; rename 'Arrays'; change tab color independently.

_____Using *Figure 92* as an example, students build arrays by coloring blocks and adding cell borders to answer relevant math problems.

_____Students have used spreadsheets since 1st grade. Ask them to work as independently as possible (or in small groups) using their problem solving strategies to go through as many steps as possible on their own.

_____Be sure to show students how to set column width so cells are square.

Figure 92—Arrays with spreadsheets

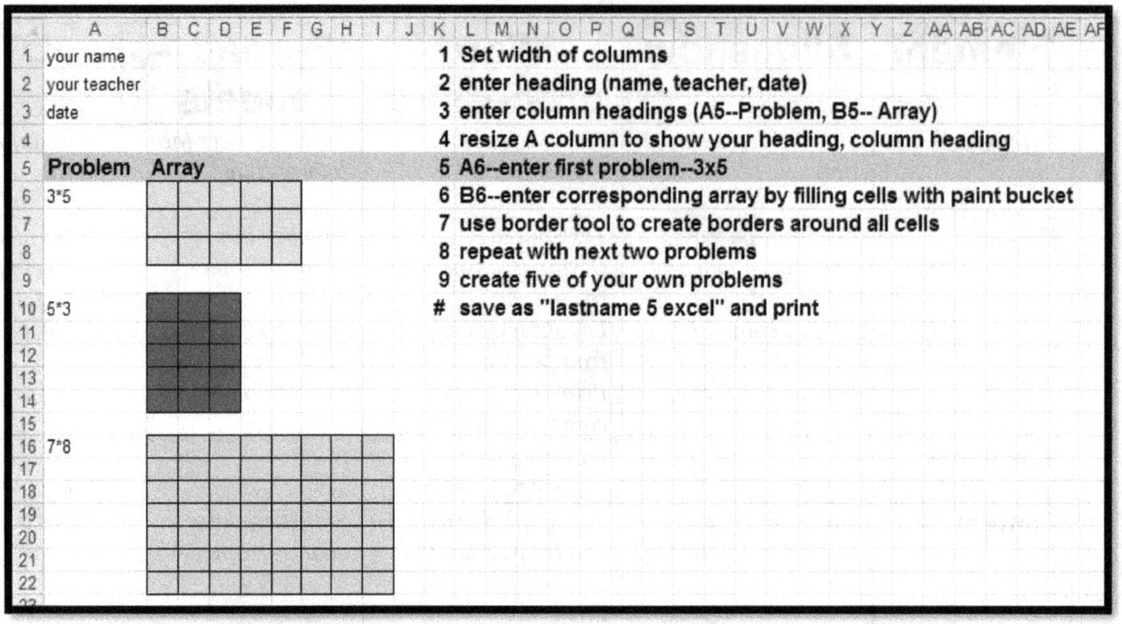

_____ When done, save/print/share/publish, as is the custom in your classroom.

Automath

_____ This is a review of skills introduced in 3rd grade. Students should work as independently as possible, only requesting teacher assistance after they've exhausted their problem-solving strategies (from an earlier unit).

_____ Follow directions on the right side of *Figure 93* under 'Instructions'.

Figure 93—Automath with spreadsheets

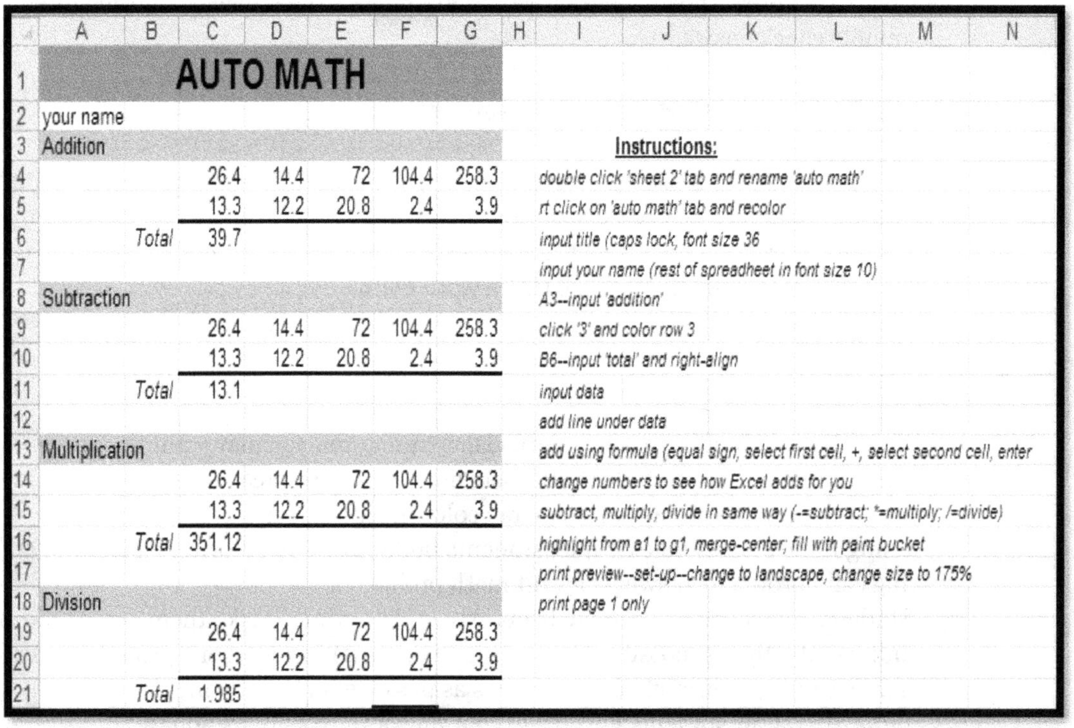

_____If students have workbooks, have them turn to that page as they work.
_____A1—add title (Auto Math), font size 36; merge-center cells A1-G1 (new skill for fifth grade); color with paint bucket.
_____A2—add student name.
_____A3—type 'Addition'; click on row 3 to select entire row; use paint bucket to color. Or, select A3-G3 and color with paint bucket.
_____Before inputting numbers, discuss place value. Show students how to format cells for multiple decimal places.
_____Add line beneath bottom row of data.
_____In cell beneath line, use formula to solve math problem. The easiest way to create a formula is (see *Figures 94a-c*):

- type =
- select first cell you want
- input function —,+, /,*
- select second cell you want to use
- push enter for answer

Figure 94a-c: Deconstructing spreadsheet formulae

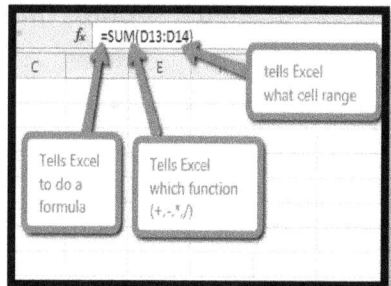 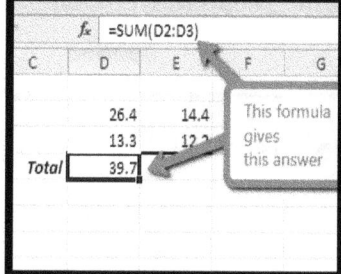 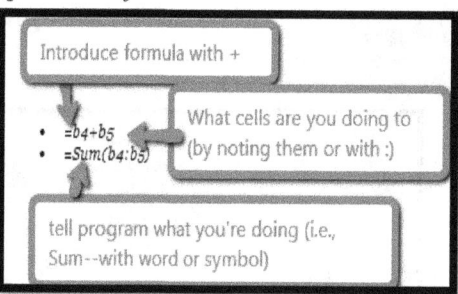

_____In short: A formula is built from four parts:

- = (*introduce formula*)
- **Function** (*add, subtract, multiply, divide*)
- **Location** (*cells that function applies to*)
- *( )* (*group numbers*)

_____Resulting formula will look like *Figure 94c*.
_____Add 'Total' next to the answers; right-align in cell. Complete at least five problems by inputting the formula (not answers) into the spreadsheet.
_____Before entering answer formula, try to get the answer with mental math. This can be done several ways:

- poll class for answer
- race the spreadsheet—will you or program get answer first?
- work in pairs—one student mentally calculates answer while second uses formula

_____Finish problems for other functions in similar fashion using:

- **+ = add**
- **- = subtract**
- *** = multiply**
- **/ = divide**

_____In spreadsheet, analyze relationship between these two variables. Identify which are 1) dependent, and 2) independent variables. How does changing one affect the other?

_____Look both for general methods and shortcuts. For example, copy formula =b4+b5 and replace addition symbol with * for multiplication. Why does this work?

_____When answer shows up, does it look correct:

- eyeball to determine if it is accurate
- use mental math
- guess-and-check
- use algorithm from class

_____This can be done in small groups.

_____If students are expected to print, have them switch to 'landscape'; adjust size to fit one page. Share/publish as required.

_____Throughout class, check for understanding.

Class exit ticket: Have students 1) line up in arrays), or 2) change data in three cells and watch the program recalculate—depending upon which option you selected.

Differentiation

- Do one set of numbers with decimal places, another rounding to next whole number. Evaluate difference between answers.
- Have students use a spreadsheet to complete math homework.
- Early finishers: visit class internet start page for math websites.

I cannot conceive that anybody will require multiplications at the rate of 40,000 or even 4,000 per hour.

— F. H. Wales, 1936

Lesson #18 More Spreadsheet Formulae

Vocabulary	Problem solving	Skills
• Alt+F4 • Autosum • Calculation • Cell address • Cells • Count • Expressions • F row • Formula • Max • Min	• I can't find my document/file (Start-search) • I can't remember how to create a graph (highlight data, F11) • My formula doesn't work (did you start with =?) • Numbers didn't add (is there text in cell instead of a number?) • How do I color tab? (right click) • How do I center (same tools as used in Word)	**New** Formulae for mean, median, mode, count, max, min **Scaffolded** Spreadsheets Formulas graphs
Academic Applications Math, any class that requires data evaluation (i.e., a student invention project)	**Materials Required** Problem-solving Board rubric, Evidence Board badges, spreadsheet program, sample data to evaluate, student workbooks (if using)	**Standards** CCSS: Math.Content.5.OA NETS: 1d, 3c, 5a-b

Essential Question

How do I evaluate data objectively so others understand?

Big Idea

Spreadsheets can turn dull data into intriguing information

Teacher Preparation

- Is class shorter than 45 minutes? Highlight items that must be completed and leave the rest for 'later'.
- Be prepared to use domain-specific tech vocabulary.
- Know if you need extra time to complete this lesson.
- Know which tasks weren't completed last week and whether they are necessary to move forward.
- Ask grade-level team and parents if there are any tech problems you can assist students with.
- Continue to collect words students don't understand for Speak Like a Geek Board presentations.
- If you offer afterschool tech help and it's manned by students, verify they will be there.

Assessment Strategies

- Anecdotal
- Understood relationship of formulae to data
- Completed exit ticket
- Completed spreadsheet
- [tried to] solve own problems
- Decisions followed class rules
- Left room as student found it
- Joined class conversations
- Higher order thinking: analysis, evaluation, synthesis
- Habits of mind observed

Steps

Time required: 45 minutes in one sitting or spread throughout week, setting aside 10 minutes to compare-contrast and 25 minutes for core project.

Class warm-up: None

_____ Continue Google Earth Board presentations.
_____ For this project, use Numbers, Excel, or Google Spreadsheets on PC or Mac computers. If you have Chromebooks, use the online version (Office 365 and Google Drive). If you have iPads, use MS Office or Mac app, but know the differences from the fully-featured program and adapt the

project to accommodate them.

_____Open spreadsheet tool. Today, students will learn new formulae and apply them to an authentic situation they will face in class.

_____Rename worksheet 'speed quiz'; color to preference (remember doing this in 3rd grade). Expect students to do this independently by following directions on the right side of *Figure 95*. If they have workbooks, students can follow along there:

Figure 95—Spreadsheet project

	A	B	C	D	E	F	G
1	**T2 SPEED QUIZ**						
2		WPM	Grade		Teach this with each speed quiz:		
3	1	22	9		rename tab	font size	
4	2	21	10		recolor tab	fill	
5	3	19	6		enter data	merge cells	
6	4	14	8		average column		
7	5	21	8		Teach this with 3-week training		
8	6	24	8		add count, min, max, median, mode		
9	7	29	10		add label for WPM and Grade		
10	8	28	10		add labels for formulas		
11	9	19	9		click on cells and see the formula		
12	10	21	10		add separater line under data		
13	11	15	8		B/I rows 21-24		
14	12	17	10		F11 graph		
15	13	16	10			Who's the slowest	
16	14	19	10			Who's the fastest	
17	15	20	10			Who got the highest grade	
18	16	18	10			Who got the lowest grade	
19	17	14	10		Format Graph		
20	18	20	10			rt click--chart options	
21	average	19.83333	9.222222			explore chart options	
22	median	19.5	10			rt-click--chart type	
23	mode	21	10			change colors	
24	count	18	18			change background	
25	max	29	10				
26	min	14	6				
27							

_____Go to **A1**—add a title (for example, *T2 Speed Quiz*).

_____Go to **A2**—enter column headings ('WPM' and 'Grade' in *Figure 95*).

_____Go to **A3**—enter data. Remind students: *Enter* moves down column; *tab* moves to the next column; *Shift+tab* moves to previous column. Display input on the class screen.

_____Remind students: Only put numbers in cells—spreadsheets can't evaluate letters or symbols.

_____Discuss meaning of mean, median, mode. Explain how to calculate:

- *highlight data; use autosum to average*
- *notice formula in the cell: =AVERAGE(H8:H15)*
- *copy/paste formula and replace AVERAGE with Mean, median, or mode*

_____Relate these formulas to numerical expressions, operations, and algebraic thinking inquiry.

_____What conclusions can you draw from spreadsheet information?

_____Save to student digital portfolio.
_____Throughout class, check for understanding.

Class exit ticket: ***Students share a screenshot of their spreadsheet with you.***

Differentiation

- *Because this is a review, use this lesson as a formative assessment of spreadsheet skills.*
- *Try other formulas that interest students (turn a cell red, if-then).*
- *Try Excel games from Mashable*
- *Play Excel Battleship! (check Ask a Tech Teacher resource page, Games)*
- *Try these Google Spreadsheet tricks from Ask the Gooru.*
- *Play Lemonade Stand (Google for address). Evaluate data with a spreadsheet.*
- *Have students practice keyboarding with good posture and hand position.*

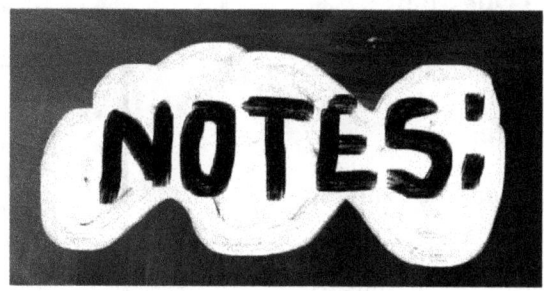

5th Grade Technology Curriculum: Teacher Manual

Lesson #19 Graphs

Vocabulary	Problem solving	Skills
• Autosum • Axis • F11 • Format • Formula • Legend • Workbook • Worksheet	• I can't find my file folder (are you logged in correctly?) • I can't find my file (did you save to your digital portfolio?) • Graph is empty (data highlighted) • Making charts is confusing (F11) • What's the difference between save and 'save-as'?	**New** Analyzing data from charts and graphs **Scaffolded** Tables Charts Graphs
Academic Applications Any class that requires modeling of data	**Materials Required** spreadsheet rubric, Google Earth rubric, keyboarding program, Evidence Board badges	**Standards** CCSS.Math.Practice.MP4 NETS: 1d, 5a, 6d

Essential Question

How do I visually display a data set?

Big Idea

A graph will visually display a data set.

Teacher Preparation

- Talk with grade-level team about spreadsheet skills essential to fifth grade (formulas, formatting, graphs, etc.).
- Know whether you need extra time for this lesson.
- Know which tasks weren't completed last week and whether they are necessary to move forward.
- Be prepared to integrate domain-specific vocabulary.
- Continue to collect words for Speak Like a Geek Board presentations.
- If you offer afterschool tech help and it's manned by students, verify they will be there.

Assessment Strategies

- Anecdotal
- Decisions followed class rules
- Completed project
- Followed directions
- Completed warm-up, exit ticket
- Joined class discussion
- Able to interpret data
- Left room as student found it
- Higher order thinking: analysis, evaluation, synthesis
- Habits of mind observed

Steps

Time required: 45 minutes in one sitting or spread throughout the week with 10 minutes for keyboarding warm-up and 35 minutes for graphs

Class warm-up: Keyboarding practice with good posture, hand position, eyes on screen.

_____ Google Earth Board presentations finish today. Anyone who hasn't, will present today.
_____ Any evidence of learning for Evidence Board?
_____ For this project, you can use Numbers, Excel, or Google Spreadsheets on PC or Mac computers. If you have Chromebooks, you can use online versions (Office 365 or Google Apps). If you have iPads, you can use the MS Office or Mac app, but know how they differ from the fully-featured program so you can adapt the project to accommodate them.

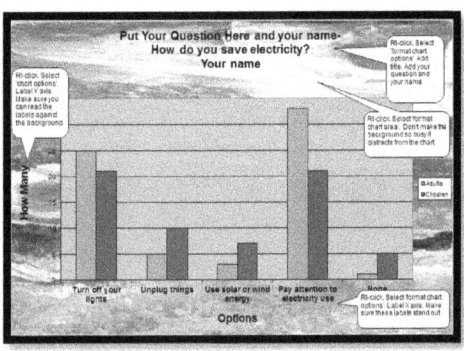

163

_____If a web-based tool works best for you, try Lucid Chart or another from the Ask a Tech Teacher resource pages for *Visual Learning*.

_____Have students open their spreadsheet workbook (keep all spreadsheet practice in the same workbook by adding new tabs for new worksheets). If necessary, demonstrate on the class screen. Today: Take a classroom poll and turn it into a graph. This may be adapted to any topic that fits inquiry in the classroom.

Figure 96—Turn data into a graph

	A	B	C	D	E	F	G	H	I
1	**HOW DO I LEARN**								
2	your name					Instructions:			
3	date (use shortkey)				1	double click 'sheet 3' tab and rename 'survey data'			
4		Boys	Girls		2	rt click on 'survey data' tab and recolor			
5	Reading	0	4		3	A1--input title (caps lock, font size 12)			
6	Writing	2	2		4	A2--input your name (rest of spreadheet in font size 10)			
7	Listening	5	0		5	A3--date (Ctrl+;)			
8	Talking	0	5		6	B3/B4, input 'boys', 'girls'			
9					7	A4-A8--input subjects			
10					8	survey class to collect data			
11					9	highlight from a1 to c1, merge-center, fill with paint bucket			
12					10	highlight from A4-c8; f11			
13	**WHEN I DO HOMEWORK**								
14		Boys	Girls		11	format chart			
15	Do early				12	add title, x and y labels			
16	Do on time				13	add backgrounds			
17	Do late				14	print preview--set-up--change to landscape, size to 175%			
18	Don't do				15	Print page 1 only			

_____*Figure 96* has a list of instructions (right side, under 'Instructions). Many of the skills students already know from 2nd-4th grade. They can work independently or in small groups until they reach 'survey class to collect data'.

- A1—add title (i.e., *How Do I learn*)
- A2—add student name
- A3—add date
- B4-C4—add column headings (i.e., *boys* and *girls*)
- A5-A8—add categories (i.e., *reading, writing, listening, talking*, or your own)

_____Collect data as a class with a call for hands.
_____Highlight A4-C8. Push F11 to make graph.
_____Format graph:

- *add title; add x and y labels*
- *add a background if desired; format plot area*
- *add student name*

_____In *Figures 97a-b*, discuss the differences between how a graph and table represent data. Is one better or worse than the other? Clearer or more confusing? How about interpretation of data—is there a danger in allowing the graph to interpret data for us—that we won't draw our own conclusions?

Figure 97a-b: Table vs. Graph

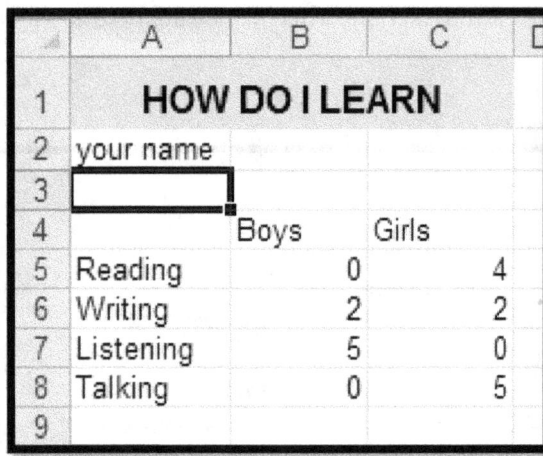 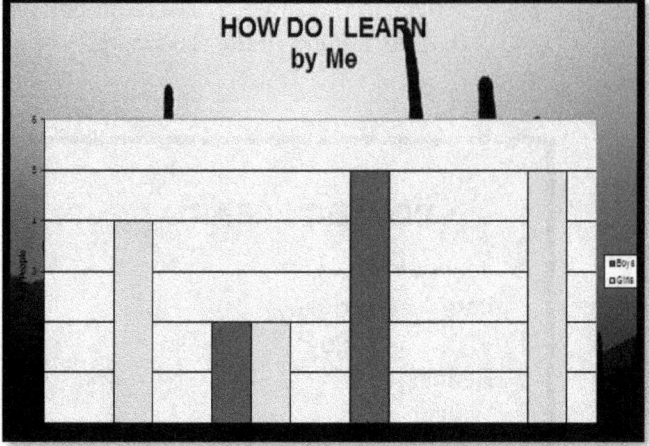

_____Ask students to re-form graph as a line graph, a 3D graph, or other options (*Figure 98a* is in MS Word; *Figure 98b* is in Google Spreadsheets).

Figure 98a-b: Graph options in Excel and Spreadsheet

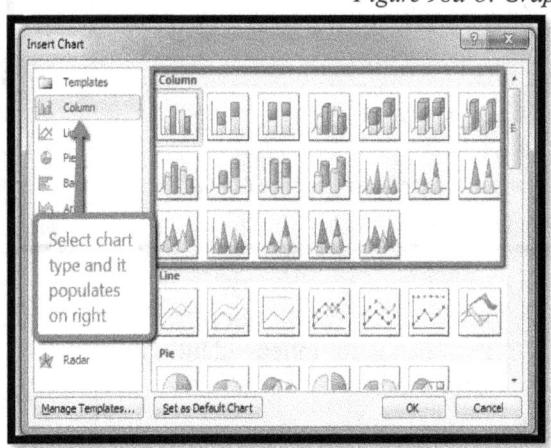 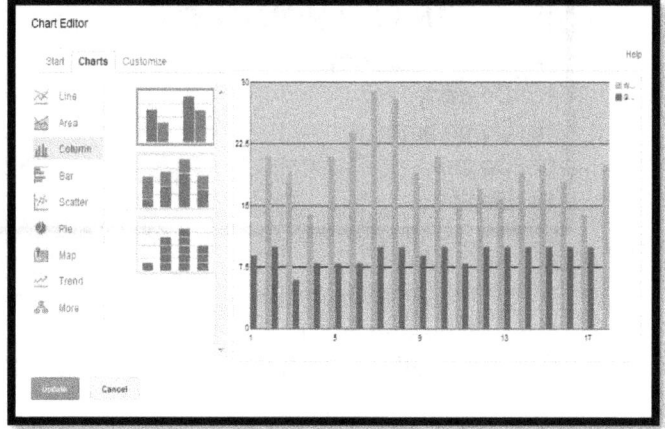

_____The graphs in *Figures 99a-b* represent the same data. Which is clearer?

Figure 99a-b: Two types of graphs

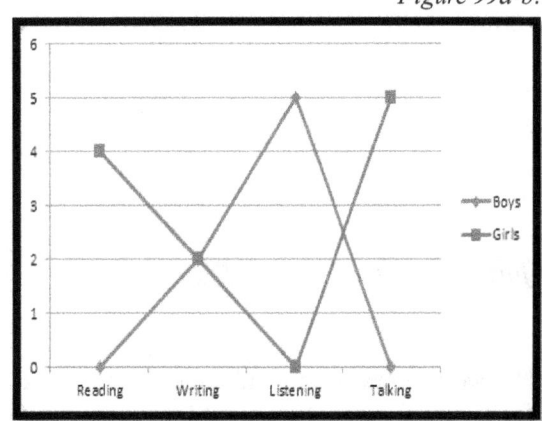 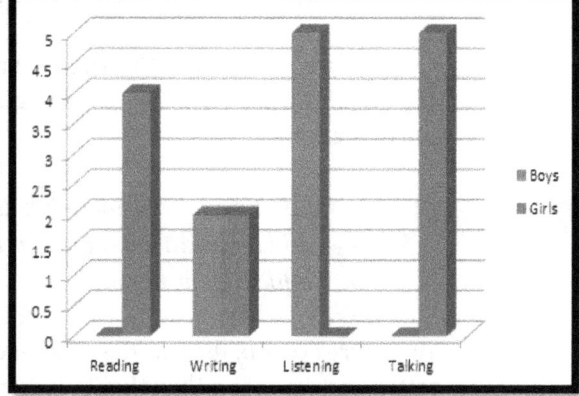

_____With graph on class screen, ask students about what they observe:

- *Which subject did girls like best?*
- *If girls 'writing' results were redistributed equally among other three choices, which would be the favorite?*
- *By what percent did girls like writing more than boys liked talking?*

_____Save to digital portfolio. Print/publish/share as desired.
_____Throughout class, check for understanding.
_____Remind students to transfer knowledge to classroom or home.

Class exit ticket: ***Change the data in the table and observe how it changes the graph.***

Differentiation

- Add spreadsheet summative assessment (coming up next week) date to class calendar.
- If homework is due, add to class calendar.
- Blog about student Fascinating Fact—at least one sentence. These will be used for Google Earth Tour lesson. If you don't use blogs, do this on a Discussion Board.
- Early finishers: Visit graphing websites, i.e. the National Library of Virtual Manipulatives).

_____

_____

_____

_____

_____

_____

5th Grade Technology Curriculum: Teacher Manual

Lesson #20 Spreadsheet Summative

Vocabulary	Problem solving	Skills
• Data • Format • Formula • Function • Hyperlink • Quantitative	• My cell says **** (widen column) • Can't find hyperlink tool (use Ctrl+K instead) • I put data in, but it didn't take (push enter) • My formula doesn't work (start with =?)	**New** **Scaffolded** Spreadsheet skills
Academic Applications Assessment of student tech skills; math	**Materials Required** spreadsheet program and assessment, keyboarding program, Speak Like a Geek sign-ups, student workbooks (if using), companion site	**Standards** CCSS: Math.Practice.MP5 NETS: 5a-d, 6a

Essential Question

Do spreadsheets help me share information?

Big Idea

Use spreadsheets to share number-oriented information.

Teacher Preparation

- Talk with grade-level team about spreadsheet skills.
- Be prepared to use domain-specific tech vocabulary.
- Know whether you need extra time to complete lesson.
- Have websites on class start page for early finishers.
- Is class shorter than 45 minutes? Highlight items most important to your integration with classroom studies.
- Know which tasks weren't completed last week.
- If you offer afterschool tech help manned by students, verify they will be there.

Assessment Strategies

- Anecdotal
- Completed assessment
- Used test taking strategies
- Employed Common Core skills
- [tried to] solve own problems
- Decisions followed class rules
- Left room as student found it
- Completed warm-up
- Joined classroom conversations
- Higher order thinking: analysis, evaluation, synthesis
- Habits of mind observed

Steps

Time required: 45 minutes in one sitting with 30 minutes set aside for assessment
Class warm-up: Sign up for Speak Like a Geek Presentation Board

_____Speak Like a Geek Board starts next week. This is the last Presentation Board. Sign-up via:

- *Google Calendar*
- *Google Forms*
- *Google Spreadsheet*
- *Padlet calendar*

_____These words are the ones you've collected all year. Add to them with words mentioned by parents, grade-level team, and students themselves. Find all the vocabulary included in the K-5 technology curricula at the free companion website mentioned earlier in this book (*Fig. 100*):

Figure 100—Glossary on class resource website

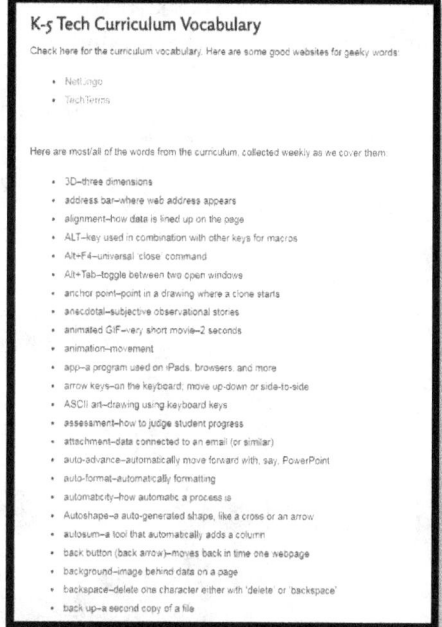

_____Review grading in *Assessment 18* (same as prior boards).

Assessment 18—Speak Like a Geek presentation rubric

_____Students can get a geek word definitions from family, friends, neighbors, or teacher as a last

5th Grade Technology Curriculum: Teacher Manual

resort. Students teach classmates definition and use it in a sentence that shows they understand the meaning (i.e., *I like formatting* is **not** good; *I format my letter by adding borders and pictures* **is** good).

_____Open current spreadsheet workbook. If students can't find it, review *Figure 101* (full-size poster in appendix) on strategies for finding a lost file:

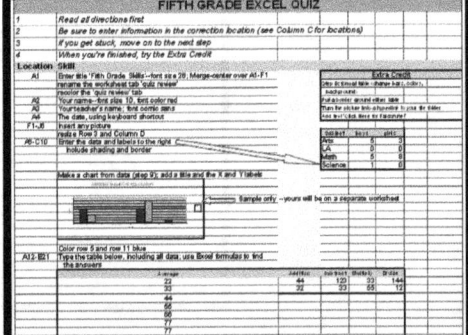

Figure 101—I can't find my file

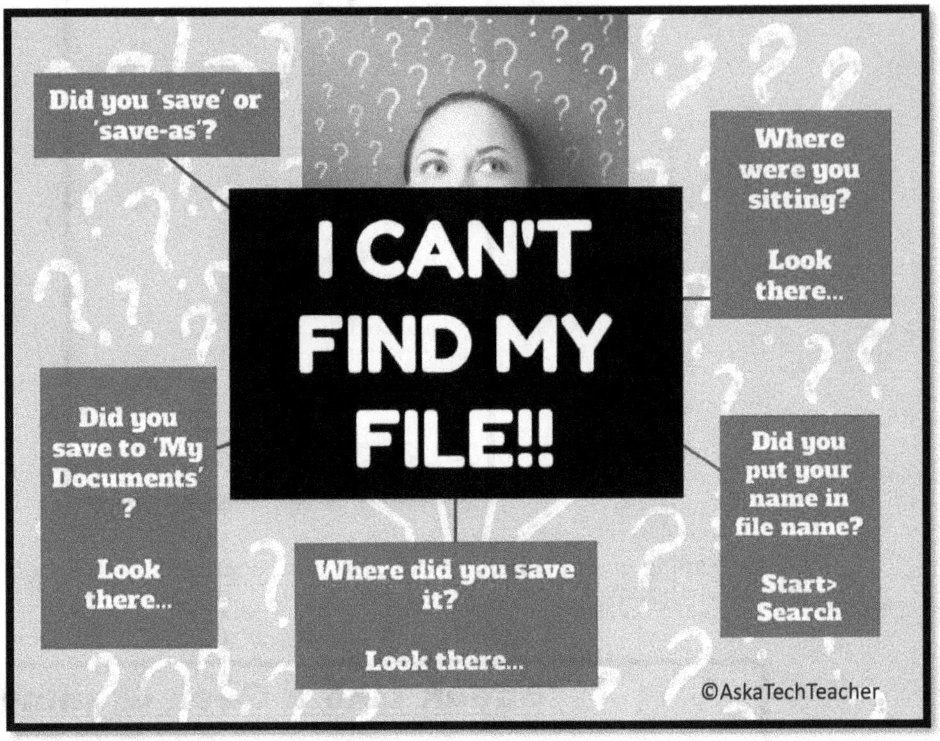

_____It's OK for them to use their prior work as a test-taking resource. You may choose to have students open a new workbook.

_____Add new worksheet named '*Assessment*'. Recolor tab.

_____Today, assess student general spreadsheet knowledge. Have students follow directions on assessment. All skills have been covered between 2nd and 5th grade. Adjust assessment as needed to satisfy your circumstances. You may choose to make this a collaborative exercise or individual.

_____*Figure 102* is a thumbnail of the assessment. There is a full-size sample at the end of the lesson as well as a spreadsheet to collate student skills. It doesn't matter if you assess more or less skills than you see on the example; it matters that it's authentic.

Figure 8--*Spreadsheet summative*

_____Remind students:

- *put data in correct cells*
- *push 'enter' to input data*
- *start each formula with an = sign*
- *+ = add, - = subtract, * = multiply, / = divide*
- *when finished, try Extra Credit*

_____Review test-taking strategies:

169

- *Answer questions you know first—go back for others.*
- *Check work when done.*
- *If a skill is difficult, see if you can find help in another question.*

_____Use class cumulative grades (*Assessment 20*) to find holes in learning. Record skills accomplished by students and add them at the bottom. Are there skills that lots of students missed? Evaluate this for next year.

_____When finished, students upload quiz to drop box or save to digital portfolios. No printing. **Mulligan Rule** in effect.

Class exit ticket: **None**

Differentiation

- *Assessment takes longer than thirty minutes? Adjust requirements and grading.*
- *Show how to use Google's **define:[the word]** to find definition for Speak Like a Geek, but caution students not to use terminology they don't understand.*
- *Review spreadsheet skills first as a class, then as an assessment. You might even do the assessment as a class.*
- *Those who finish can practice keyboarding.*

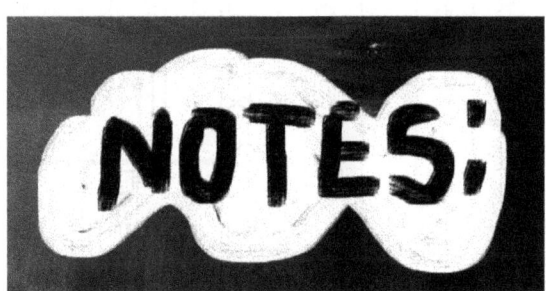

_____
_____
_____
_____
_____
_____

Assessment 19—Spreadsheet summative

FIFTH GRADE EXCEL QUIZ

1. Read all directions first
2. Be sure to enter information in the correction location (see Column C for locations)
3. If you get stuck, move on to the next step
4. When you're finished, try the Extra Credit

Location	Skill
A1	Enter title "Fifth Grade Skills"--font size 26; Merge-center over A1-F1; rename the worksheet tab 'quiz review'; recolor the 'quiz review' tab
A2	Your name--font size 10, font color red
A3	Your teacher's name; font comic sans
A4	The date, using keyboard shortcut
F1-J6	Insert any picture; resize Row 3 and Column D
A6-C10	Enter the data and labels to the right; include shading and border
	Make a chart from data (step 9); add a title and the X and Y labels
A12-E21	Color row 5 and row 11 blue; Type the table below, including all data; use Excel formulas to find the answers

Extra Credit

Step 8: format table (change bars, colors, background)
Pull a border around either table
Turn the picture into a hyperlink to your file folder
Add text 'click here for Falconer!'

Subject	boys	girls
Arts	5	3
LA	0	0
Math	5	8
Science	1	0

Sample only --yours will be on a separate worksheet

	Addition	Subtract	Multiply	Divide
	44	123	33	144
	32	33	55	12

Average
22
33
44
55
66
77
77
88

Assessment 20—Spreadsheet quiz grade curation

Grade Sheet for Spreadsheet Assessment

STUDENT Question		1	2	3	4	5	6	7	8	9	10	11	12	13	14	15	16	17	18	19	20
1	Spelling																				
2	Grammar																				
3	Rename tab																				
4	Recolor tab																				
5	Title																				
	Font 26																				
	Merge-center																				
6	Student name																				
	Font 10																				
	Color: red																				
7	Teacher																				
	Font: CS																				
6	Date (shortkey)																				
7	Image																				
	In G1-J6?																				
8	Table—data																				
	Shading?																				
	Border?																				
	All data?																				
9	Chart																				
	Title?																				
	X/Y labels?																				
10	Row 1—blue																				
11	Row 5—blue																				
12	Table																				
	Answers?																				
	Use formulas?																				
13	Cells right?																				
	Time in A4																				
	Image linked																				
14	Link has text																				
	Chart format																				
Total		0	0	0	0	0	0	0	0	0	0	0	0	0	0	0	0	0	0	0	0

5th Grade Technology Curriculum: Teacher Manual

Lesson #21 Google Earth Tour

Vocabulary	Problem solving	Skills
• Climate • Dialogue box • Geolocation • Grid • IDL • Lats and longs • Layers • Placemark • Tour	• Placemarks aren't in my folder (copy-paste location from wrong spot to right) • Project wasn't saved—just a location • How do I play GE tour? • I can't drag globe (use arrow keys) • Can't see borders (zoom in) • I don't have 3D (is 3D layer checked?) • Where's Street View (drag yellow guy onto a blue street)	**New** Google Earth tour Personalized placemarks **Scaffolded** Google Earth basics Speaking/listening Keyboarding
Academic Applications History, literacy, geography, research	**Materials Required** Google Earth and tours, Board badges, keyboard program, spreadsheet assessment results, Speak Like a Geek rubrics, student workbooks (if using)	**Standards** CCSS.SL.5.4-5 NETS: 3c-d,

Essential Question

How can I present geographic information and supporting evidence in a way listeners understand?

Big Idea

I can present geographic information, findings, and supporting evidence in a way that listeners understand.

Teacher Preparation

- Talk with grade-level team so you tie into conversations.
- Is class shorter than 45 minutes? Highlight items you must cover and leave the rest for 'later'.
- Have spreadsheet assessments graded and analyzed.
- Know which tasks weren't completed last week.
- Be prepared to integrate domain-specific tech vocab.
- Know whether you need extra time to complete lesson.
- If you offer afterschool tech help and it's manned by students, verify they will be there.

Assessment Strategies

- Used good keyboarding habits
- Followed directions
- Completed tour
- Solved simple problems
- Exhibited critical thinking
- Worked well with partner
- [tried to] solve own problems
- Decisions followed class rules
- Left room as student found it
- Completed warm-up, exit ticket
- Joined classroom conversations
- Exhibited higher order thinking: analysis, evaluation, synthesis
- Habits of mind observed

Steps

Time required: 45 minutes in one sitting or spread throughout the week, with a block of 35 minutes to complete Google Earth tour

Class warm-up: keyboarding on school typing tool. Remind students to keep elbows at side, use proper hand position and all fingers with no flying hands.

_____Start Speak Like a Geek presentations. Review expectations and grading.

_____Any students have tech problems to share? Any evidence of learning for Evidence Board?

_____Review results of spreadsheet assessment. Point out common problems and how to do them. Answer student questions.

5th Grade Technology Curriculum: Teacher Manual

_____Open Google Earth on your PC or Mac. IPads: Access app, but be aware there are differences between the app and the full-featured program. Accommodate these to project requirements.

_____If you don't have Google Earth, adapt this lesson to Google Maps. Many of the map-reading skills and geographic exploration are available through a mapping program.

_____Ask students what they remember about Google Earth from prior years (*Figure 103a* is kindergarten, *Figure 103b* is 1st grade; *Figure 103c* is 2nd grade, *Figure 103d* is 3/4th grade)—if you've been using the SL technology curriculum.

Figure 103a-d: Google Earth projects in K-4

   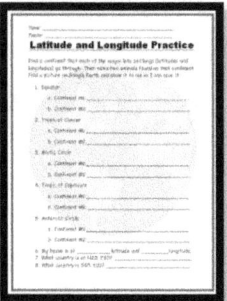

_____Discuss 'geolocation'. How does it impact online activity?

_____Open Google Earth on class screen and on student computers. Discuss Google Earth's toolbars. Explain locations under 'My Places'; explain layers (make sure 3D Buildings and Street View are on). This is a review of previous skills so shouldn't take much time.

Figure 9--GE Tour

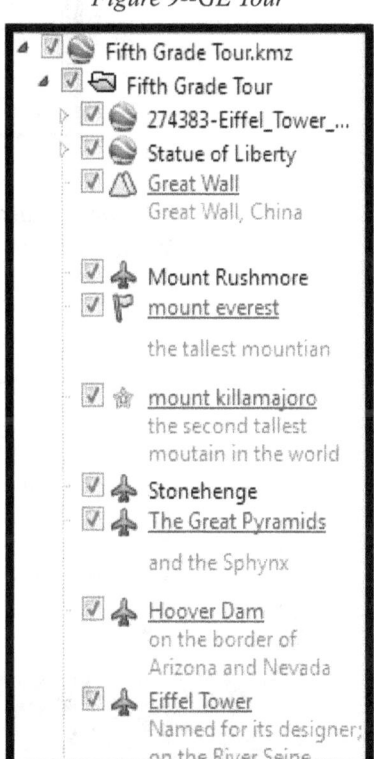

_____For this project, students will create a tour of five Google Earth locations presented during the Google Earth Board (*Figure 104*). The goal (based on CCSS.ELA-Literacy.CCRA.SL.5.4-5): *Present information and supporting evidence such that listeners can follow the reasoning and organization of the tour. Overall style is specific to purpose and audience.*

_____To this end, students will:

- placemark five sites (or what works for your student group)
- add to each a Fascinating Fact presented on the Google Earth Board. **This requires no research!** Refer to the blogs or discussion postings students made about their Fascinating Fact.

_____Show projects completed by last year fifth graders.

_____Have students follow along as you create a tour.

- Create a folder under 'My Places'. Name it student's last name. This is where s/he will collect the five placemarks.
- Search for first location. Make sure 3D is selected in layers so students can 'walk around' location for a better look. Many locations have amazing views using this tool—for example, Stonehenge, Statue of Liberty, and Hoover Dam.

174

- *Right-click on location in 'My Places' and select 'Properties'. Add a Fascinating Fact to dialogue box (see Figure 105).*
- *Demonstrate how to customize placemark (Figure 105 shows a camera as unique placemark). This organizes tour locations under student unique placemark.*

Figure 105—GE dialogue box

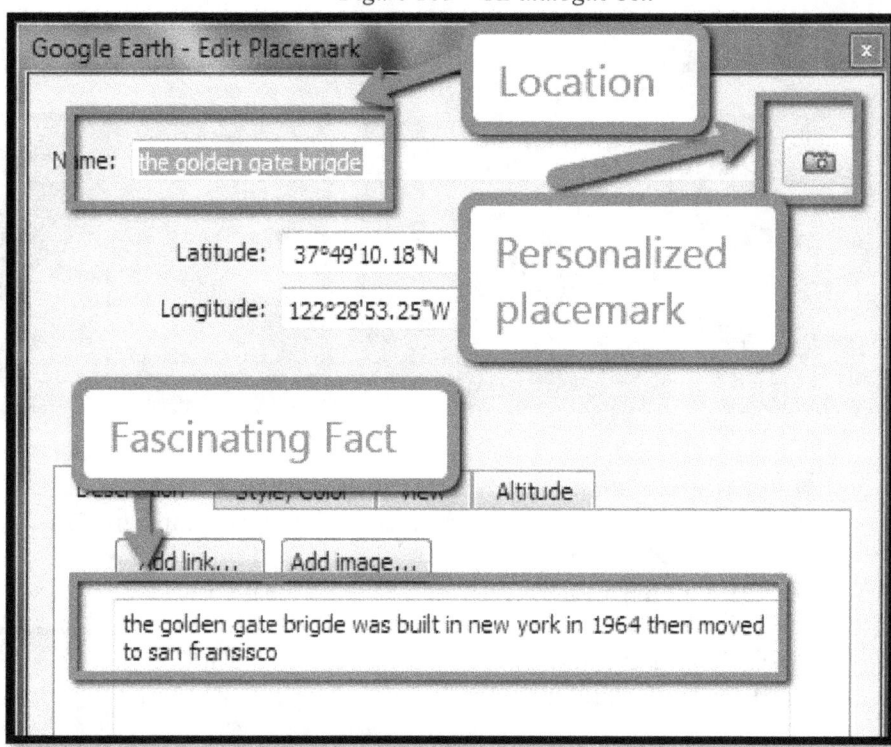

_____Make sure placemark ends up under 'My Tour'. If not, cut and paste into the folder.

_____Mark four more locations from the Google Earth Board in the same manner. Each placemark will look like *Figure 106a*. *Figure 106b* shows entire tour:

Figure 106a—GE placemark; 106b: GE tour

_____Students may work in groups.

_____When done, students work with a partner to complete *Assessment 21*. If using workbooks, they can complete the rubric there and share a screenshot with teacher:

Assessment 21—Google Earth tour rubric

Google Earth Tour Rubric

Your name:_____

Teacher:_____

GE Tour	1 points
o Folder w/ student name	
o Tour runs	

Sufficient Placemarks	15 points
o Five locations	
o Locations include fact	

Each Placemark...	3 points
o Placed geographically	
o Labeled correctly	
o Placemark customized	

| Professional Look | 1 points |

_____Save tour. Save-as to student digital portfolio as back-up. Demonstrate how to do this (it's a bit tricky in Google Earth).

_____Throughout class, check for understanding.

_____Remind students to transfer knowledge to the classroom or home.

Class exit ticket: ***Visit two classmate tours before leaving***

Differentiation

- Play tours on the class screen in classroom—for parents, for other students.
- Not enough time? Have students include fewer locations.
- Add student home as first location on tour.
- Instead of Google Earth Board locations, tie into class inquiry. For example, the Google Earth Tour—From England to the Colonies (Assessment 22, at end of lesson) is a step-by-step worksheet on a tour focusing on colonial America. This can even be a story or places students visited during the school year.
- Have students set tour up on their computer. Then, have students travel around the classroom and view classmate tours.
- Replace this lesson with 5th Grade Lesson #4 Google Earth Literary Tour in curriculum extenders (available from Ask a Tech Teacher).
- Early finishers: visit class internet start page for websites that tie into classwork.

Assessment 22—Google Earth tour notes

Google Earth Tour
From England to the Colonies

Tour locations include these spots and this information:

1. Your home in England
   a. Introduce yourself; tell us why you're leaving England
   b. Share your hopes and dreams
   c. Include distance from your home in England to the Colonies_____
2. Jamestown
   a. Tell me what would draw colonists to settle in each of these areas
   b. Tell me about the jobs
   c. Tell me about the geography and climate
   d. Tell me about the organization of Jamestown
3. The Hudson Bay
   a. What is its impact on colonization and life in this area?
   b. Include width of Hudson Bay_____
4. The Appalachian Mountains
   a. What is its impact on colonization and life in this area?
5. Plymouth Rock
   a. What is its impact on colonization and life in this area?
6. Chesapeake River/Bay
   a. What is its impact on colonization and life in this area?
   b. Include length of Chesapeake River_____
7. The Potomac River
   a. What is its impact on colonization and life in this area?
   b. Include length of Potomac River_____
8. A colony from each region of colonies (northern, middle, southern)
   a. Tell me what would draw colonists to settle in each of these areas
   b. Tell me about the jobs
   c. Tell me about the geography and climate
   d. Tell me about the colonial organization of each area

Setup:

1. Set up a file folder in Google Earth, My Places, with your name
2. Customize the placemark to be your picture
3. Copy-paste each placemark for each location into this file folder
4. To edit a placemark, right click on it and go to **Properties**
5. Save this folder to your network file folder

Lesson #22 Graphics in Word Processing

Vocabulary	Problem solving	Skills
• Aligned • Autoshape • Background • Crop • Fill • Layout • Styles • Washout	• My project disappeared (use search under Start button) • My computer crashed (did you save early save often?) • When I copy-paste, it replaces image (make sure image isn't selected) • Project takes more than a page (resize graphics)	**New** Image editing in a variety of image editors **Scaffolded** Keyboarding Digital citizenship Word processing
Academic Applications Any subject that uses images; digital storytelling	**Materials Required** word processing program with graphics editing, row graphics	**Standards** CCSS.RI.5.7 NETS: 1a, 6a

Essential Question

How can I manipulate images to better-reflect my words and ideas?

Big Idea

Basic photo editing tools can be incorporated into word processing projects

Teacher Preparation

- Talk with grade-level team so you tie into conversations.
- Have several row graphics in a file for students to select.
- Be prepared to use tech vocabulary while you teach.
- Know whether you need extra time to complete lesson.
- Know which tasks weren't completed last week.
- Ask grade-level team and parents if there are any tech problems students are having difficulty with. Cover them during tech lessons.
- If you offer afterschool tech help and it's manned by students, verify they will be there.

Assessment Strategies

- Anecdotal
- Followed directions
- Employed risk-taking and discovery
- Completed image editing
- [tried to] solve own problems
- Decisions followed class rules
- Left room as student found it
- Completed warm-up, exit ticket
- Joined class conversations
- Higher order thinking: analysis, evaluation, synthesis
- Habits of mind observed

Steps

Time required: 45 minutes in one sitting or spread throughout the week, setting aside 20 minutes for activity.

Class warm-up: Keyboarding with software or website. Remind students to pay attention to correct posture—hands curved over home row, pointers on f, j.

_____ Keyboard homework due monthly.
_____ Continue Speak Like a Geek presentations.
_____ Any evidence of learning to post?
_____ Choose a word processing program that has graphic editing facility. This includes MS Word and Google Docs (through an add-on). If you are using Chromebooks, try Office 365.
_____ If you don't have a word processing program that can edit images, use an online graphic editing tool. If you don't have a favorite, visit the Ask a Tech Teacher resource pages.

5th Grade Technology Curriculum: Teacher Manual

_____Whichever you select, you likely will need to adapt the skills in this lesson to what's available with your tool. That's fine because the goal this week is to show how to **manipulate images to better-reflect what students want to communicate,** not to learn specific skills.

_____Open the image editing tool used in your school. Demonstrate the graphics editing tools available, such as:

- o *color*
- o *artistic effects*
- o *background*
- o *styles*
- o *border*
- o *fill*
- o *rotation*

_____Students will use several images, one for each tool. They might also use a row graphic (*Figure 107a*), use their cropping skills to separate each image (or teach them how to crop with your classroom tool), and then apply a different formatting tool for each image from the row graphic.

_____When done, arrange the images artistically on page. *Figure 107b* uses MS Word; *Figure 107c* uses Google Docs with the Pixlr app:

Figure 107a-c—Image editing in Word and Docs

_____You might also use an app like PicMonkey (*Figure 108*):

179

Figure 108—Image editing in PicMonkey

_____As students experiment with effects, guide them, don't teach. This is about exploration and risk-taking.
_____Throughout class, check for understanding.
_____If students are printing, go to print preview to be sure all images fit on one page.
_____Save to student digital portfolio.
_____Remind students to transfer knowledge to classroom or home.

Class exit ticket: ***Upload edited picture to student blog or class website to share.***

Differentiation

- *Early finishers: Try another picture that you select.*
- *Add a color block or shape behind cropped images (Figure 109).*
- *Replace this with 3rd Grade Lesson #2 Puzzle Maker to Prepare for Tests in* <u>curriculum extenders</u> *(available from Structured Learning).*

Figure 10--Image with color block

Lesson #23 Writing With Graphics

Vocabulary	Problem solving	Skills
• Bmp • Crop • Fill • Gif • Jpg • Layering • Ribbon • Tiff	• MS Word ribbon is different for some images (true. Show how to adapt) • Can't find image editing tools (click 'Picture Tools' at page top) • Picture won't move (check wrap) • Picture is behind another (layering) • How do I publish as a PDF? (use Word or stand-alone program)	**New** Citations **Scaffolded** Graphics in writing Speaking and listening Keyboarding Digital citizenship
Academic Applications Writing, digital storytelling	**Materials Required** word processing program with graphics editing, Speak Like a Geek rubrics, Evidence Board badges	**Standards** CCSS.W.5.6 NETS: 1a, 6a

Essential Question

How can I edit a photo so it reinforces my writing?

Big Idea

Basic photo editing tools can be incorporated into word processing projects to communicate ideas

Teacher Preparation

- Talk with grade-level team to tie into conversations.
- Know which tasks weren't completed last week and whether they are necessary to move forward.
- Ask grade-level team and parents for tech problems students need help with.
- Be prepared to use domain-specific tech vocabulary.
- Know whether you need extra time for this lesson.
- If you offer afterschool tech help manned by students, verify they will be there.

Assessment Strategies

- Typed multiple pages in one sitting
- Completed typing assessment
- Board presentation
- Used image editing skills
- Understood how images communicate ideas effectively
- Completed warm-up, exit ticket
- Completed project
- Worked well in groups
- [tried to] solve own problems
- Left room as student found it
- Higher order thinking: analysis, evaluation, synthesis
- Habits of mind observed

Steps

Time required: 45 minutes in one sitting or spread throughout the week, setting aside 15 minutes for typing warm-up and assessment, 10 min. for Speak Like a Geek and Evidence Board, and 20 minutes for writing with images

Class warm-up: Keyboarding practice. Remember correct posture, hands curved over home row, eyes on monitor, keyboard in front of body.

_____After ten minutes of keyboarding warm-up, go to TypingTest.com. Take three-minute speed/accuracy assessment in preparation for next week's quiz. Are students reaching their grade-level goal of net 30 wpm? Point out this program deducts wpm for mistakes. Notice speed and accuracy; take a second speed test. If there were more than five mistakes on the first test, slow down to improve accuracy. If less than five mistakes, push to type faster. Remind students they know where the keys are. Keep their eyes on the screen and be risk-takers!

Figure 110—Hand position for keyboarding

_____Continue Speak Like a Geek presentations.
_____Any evidence of learning to post on Evidence Board?
_____Today, students place 3-5 images in a report/essay/project created in class. Each image must:

- *reinforce paper's purpose*
- *contribute relevant information not contained in text*

_____If students are going to orally present these reports, consider this Common Core Standard:

Include multimedia components (e.g., graphics, sound) and visual displays in presentations when appropriate to enhance the development of main ideas or themes.

_____Open word processing program used last week (with graphic editing capabilities) on class screen. If you don't have a word processing program with image editing tools, use an image editor, and then embed the formatted image into your word processing program.
_____If you have iPads, here are good text-image mash-up programs your students will like:

- *Adobe Spark*
- *Book Creator*
- *Book Writer*

You can find these by an internet search or visit the Ask a Tech Teacher resource pages under *Digital Storytelling*.
_____Ask one of the students to quickly review image editing skills covered last week.
_____Discuss types of image files (by extension)—gif, jpg, tiff, bmp. Any others students have seen? Each has somewhat different presentation and editing functions.
_____If document is a hard copy, expect students to type it quickly and efficiently. Which student can tell the class how long a 300-word story would take to type?
_____Add pictures from student personal folder, a search engine, or a collection you've provided. Add citations if needed. If using Google Docs, review how this can be completed. See *Figure 111* for a summation:

Figure 111—Citations

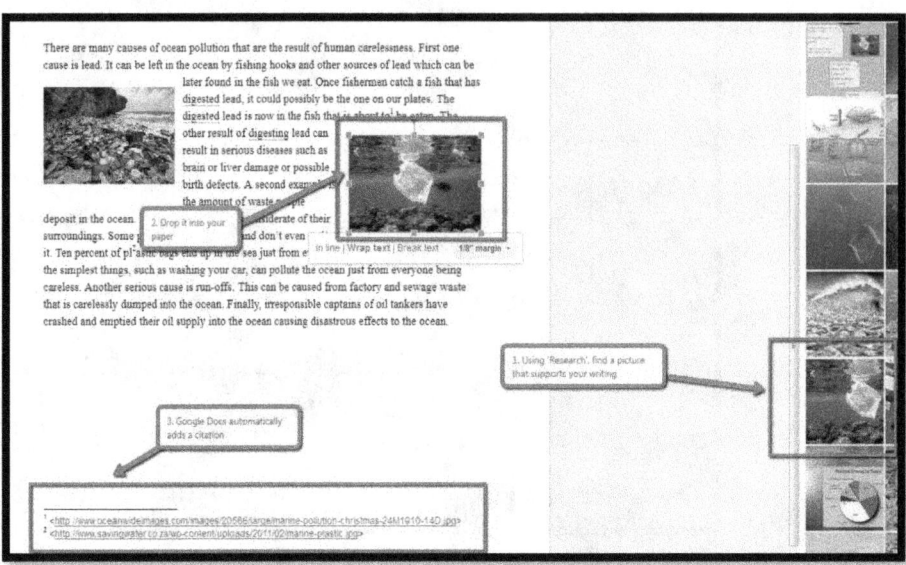

_____Review copyright provisions that apply to the use of Internet images if necessary. What can be used? Cannot? How do you know? Review this rephrased summary of the law:

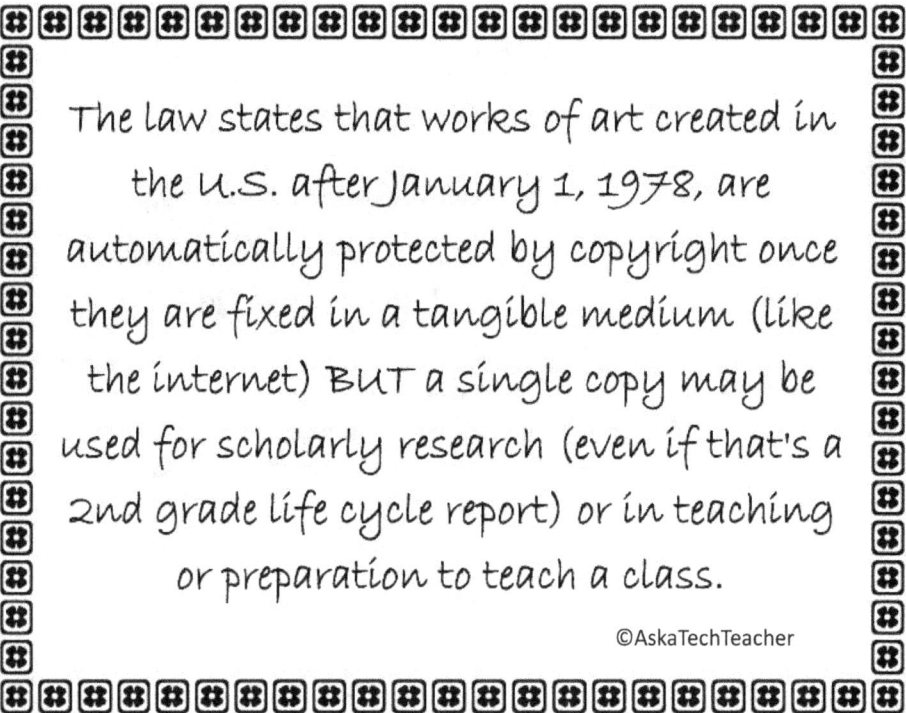

_____When finished, share document with neighbor. Ask him/her to confirm images support writing.
_____Throughout class, check for understanding.
_____Go to 'Print preview'—be sure everything fits on one page. Resize as needed.
_____Print (Ctrl+P) if necessary; save (Ctrl+S) to digital portfolio. Should students 'save' or 'save-as'? Does it depend upon where they opened document?
_____Remind students to transfer knowledge to classroom or home.

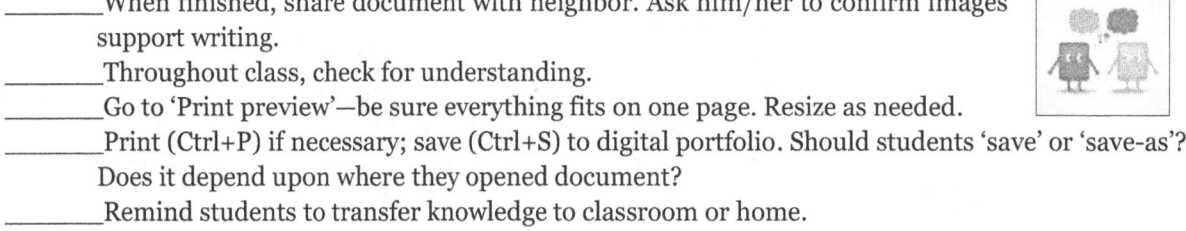

Class exit ticket: Create a form in Google Forms that asks students to share one thought about how images contributed to a better understanding of the topic. Display the collection spreadsheet on the class screen so it's clear who's finished and who can leave.

Differentiation

- Add speed quiz to calendar of class events.
- If homework is due, add to class calendar.
- Early finishers: visit class internet start page for websites that tie into classwork.
- Publish document as a PDF and share on class website, blog, wiki.
- Replace this lesson with 3rd Grade Lesson #3 Create a Timeline of Events in curriculum extenders (available from Structured Learning)

Titanic Virus:
Your computer goes down.

Alzheimer Virus:
Your computer forgets where it put your files.

Child Virus:
Your computer constantly does annoying things, but is too cute to get rid of.

Disney Virus:
Everything in your computer goes Goofy

Lesson #24 Image Editing I

Vocabulary	Problem solving	Skills
• Append • Autofix • Canvas • Crop • Foreground • Hoax • Lasso • Magic wand • Photoshopped • Pixels • Scale • Transform • Workspace	• Can't edit picture (check layers) • I'm drawing but nothing happens (are you in right layer?) • I'm editing, but nothing happens (is layer locked?) • Magic wand selected too much (change tolerance) • I forgot to name my drawing (name it when you save) • I want my canvas sized for a clipboard image (it does that automatically) • Can't change color (use 'foreground' or 'color' in right sidebar)	**New** Cropping Website scams **Scaffolded** Drawing Speaking and listening Keyboarding Digital citizenship
Academic Applications Digital citizenship, art, writing, digital storytelling	**Materials Required** Image editor, keyboarding program, speed quiz, Speak Like a Geek rubric, Evidence Board badges	**Standards** CCSS.RI.5.7 NETS: 1b, 6b

Essential Question

What photo editing skills help me better communicate ideas?

Big Idea

Images communicate big ideas, but may require tweaking

Teacher Preparation

- Have speed quiz available.
- Talk with grade-level team so you tie into conversations.
- Have links to 'fake' online images/videos.
- Be prepared to integrate domain-specific tech vocabulary.
- Know whether you need extra time to complete lesson.
- Know which tasks weren't completed last week and whether they are necessary to move forward.
- If you offer afterschool tech help manned by students, verify they will be there.

Assessment Strategies

- Anecdotal
- Cropped picture
- Was a risk-taker with new skills
- [tried to] solve own problems
- Decisions followed class rules
- Left room as student found it
- Completed warm-up, exit ticket
- Joined classroom conversations
- Finished speed quiz
- Higher order thinking: analysis, evaluation, synthesis
- Habits of mind observed

Steps

Time required: 45 minutes either in one sitting or spread throughout the week
Class warm-up: Keyboard with good habits like correct posture

_____Continue Speak Like a Geek presentations.
_____Any evidence of learning to post on Evidence Board?
_____Final speed quiz of the year today. Students should be able to independently take quiz, save/share/print, and be ready for the next activity.
_____Next week: Final blank keyboard quiz of the year.
_____Introduce the image editor you use in your school. It might be:

- *Photoshop*
- *Gimp (a free version of Photoshop)*
- *Photoshop Elements*

_____Good online image editors and apps are also available:

- Adobe Photoshop through Adobe's Creative Cloud for Education
- Adobe Photoshop Express
- Adobe Photoshop Touch

Do an internet search for these addresses. If you can't find them, visit the Ask a Tech Teacher resource pages, Image editors.

_____Whatever you use is fine. The goal of this series of lessons is to show how to edit/format/change photos using the tools native to your classroom. You will have to make some adjustments of steps/skills, but not in the big idea and overall goal.

_____What is photo editing? What are examples of this skill? The following four image editing activities are commonly applied in magazines, fliers, and anywhere you see the use of photos:

- *Collages (Figure 112):*

Figure 112—Collage of edited images

- *Fixing photos that are too dark/shadowy (Figures 113a-b):*

Figure 113a-b—Color adjustment

- *Fixing mistakes (Figures 114a-b—removing pole in middle of picture):*

Figure 114a-b—Removing distractions from an image

- *Touching up portraits (Figures 115a-b):*

Figure 115a-b: Touch up portraits

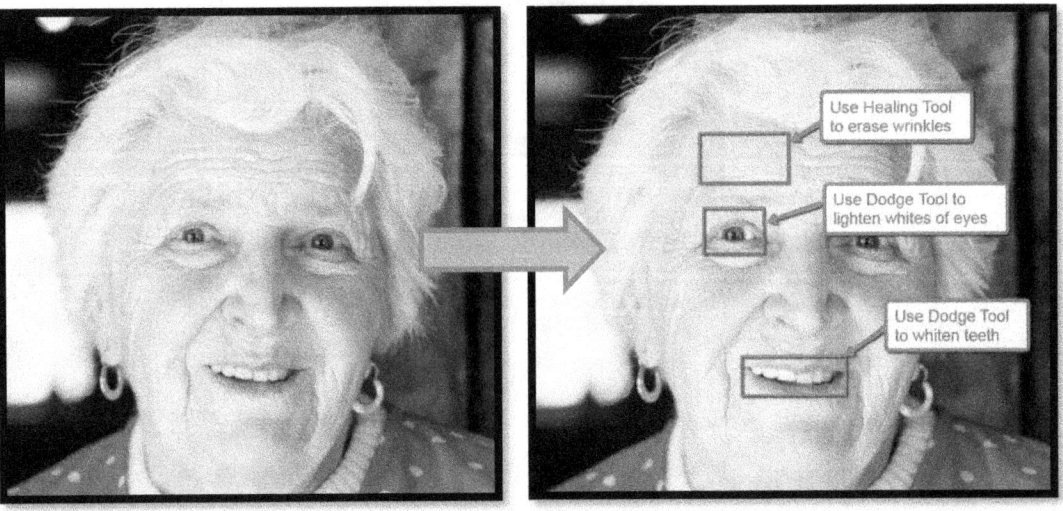

- *Changing the appearance of things (Figures 116a-b):*

Figure 116a-b: Change color in car

- *Changing the location. Check out where Casey the Lab has been in Figure 117:*

Figure 117—Put individuals in different backgrounds

_____Image editors can change reality. Photoshop (the gold standard among image editors) is so powerful, its name has become a verb—*I Photoshopped the car's color*:

Figure 118—Definition of Photoshop

_____Visit Internet hoax websites. If you don't have a favorite, visit Ask a Tech Teacher resource pages, *Digital Citizenship>Internet Hoaxes*.
_____If necessary, before visiting sites, circle back on discussions about Internet safety.
_____Look at images like *Figure 119*. Did President Roosevelt really ride a moose across a river?

Figure 119—Real or a hoax?

In *Figures 120a-b,* was the tree added to or erased from the original photo?

Figure 120a-b: Add or remove pieces from a photo

_____Discuss as a class whether *Figures 119-120* are accurate—and how do you know? It's no surprise photos are not accepted as proof in court.

_____Demonstrate the class image editor on the class screen while students work at their computer. Adapt the steps in this lesson to fit your image editing tool. The project goals remain the same as the Big Idea at the start of the Lesson.

_____We use Photoshop for the examples. Photoshop is for professionals but has many tools simple enough for students. When done, students will appreciate the power, creativity, and fun that technology brings to image editing.

_____Review screen layout and toolbars of your tool. Students can explore while you demonstrate.

- *overview of screen layout*
- *overview of toolbars; point out those you will cover*

_____Open an image. Zoom in on pixels. Show the layers. Review layout of left sidebar. See how top tools change as you select a tool.

_____Go to *File>new* to create a new drawing canvas. A dialogue box opens (see *Figure 121*) asking for decisions about your new canvas. What do these mean:

- *title box*
- *inches vs. pixels*
- *size of image*

Figure 121—Image editor dialogue box

_____This lesson includes two projects:

- *drawing from scratch*
- *cropping*

Drawing from Scratch

_____Why is it important to have a basic understanding of how to create pictures:

- *to personalize a picture to a need*
- *to understand why creative work is copyrighted*
- *to realize how easy a talented image editor can change a picture to convey any message they want*
- *to have no worries about illegally using someone else's work*

_____Today: Draw a picture in the image editing tool using a paint brush. *Figure 122a* is an example of available brushes. *Figures 122b-c* are two drawings students might create:

Figure 122a-c—Drawing in an image editor

_____Select brush and size from toolbar. Select a traditional brush first, then others.
_____Leave 'opacity' and 'flow' for later.
_____Go to Channel (if available)—-hide some of the channels.
_____Go to history; go back in time. Or, use Ctrl+Z to go back one step at a time.
_____Save to digital portfolio. Print/publish/share as is the custom in your classroom.

Cropping

_____Today's second project is to crop a picture and drop it in a new background (i.e., *Figure 124c* where I dropped a lizard into the Coliseum). What is 'cropping'?

_____There are three ways we will crop:

- **marquis**—*crops as a square or rectangle (Figure 123a)*
- **lasso**—*crops freehand—drag the mouse around what you want to crop (Fig. 123b)*
- **magic wand**—*selects pixels close in color (Figure 123c)*

Figure 123a-c: 3 ways to crop

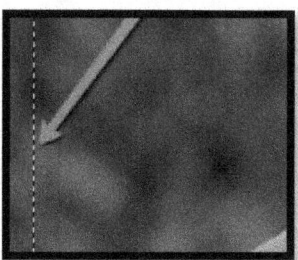  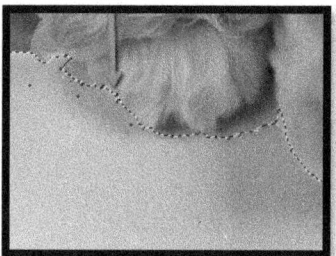

_____Your image editor may have one of these or all three. Try as many as you have, then drop the cropped image into a new background. *Figures 124a-c* crops a lizard and puts him in the Coliseum. Which cropping tool works best for this situation? Use top toolbar to fine tune:

Figure 124a-c: Cropping

_____Check out where Casey the Labrador has been (*Figures 125a-d*). He's brave!

Figure 125a-d: Place individual in different backgrounds

_____Throughout class, check for understanding.
_____Remind students to transfer knowledge to classroom or home.

Class exit ticket: *Student shows their cropped project to ten people. Do they think it's real?*

> **Differentiation**
> - *Add blank keyboard quiz to class calendar for next week.*
> - *Early finishers: Help classmates struggling with an image editing tool.*

Lesson #25 Image Editing II

Vocabulary	Problem solving	Skills
• .jpg • .psd • Anchor point • Clone • Crop • Filter • History button • Marquee • Photoshopped • Pixels	• I can't find last week's project (where did you save it?) • How do I undo? (go to history) • My toolbars disappeared • I forgot my presentation (is there a later date you can take?) • I can't clone (use Alt) • Can't clone between pictures (are you on the right picture and layer?) • Where's camera (click history button)	**New** Cloning **Scaffolded** Cropping Speaking and listening Keyboarding Digital citizenship
Academic Applications Art, writing, digital storytelling	**Materials Required** Image editor, keyboarding program, Speak Like a Geek rubric, keyboard quiz, student workbooks (if using), Evidence Board badges	**Standards** CCSS.RI.5.7 NETS: 1b, 6b

Essential Question

What are photo editing skills that help me tweak an image to communicate ideas?

Big Idea

Images can communicate big ideas, but may require tweaking

Teacher Preparation

- Have hard copies of keyboard quiz if no workbooks.
- Talk with grade-level team so you tie into inquiry.
- Know which tasks weren't completed last week and whether they are necessary to move forward.
- Be prepared to integrate domain-specific tech vocabulary.
- Know whether you need extra time for this lesson.
- If you offer afterschool tech help manned by students, verify they will be there.

Assessment Strategies

- Anecdotal
- Annotated workbooks (if using)
- Completed cloning projects
- Followed directions
- Showed curiosity
- [tried to] solve own problems
- Decisions followed class rules
- Left room as student found it
- Completed warm-up, exit ticket
- Joined classroom conversations
- Completed blank keyboard quiz
- Higher order thinking: analysis, evaluation, synthesis
- Habits of mind observed

Steps

Time required: 45 minutes in one sitting or spread throughout the week will a block of 10 minutes for blank keyboard quiz and 25 minutes for image editing project.

Class warm-up: Keyboarding practice. Remember correct posture—body centered in front of keyboard, fingers curved over home row, anchored to f and j

_____Any evidence of learning to post on Evidence Board?
_____Continue Speak Like a Geek presentations.
_____Final blank keyboard quiz of the year. As before, it can be taken in groups, but give only 5-10 minutes to complete. They should know key placement by now.

_____If students have workbooks, they can fill out the blank keyboard template there, take a screenshot, and share it with you.
_____Open the class image editor.
_____Discuss cloning. What does it mean? Anyone heard of cloning pets? Star Wars clones?
_____Open a field of flowers. Demonstrate how to use the image editor to clone **within a picture** while students follow along on their programs (*Figure 126*):

- *Add flowers or get rid of flowers by cloning flowers or green verdure.*
- *If you place the anchor point over green, that will be cloned. If you place it over flowers, that will be cloned.*
- *Notice where the anchor point is moving. It shows what's being cloned. Make colors match as closely as possible.*

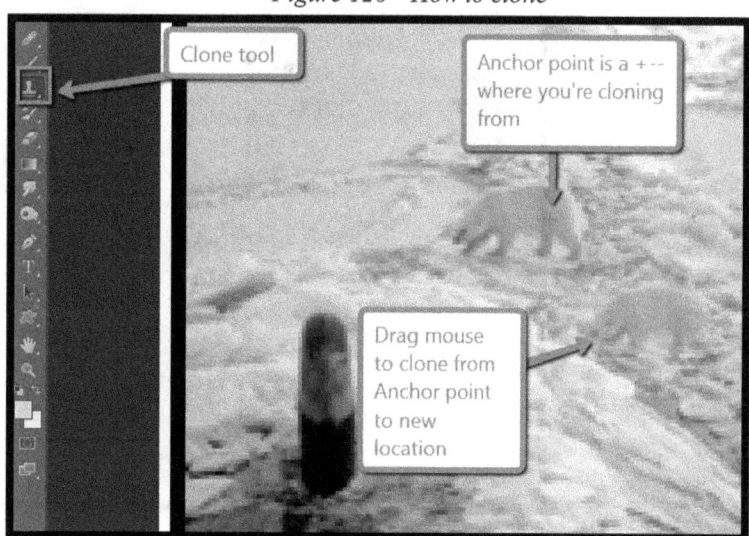

Figure 126—How to clone

_____Do you notice how pixelated *Figure 126* is? Why? (Hint: Student zoomed in to grab the right pixels for cloning).
_____Can students tell which is the original in *Figures 127a-c*:

Figure 127a-c: Cloning

_____Now clone between two pictures. It's the same concept. See if students can figure it out without a demonstration (see *Figures 128a-c*):

- Open two pictures.
- Create anchor point in one picture (the polar bears on an Arctic ice flow). Cursor becomes a cross to show where you're cloning from.
- Clone to another picture (the sea cave).
- Make edges match naturally. Work patiently. Zoom in to pixels if necessary.
- Show students how to use camera (lower right of history button) to keep a copy of a picture before further editing.

_____Look at *Figure 128c*. Can you tell which pieces were cloned from another picture? Why?

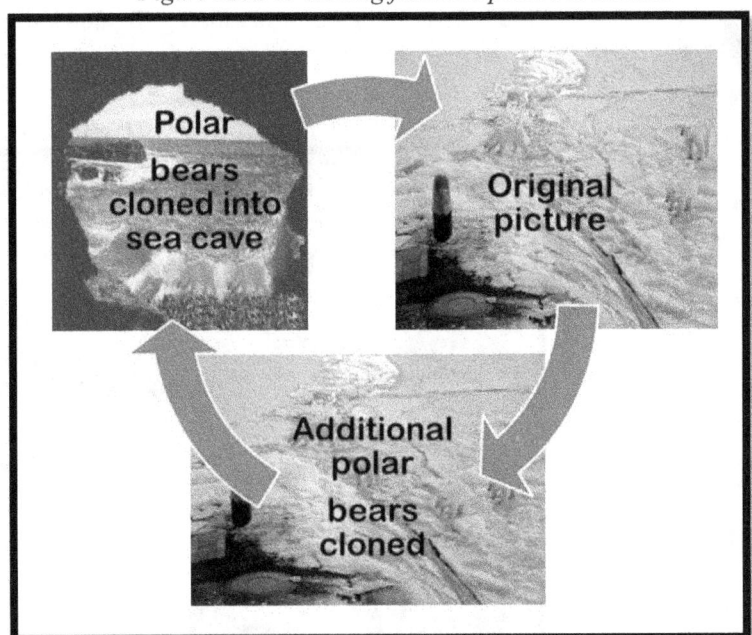

Figure 128a-c: Cloning from one picture to another

_____Now experiment between **cropping and coning**:

Figure 129a-b: Cropping or cloning

- Open a picture (i.e., astronauts). Open another with a focal image (i.e., a dog).
- To place the dog among the astronauts (Figure 129a), would you crop or clone?
- To swap heads between a dog and a person, would you crop or clone (Figure 129b)?
- What are advantages and disadvantages of doing either?

_____Throughout class, check for understanding.
_____Save file to digital portfolio as both a .psd (Photoshop's default file. It will keep all layers for later editing) and a .jpg (usable in many programs and on Internet).
_____Remind students to transfer knowledge to classroom or home.

Class exit ticket: **Print the cloned picture and the original. Ask ten people if they can tell which is Photoshopped.**

Differentiation

- *Early finishers: Have image editing websites for interested students. Scroll to 'Image Editing' for examples on Ask a Tech Teacher's resource pages.*

Lesson #26—Image Editing III

Vocabulary	Problem solving	Skills
• Ants • Append • Color palette • Foreground • Inverse • Magic wand • Medium • Pixel • Tolerance • Warp	• Computer didn't save my project (Did you save to 'My Documents'?) • I can't find last week's project (did you save as PSD rather than jpg?) • When I add brushes, it deletes old ones (did you append?) • Magic wand doesn't work well (try magnetic lasso or lasso) • I liked the Filter, but then I didn't (Ctrl+Z to undo and try again)	**New** **Scaffolded** A card mixing text, pictures, and multimedia Speaking and listening Digital citizenship
Academic Applications Life, art, digital storytelling	**Materials Required** Image editor, keyboarding program, Speak Like a Geek rubric, Evidence Board badges	**Standards** CCSS.RI.5.7 NETS: 1b, 6b

Essential Question

How can image editing become that 'killer app' that entices reluctant students into technology?

Big Idea

Image editing makes technology fun

Teacher Preparation

- Talk with grade-level team so you tie into inquiry
- Know which tasks weren't completed last week and whether they are necessary to move forward
- Be prepared to use domain-specific tech vocabulary
- Know whether you need extra time to complete lesson.
- If you offer afterschool tech help and it's manned by students, verify they will be there.

Assessment Strategies

- Anecdotal
- Completed project
- [tried to] solve own problems
- Decisions followed class rules
- Left room as student found it
- Completed warm-up
- Joined classroom conversations
- Higher order thinking: analysis, evaluation, synthesis
- Habits of mind observed

Steps

Time required: 45 minutes in one sitting or spread throughout the week, setting aside 35 minutes for image editing project

Class warm-up: Have a Google Form on class screen. Ask students to share which picture their ten friends selected as 'original' or 'Photoshopped'. When everyone has voted, share results.

_____Any evidence of learning to post on Evidence Board?
_____Remember to submit homework.
_____Continue Speak Like a Geek presentations.
_____Open image editing program. Today, we'll make a greeting card for a loved one using student picture, creative background, paint brushes, and text (see *Figure 130*).

_____Open student school picture on image editor (or other). Decide which cropping tool would best delete the background. Often, with school pictures, magic wand is best. It might be necessary to reset tolerances to select correct pixels (what's 'tolerance'?).

_____Select agreeable background and foreground colors. I've selected blue and white to match a holiday theme.

_____Under the (Photoshop) *Filter* menu item, select *render>clouds* to replace background with clouds shaded to these two colors.

_____Under the (Photoshop) *Select* menu item, go to *inverse* ('ants' were moving around background. Now, they will march around person).

_____Try several filters and then select one you like.

_____Use text tool to add a greeting. Change font, size, color, and warp.

_____Use paint brush to spray leaves or something else.

Figure 130—Card from an image editor

_____Save as .jpg and .psd. Print with preview—check box to fit picture to medium.

_____Throughout class, check for understanding.

_____Remind students to transfer knowledge to classroom or home.

Class exit ticket: *None*

Differentiation

- *If homework is due, add to class calendar.*
- *Early finishers: visit class start page for websites on image editing.*

Lesson #27 Image Editing IV

Vocabulary	Problem solving	Skills
• Actions tab • Anchor • Blur tool • Clouds • Filter • Foreground • Gradient tool • History tab • Layers • Quadrant • Render • Smudge tool • Styles • Variegated	• I can't edit text (are you in text layer?) • I can't find image editor (Search on Start button) • I saved a picture and it won't open (did you save as PSD or JPG?) • I'm painting but nothing is happening (are you in correct layer?) • Clouds are the wrong color (did you change foreground/background?) • Styles layer won't show (are you in a new layer and the paint bucket?) • Picture got weird (use corner handles) • When I paint with History brush, I get white (did you anchor to picture?)	**New** Layering backgrounds Filters History brush Blurring Hue and saturation Actions Gradient **Scaffolded** Paint bucket Speaking and listening Keyboarding Digital citizenship
Academic Applications Art, digital storytelling	**Materials Required** Image editor, keyboarding program, Speak Like a Geek rubric, Evidence Board badges	**Standards** CCSS.RI.5.7 NETS: 1b, 6b

Essential Question

Can image editing pull reluctant students into technology?

Big Idea

Images can communicate big ideas, but may require tweaking

Teacher Preparation

- Talk with grade-level team so you tie into inquiry.
- Know which tasks weren't completed last week.
- Be prepared to integrate domain-specific tech vocabulary.
- Know whether you need extra time to complete lesson.
- If you offer afterschool tech help and it's manned by students, verify they will be there.

Assessment Strategies

- Anecdotal
- Completed project
- Displayed inquiry and curiosity
- [tried to] solve own problems
- Decisions followed class rules
- Left room as student found it
- Completed warm-up, exit ticket
- Joined classroom conversations
- Higher order thinking: analysis, evaluation, synthesis
- Habits of mind observed

Steps

Time required: 45 minutes either in one sitting or spread throughout the week
Class warm-up: Open a picture students would like to work with today

_____Any evidence of learning to post on Evidence Board?
_____Remember to turn in homework.
_____Continue Speak Like a Geek presentations.
_____Open a picture in image editor. You'll use four tools today. All of these may not work with your school image editor. Pick those that do. All are easy for fifth graders to use:

- *Blur (several ways)*

- *Hue and saturation*
- *History brush*
- *Actions*

Blur

_____Demonstrate **blur tool**. In Photoshop, there are several ways to blur, including *Filters>Blur* (*Figure 131a*) or 'Blur' on the left toolbar (*Figure 131b*). You can blur the entire picture or just part of it. This is a common effect used to make a focal point stand out (as the runner stands out in *Figure 131b*). Your eye immediately goes to the nonblurred focal point.

Figure 131a-b: Blurring an image

_____Use image editor camera tool to take a picture (if available).
_____Return to the original picture and try a different way to blur part of the image—the **smudge tool** on the toolbar. What's the difference? When might you use one or the other?

Hue and Saturation

_____A popular effect in photography is to change the color emphasis in an image, or remove the color entirely. Here's how that is done in Photoshop—*Figure 132a* is the original picture:

- go to *Image>Adjustments>Hue&Saturation*
- move the *Saturation* slider and the *Hue* slider to new positions and get an image like *Figure 132b*
- move the *Saturation* slider all the way to the left so the color washes out like *Figure 132c*

Figure 132a-c: Changing hue and saturation

History brush

_____The History brush can be used any time you want to return an image to what it was in a different layer. It depends on what the History brush is anchored to. Here's how it's done:

- Anchor 'history' to the layer you wish to 'paint back to. See *Figure 133*:

Figure 133—Using the History brush

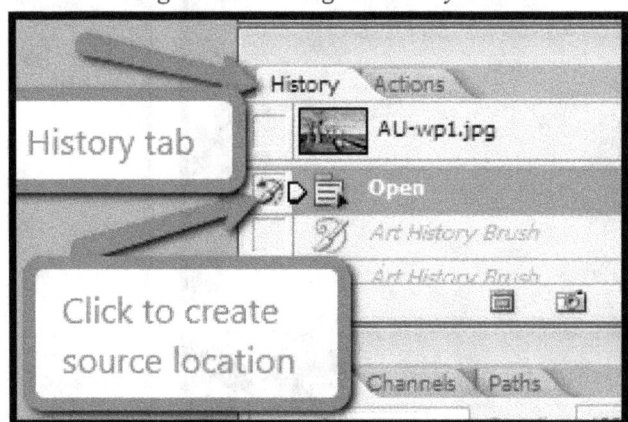

- For example: Bring color back to a desaturated focal point by painting over that part of the image with the History brush. In the images below: *Figure 134a* is original picture, *Figure 134b* and *134d* are desaturated, *Figure 134c* and *134e* show a focal point 'painted back' to original.

Figure 134a-e: Images with history tool

Actions

_____Return to original picture. Go to '**Actions**' (if it isn't available in Photoshop, click Alt+F9).

_____You'll see a list of popular multi-step formatting effects that Photoshop has automated. This includes borders, reflections, sepia tone, video, and star trails. These can be applied to the entire picture or to just a part you select with the marquis tool. All you do is select the action you want and push the 'go' arrow at the bottom.

_____Experiment with as many *Actions* as you have time for. See *Figures 135a-c* for examples:

Figure 135a-c: Actions in image editor

Backgrounds

_____Open a new canvas in the image editor. Today, we create backgrounds using (see *Figure 136*):

- *paint bucket*
- *patterns*
- *styles*
- *gradient*
- *clouds*

_____**First: Paint Bucket**—add a layer over background layer (never use background). Double click layer name and call it 'paint bucket'. Change foreground and background colors on left toolbar to new colors. Select Paint Bucket. Make sure 'fill' on top toolbar says 'foreground'. Pour. It will be foreground color as selected.

_____**Second: Patterns**—add a layer on top. Double click name and rename 'patterns'. Again, select paint bucket. This time, make sure 'fill' (in top toolbar) says 'pattern' and select one from drop down box. Pour.

_____**Third: Styles**—add a layer called 'styles'. Again, select paint bucket; select a style (on right toolbar). Pour onto new layer. Don't like it? Pour another.

_____**Fourth: Gradient**—add a layer called 'Gradient'. Select gradient tool nested under paint bucket. Drag the mouse across the screen to create a variegated background.

_____**Fifth: Clouds**—add a layer called 'Clouds'. Select two coordinating (or not) foreground/background colors (as done in greeting card). Go to *Filter>render>clouds* and layer fills with clouds colored to foreground/background colors.

_____Have students drag favorite background layer to top of stack. Then, drill through each layer, one at a time, until all five backgrounds are displayed:

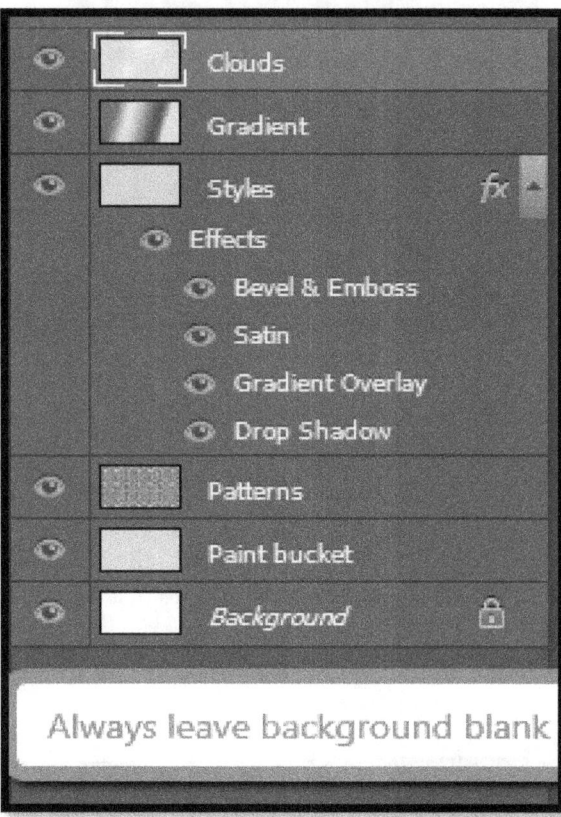

Figure 11--Background layers

- *use marquee tool to select, then delete.*
- *make sure you are on correct layer*

_____The finished image will be similar to *Figure 137a*:

Figure 137a-b: Drill through background layers

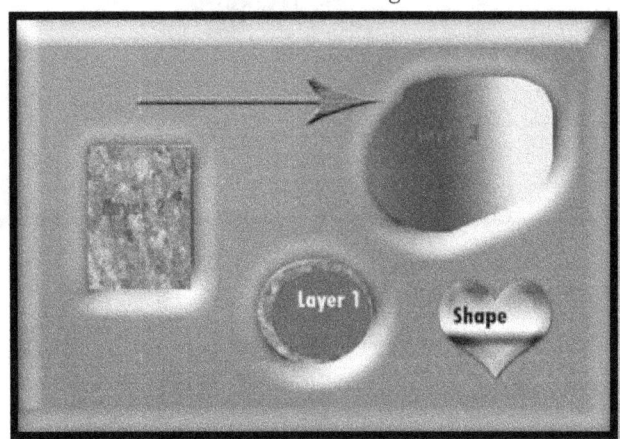 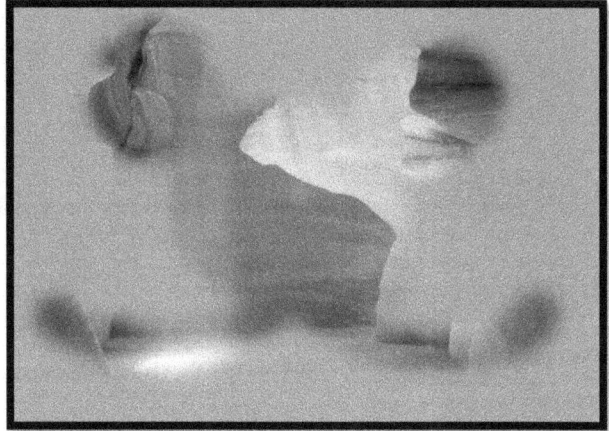

_____If you are pressed for time, you might use just two layers, as shown in *Figure 137b*.
_____Save as a .psd and a .jpg. Share on blog, class website, or other. What's the difference between the two file types?
_____Remind students to transfer knowledge to the classroom or home.

Class exit ticket: *How are the many image effects in Figure 138 made with your image editing tool:*

Figure 138—Can you do each of these?

Differentiation

- *Have image editing websites for interested students. Scroll to 'Image Editing' at Ask a Tech Teacher's resource pages.*

5th Grade Technology Curriculum: Teacher Manual

Lesson #28 Photoshop Tennis

Vocabulary	Problem solving	Skills
• Action • Crop • Filter • Hue • Photoshop tennis • Saturation	• I can't work well in a group • I don't remember how to do the skills • I'm the worst image editor on my team. • One of the team members never talks to anyone	**New** **Scaffolded** All image editing skills Speaking and listening Digital citizenship
Academic Applications Image editing, game-based learning, digital storytelling	**Materials Required** Image editor, image	**Standards** CCSS.SL.5.1 NETS: 1b, 6b

Essential Question

What photo editing skills help to communicate ideas?

Big Idea

Images communicate big ideas, but some require tweaking

Teacher Preparation

- Talk with grade-level team so you tie into inquiry.
- Be prepared to use domain-specific tech vocabulary.
- Know if you need extra time for this lesson.
- Know which tasks weren't completed last week and whether they are necessary to move forward.
- If you offer afterschool tech help and it's manned by students, verify they will be there.

Assessment Strategies
- [tried to] solve own problems
- Decisions followed class rules
- Completed project
- Worked well in a group
- Finished exit ticket
- Left room as student found it
- Higher order thinking: analysis, evaluation, synthesis
- Habits of mind observed

Steps

Time required: 45 minutes spread throughout the week
Class warm-up: None

_____**Photoshop tennis** is named after Photoshop but can use any image editing tool. It is played through sequential alternating editing of an image. Pick a starting image. One team member alters the image using one skill learned during class image editing unit and sends the altered image to the next team member. That person does the same—edits and passes it on. This continues until all team members have edited the image and all learned skills are represented.

_____All edits must comply with the assigned theme (you share that with students—history, science, fiction, or one of your choice) and use only the skills learned the last several weeks. Here's a list from these past lesson plans. Yours will vary, depending upon the image editing tool used:

- action
- blur
- clone
- crop
- filters
- history brush
- hue and saturation
- layers
- miscellaneous other skills

_____Before submitting, the team annotates the image (see *Assessment 23*) showing where editing tools were used and by whom.

205

_____This project is not done during class time. Rather, it is assigned this week and due next week. The first team member may be given time during class to get it started, but maybe not. It's up to you.

_____During class today, students:

- break into groups of nine (size varies by the number of skills to be represented)
- agree on a starting picture
- decide who will do which skill
- discuss how this will be done outside of class, during student free time
- decide how to verify as a group the completed image meets all requirements

_____As students work today in their groups, remind them to:

- listen to others
- take turns speaking
- brush up on personal image editing skills so they can participate fully in the project
- build on the contributions of others

_____Assessment 23 is an example of a Photoshop Tennis image that started as a playground:

Assessment 23—Photoshop Tennis

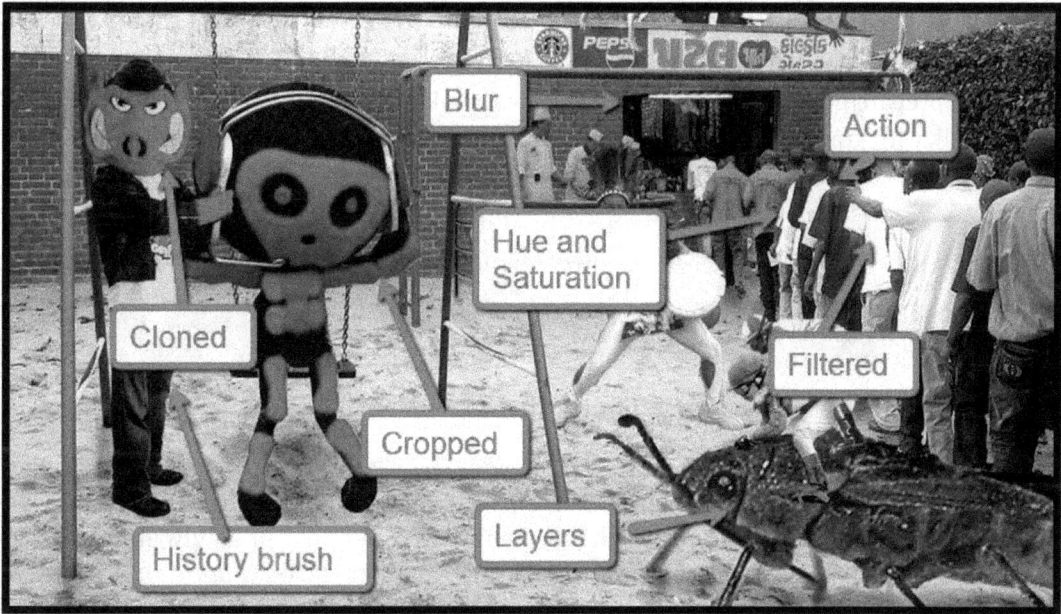

Class exit ticket: ***Each group tells you its members and what picture they're using.***

Differentiation

- *Add the due date for the Photoshop Tennis image to class calendar.*
- *Search YouTube for video of people playing Photoshop Tennis*

5th Grade Technology Curriculum: Teacher Manual

Lesson #29 Keyboarding and Science

Vocabulary	Problem solving	Skills
• Compare-contrast • Critical thinking • Digital device • Hypothesis • Scientific Method	• I don't understand this program (is it like another you do understand?) • My science teacher uses a different Scientific Method (explain why to students)	**New** **Scaffolded** Scientific Method Keyboarding
Academic Applications Experimentation, Scientific Method, research	**Materials Required** Hard copy of typing quiz, school Scientific Method, student workbooks (if using)	**Standards** CCSS.SL.5.1 NETS: 6a, 6b

Essential Question

How can I use technology to evaluate choices?

Big Idea

Knowledge is meant to be transferred to new situations

Teacher Preparation

- Know whether you need extra time to complete lesson.
- Be prepared to use domain-specific tech vocabulary.
- Talk with grade-level team to use their scientific method.
- Know which tasks weren't completed last week and whether they are necessary to move forward.
- Ask grade-level team and parents if there are any tech problems students need help with.
- If you offer afterschool tech help manned by students, verify they will be there.

Assessment Strategies

- Anecdotal
- [tried to] solve own problems
- Completed experiment thoughtfully
- Left room as student found it
- Joined classroom conversations
- Higher order thinking: analysis, evaluation, synthesis
- Habits of mind observed

Steps

Time required: 45 minutes in one sitting
Class warm-up: None

_____This week: Students compare and contrast **typing vs. handwriting speed**. Discuss as a group which they think is faster—typing or handwriting.
_____Circle back on science class and the scientific method (*Figure 139*):

Note: There are varying examples of the scientific method. Talk to your science teacher and adapt this experiment to theirs.

_____Discuss its steps and applicability to general problem solving (such as this issue). Review Problem-solving lesson from earlier this year.
_____Apply to the comparison of handwriting and typing speed as follows (this is done as a group):

- **Ask a question**: *Is handwriting or keyboarding faster?*
- **Do background research:** Discuss why students think they handwrite faster/slower than they type. Curious students might even research the topic by Googling, *Is keyboarding faster than handwriting?*

207

- **Construct a hypothesis:** Student states her/his informed conclusion: i.e.: *Fifth graders in Mr. X's class handwrite faster than they type.*
- **Test hypothesis**: Do an experiment to see if handwriting or typing is faster. Pass out a copy of the typing speed quiz students took. Have them handwrite it for the same length of time they typed it (three-five minutes). Count and record the words.
- **Analyze data:** Compare student personal handwriting speed to their typing speed. Which is faster? Discuss data. Why do some students type faster and others slower? Or the reverse? What problems were faced in handwriting for three-five minutes:

    - *pencil lead broke*
    - *eraser gone*
    - *hands got tired*
    - *it got boring*

- **Draw conclusions**: What can be decided based on student personal test results?
- **Communicate results:** Share results with other classes. At what grade level do students consistently type faster than they handwrite? Are students surprised?

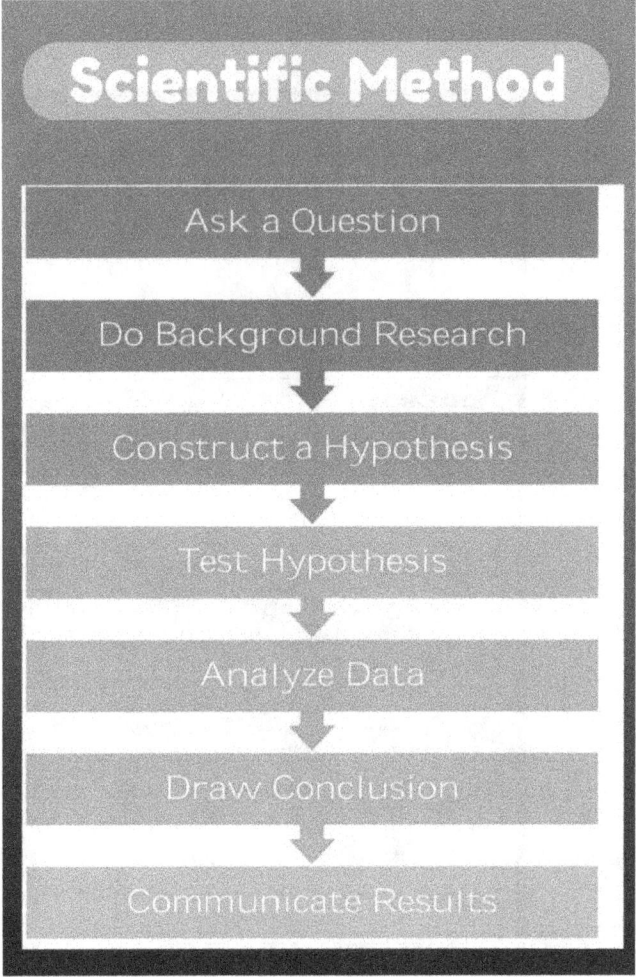

Figure 12--Scientific Method

_____If you have time, go through the same process with non-written text:

- give students a writing prompt
- give them a minute to think through the prompt organizing ideas based on your school's writing protocol, i.e., the five-paragraph essay—1) introduction, 2-4) one paragraph per point, 5) conclusion
- type response for three-five minutes
- provide a different prompt and follow the same procedure, but this time they handwrite

_____Discuss the differences between the results. Was it easier to type or handwrite from memory? Did students who type 20 wpm and faster like typing better than slower typists? What problems did students encounter?

_____You will not get through all of these experiments in forty-five minutes. You may decide to do one this year and a different one next year.

_____**Another option:** Is keyboarding on an iPad faster, the same, or slower than on a traditional keyboard? You can review Brady Cline's experiment with his class on his website by searching "iPad Typing".

_____If you'd prefer, use a **compare-contrast method rather than the Scientific Method**. Compare software and online tools (*Figure 140*):

Figure 140—Compare contrast software and online tool

	SOFTWARE	ONLINE TOOL
Examples	MS Office, KidPix, Type to Learn, Reader Rabbit	Google Drive apps, ABCYa, Dance Mat Typing
Access	Accessible only from where you installed the software	Accessible from any computer with an internet connection
Compatibility	Varies	Most are compatible across platforms (Windows, Macs, Linux, Chromebooks)
Control	You control	Someone else controls—may be moved or removed without your permission
Cost	Varies	Varies—often free versions are available
Daily use	Depends upon whether your computer works and whether the software is compatible with changes you've made to your computer	Depends upon whether your internet connection works
Limitation	Don't run on iPads, Chromebooks	Run on most computer systems
Maintenance	If it breaks, you have to fix it	If it breaks, someone online fixes it.
Security	As secure as your computer is	Depends upon the website's security
Set-up	You must install; might require adaptations to work on your system	No installation required—all you do is go to the site
Speed	Depends upon your system	Depends upon your internet connection
Updates	You do these	Managed by website; always up to date
Where it lives	On your computer (or network)	On the internet
Working with a partner	Difficult	Easy

_____Or, compare digital devices used by students (*Figure 141*):

Figure 141—Compare contrast digital devices

	Desktop	Chromebook	Laptop	iPad
Operating system	Windows or OS X	Chrome OS (Linux)	Windows or OS X	iOS
Set-up	Can be complicated	Plug in, log on, go	Can be complicated	Plug in, go
Cost	Cheap	Cheap	Expensive	Expensive
Maintenance	Virus protection, updates, software, repairs cheaper than other options	Almost nothing; hardware repair may require unit replacement	Virus protection, updates, software, repairs may be expensive	Almost nothing; hardware repair may require unit replacement
Virus and malware issues	Uses firewall, antivirus, malware protection	None	Require firewall, antivirus, malware protection	None
Boot-up time	Average	Fast	Average	Fast
Speed while using	Depends upon install	Fast	Depends upon install	Fast
Keyboard	User selected—standard to gamer	Standard; can upgrade	Standard; can upgrade	Virtual; some schools use external keyboard
Popular programs	Compatible with most	Only online and apps; availability a work in progress	Compatible with most	Only apps; availability a work in progress
Ease of printing	Easy	Requires Google Chrome and Google Cloud printing	Easy	Requires Airprint-enabled printer
Switch between programs	Dock or taskbar	Browser tabs	Dock or taskbar	Home button
Multitask	Easily runs multiple programs	Runs multiple programs as browser tabs or side-by-side windows; multitask mode available (two mouses)	Easily runs multiple programs depending upon processor speed	Use 'multitasking gestures' under Settings
Update alerts	Constant—must be cleared	Rare; device restart installs updates	Constant—must be cleared	Rare
Learning curve	Moderate	Low	Moderate	Low
Portability	None	Lightweight, battery life varies (depends on usage)	Yes, but depends on device; battery depends on use	Lightweight, 10 hr. battery (depends on use)
Durability	Lots of parts, wires, plugs that can be damaged	Considered tough and durable	If one part breaks, entire device may need replacement	Shouldn't be dropped or mishandled
Peripherals	Highly adaptable	plug-and-play; compatible with USB HDMI devices; no downloads	varies with device	Limited, no downloads; must plug in via charging dock

Class exit ticket: Write a three-minute summation of this experiment on student blog or a class Discussion Board.

Differentiation

- *Another topic: Should the word 'Internet' be capitalized? Is it a place like Europe or a piece of technology like a monitor?*
- *Early finishers: visit class internet start page for websites that tie into classwork*

5th Grade Technology Curriculum: Teacher Manual

Lesson #30 What Have I Learned

Vocabulary	Problem solving	Skills
• Embed • Help files • Template • Transfer • Tutorial • Upload	• I never used this before (does it look like any you have used?) • I can't find the toolbar • Screen froze (Is dialogue box open?) • How do I use a document link (Ctrl+click) • How do I get help? (F2)	**New** **Scaffolded** Decoding new skills Speaking/listening Digital citizenship
Academic Applications Academics, life, critical thinking	**Materials Required** Speak Like a Geek rubric, Evidence of Learning badges	**Standards** CCSS: Stds for Math. Pr. NETS: 6a, 6d

Essential Question

How can I use what I've learned in another program?

Big Idea

Knowledge is meant to be transferred to new situations

Teacher Preparation

- Talk with grade-level team so you tie into inquiry.
- Know whether you need extra time to complete lesson.
- Be prepared to integrate domain-specific tech vocabulary.
- Are tasks not completed last week necessary this week.
- Have 3-4 programs available on computers that students have never before used. They can be online or software.
- If you offer afterschool tech help manned by students, verify they will be there.

Assessment Strategies

- Anecdotal
- Completed project
- Completed presentations
- [tried to] solve own problems
- Decisions followed class rules
- Left room as student found it
- Completed warm-up
- Joined classroom conversations
- Higher order thinking: analysis, evaluation, synthesis
- Habits of mind observed

Steps

Time required: 45 minutes either in one sitting or spread throughout the week
Class warm-up: Turned in final homework

_____Any evidence of learning to post on Evidence Board?
_____Speak Like a Geek—finish presentations today.
_____Today, students transfer new knowledge to new situations.
_____Give students a list of three software or online tools they've never used. They may be tools they'll need next year like **Evernote** or tools you didn't have time to get to this year. How does one start with a tool they've never seen? Have students offer suggestions. Prod gently to come up with:

- Is there a tutorial or a demo?
- Is there a Help button?
- How did we initiate other programs we used this year?
- Are tools familiar?

211

- *How about menus?*

_____Here are two ideas (*Figures 142a-b*):

- *use PrintMusic to compose music for the 5th-grade graduation ceremony*
- *use a flier program to create announcements for the 5th-grade graduation*

Figure 142a-b New 5th grade digital tools

_____Give students the rest of the class to work in a group and figure out how to create a project. Is it like a Word doc? A new Photoshop canvas?
_____When they're done, have them publish/share projects.

Class exit ticket: None.

> "There is no reason anyone would want a computer in their home."
>
> *-- Ken Olson, president, founder of Digital Equipment Corp., 1977*

Lesson #31 Hello Next Year Students

Vocabulary	Problem solving	Skills
• .jpg • Embed • QR code • Render • Screenshot • Word cloud	• I can't figure this out (try help) • I don't know how to use these tools (be a risk-taker; try something new) • I'm doing all the work in my group • I don't like making movies (pick a different option)	**New** New webtools **Scaffolded** Reading, writing, listening
Academic Applications Any topic	**Materials Required** web-based tools, digital portfolio, student workbooks (if using)	**Standards** CCSS.W.5.6 NETS: 2d, 6d

Essential Question

How can I use technology to produce and publish writing while I collaborate with others?

Big Idea

I can use technology to share my ideas with others

Teacher Preparation

- Talk with grade-level team so you tie into their inquiry.
- Integrate domain-specific tech vocabulary.
- Verify all required links are available.
- Know which tasks weren't completed last week.
- Ask grade-level team and parents if there are any tech problems students need help with.

Assessment Strategies

- Anecdotal
- Completed project
- Organized Challenge team
- [tried to] solve own problems
- Decisions followed class rules
- Left room as student found it
- Completed exit ticket
- Joined classroom conversations
- Higher order thinking: analysis, evaluation, synthesis
- Habits of mind observed

Steps

Time required: 45 minutes in one sitting or break it into 30 minutes and 15 minutes
Class warm-up: None

_____School year is almost over. Let's share what has been learned with next year's fifth graders. What was hard? Easy? Challenging? What tips do this year's students have for those following in their footsteps?

_____To share ideas, students create a project in an online tool of their choice. This is the student's chance to create a video, artwork, writing, multimedia—whatever works best for them. Then, share their advice with next year's students through the lens of that tool. While you offer a list, be ready to listen to student suggestions for what they feel would work best for their communications style (say, they'd like to use Tellagami or Minecraft). Ask them to defend their request and provide evidence.

_____Make sure the list you offer includes a wide variety of media that will suit multiple varied learning styles. You might take suggestions from students or use tools you didn't have time to get to this year. You might even use tools you'd like to learn—have the students teach you.

5th Grade Technology Curriculum: Teacher Manual

_____Here are ideas. If you have student workbooks, these options and links are available there (Google for the websites or visit Ask a Tech Teacher's resource pages):

- *Animoto video*

- *Big Huge Labs*

- *Canva (web-based or app)*

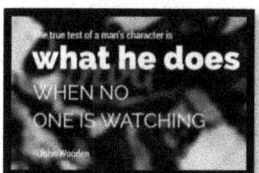

- *Comic creator*

- *Easel.ly*

- *Glogster*

- *QR Code*

- *Tagxedo*

- *Timeline (scroll to 'timelines')*

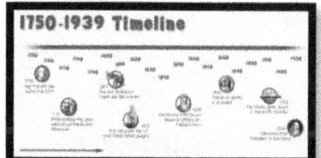

- *Voki*

_____If not using student workbooks, have websites available on class Internet start page.
_____Take one minute to review each tool on class screen (13 tools in 13 minutes—you can do it). Then, students select a tool and work in groups to finish project.
_____Give rest of class to create 'Hello, Fifth Graders!' project.

_____Publish projects to class website or blog (or another place where you curate resources for your class) using embed code or a screen shot.

_____Remind students to transfer knowledge to class or home.

_____Save last fifteen minutes of class for a dry run of next week's Challenge (see instructions under Lesson #32). This includes questions compiled from a year's worth of tech classes presented in a Jeopardy-style game. Students work in groups and challenge each other for extra credit, free dress passes, whatever the prize du jour is. It is a fun way to review what they've learned and encourage them to study.

_____Have them take this dedicated time to select a team captain and decide how their team will prepare.

Class exit ticket: ***Submit names of team members, captain, and how the group is going to prepare for the Team Challenge.***

Differentiation

- Add Team Challenge to class calendar.
- Early finishers: work with team to prepare for next week's Team Challenge
- Longer version of this project: 15 Digital Tools in 15 Days is available from Structured Learning.

5th Grade Technology Curriculum: Teacher Manual

Lesson #32 End-of-Year Challenge

Vocabulary	Problem solving	Skills
• Category • Help files • Tutorial	• How do I _____? (try Help files) • We have an odd number of students (make one the timekeeper)	**New** **Scaffolded** Year-long learning
Academic Applications Tech-in-ed	**Materials Required** challenge questions, score keeping, prizes for winners, Certificates, student workbooks (if using)	**Standards** CCSS: St. for Math. Pr. NETS: 6a, 6b

Essential Question

What did I learn this year?

Big Idea

I know more than I think I do

Teacher Preparation

- Be prepared to integrate domain-specific tech vocabulary.
- Have prizes for winners of Challenge (if using).
- Know whether you need extra time to complete this lesson.
- Know which tasks not completed last week are needed this week.

Assessment Strategies

- Came prepared for Team Challenge
- Decisions followed class rules
- Left room as student found it
- Higher order thinking: analysis, evaluation, synthesis
- Habits of mind observed

Steps

Time required: 45 minutes in one sitting with 30 minutes set aside for game and 10 minutes to pass out graduation certificates

Class warm-up: None

_____Students play a Jeopardy-style game to see who knows the most about different categories of technology. You'll develop this list of questions based on what you covered about technology this year. Yours will be different from the sample at the end of this lesson.

_____Put students into teams. Remind them about last week's practice. Pass out list of categories—not questions.

_____Assign a Timekeeper.

_____Teams go to different 'corners' of classroom. One member on each Team is Captain—s/he is the only one who can answer questions. S/he will confer with colleagues before answering.

_____Team #1 selects a category. Ask a question within that category. Give team 5 seconds to answer. If they can't, proceed to Team #2, but don't repeat question. If they don't know question or can't answer, move to Team #3 and then Team #4. If no one can answer, provide answer (because they'll be curious).

_____Next category selection goes to Team #2—even if they answered Team #1's question. This is how teams get ahead. Pose question from selected category and repeat steps above.

_____Each team selects a category their question will come from. Ask each question only once. Use each category only once.

_____Go around class until each group has a first crack at a category/question. Notice where groups have difficulties and note that the Notes section of this lesson to concentrate on next year.

_____When time runs out, count one point per correct answer. Announce winner.

_____Students love this game. If I had time, I'd play it at mid-year also.

_____Prizes? Optional. I give Free passes that include sitting where student wants, skip a homework, 5 extra credit points—prizes I know they value. You might decide no prizes.

_____Save time at the end of class to hand out Certificates—unless this will be a special ceremony.

Class exit ticket: None

Differentiation

- *Put this into a real Jeopardy template.*

_____

_____

_____

_____

_____

_____

_____

Assessment 24—End-of-year team challenge

END-OF-YEAR TEAM CHALLENGE

Review the following concepts. These are the questions that will be asked during the Team Challenge—to find the year's most tech-savvy students!

Basics
- How do you 'Print screen'
- How do you print
- How do you save
- Name 5 parts of computer
- Name four ways to save a file (.jpg, .PDF…)
- What is a local disk
- What is the network file

Classroom Tech Rules
- Name two speaking/listening skills
- Name three tech use rules
- How often should you save
- How do you print from the Internet
- What does "Respect everyone's work" mean
- When can you eat in the lab
- What Internet site can you go on
- What is proper posture at the computer
- When can you plagiarize
- When do you not have to credit info from Internet
- Who is to blame if you miss homework
- If you don't know a rule, do you have to follow it
- When is it OK to go into someone else's file folder
- What if you miss a class
- When can you touch someone else's equipment

Coding/Programming
- How do you create a macro
- How do you learn sequencing from coding
- How do you learn problem solving from coding
- How do you create a shortkey
- Name three tools for coding
- Why learn coding/programming

Digital Citizenship
- Name three netiquette rules
- Name three rules to make online search easier
- What are your digital responsibilities
- What are your digital rights
- What is a good digital citizen
- What is fair use online
- What is social media
- What is your digital footprint
- What is the digital neighborhood
- When do you share online
- What is a cyberbully
- Why use an avatar
- Why use UN and PW

Digital tools—for the classroom
- Name 5 parts of an iPad (or Chromebook)
- What digital tool takes a screenshot
- What digital tool tapes audio
- What are digital portfolios
- What is a blog
- Why use a blog
- What are Google Apps
- What is the class digital calendar
- What is the class Internet start page
- Where does the class collect weblinks
- Why use a class website
- Why use a student dropbox
- Why use Discussion Boards
- Why use email

DTP
- How do you add a border
- How do you add text
- How do you insert a page
- How do you move material to another page
- How do you add a footer
- How do you add the page number to the footer
- How do you insert a picture
- Name four projects we did in DTP
- Why use DTP instead of WP?
- What project did you use DTP in this year

5th Grade Technology Curriculum: Teacher Manual

Graphics
- How do you change a picture background
- How do you crop a picture
- How do you move an image around page
- How do you resize a picture
- How do you wrap text around a picture
- List three examples of graphic organizers
- Name two image editors you used this year
- When can you use an online image
- Why use a mindmap

Internet
- How do you attach a document to an email
- How do you copy-paste from the Internet
- How do you select the best site from a search engine
- Name 3 website extensions and what they are
- Name one address we have visited on the Internet
- Name three ways you know a site is trust-worthy
- What are the four pieces of a web address
- What is a search engine
- What is the 'Back' button
- What is the 'Forward' button
- What is the 'Home' button
- What is the 'Refresh' button
- What is the Address Bar
- What's the 'History' tool
- When can you go on the Internet at school

Keyboarding
- An A in keyboarding requires 20% of what
- Describe good keyboarding posture
- How fast should you keyboard in 5th grade
- When do you use proper keyboarding habits
- Why learn to keyboard properly

Keyboard Shortkeys
- Add a hyperlink (Ctrl+K)
- Bold (Ctrl+B)
- Bring back Internet toolbar (F11)
- Copy (Ctrl+C)
- Exdent in an outline (Shift+tab)
- Exit a program (Alt+F4)
- Find (Ctrl+F)
- Help (F1)
- Indent in an outline (tab)
- Name 5 shortkeys on an iPad/Chromebook/Mac
- Italics (Ctrl+I)
- Make a graph in spreadsheet (F11)
- New page (Ctrl+Enter)
- Paste (Ctrl+V)
- Print (Ctrl+P)
- Save (Ctrl+S)
- Toggle between tasks (Alt+Tab)
- Underline (Ctrl+U)
- Undo (Ctrl+Z)
- Zoom in on a webpage (Ctrl++)
- Zoom out of a webpage (Ctrl+-)

Presentation Tools
- Why use a presentation tool
- How do you add slides
- How do you delete slides
- How do you add animations
- How do you add transitions
- How do you add moving pictures
- How do you add GIF's
- How do you add sounds
- How do you change background
- How do you use pictures for backgrounds
- How do you insert hyperlinks
- How do you auto-advance slides

Problem Solving
- How do you find the date on the computer
- How do you fix a weird looking resized image
- How do you search for a file
- How do you take a screenshot on digital device
- If double-click doesn't work, what do you do
- Name 4 reasons you can't find your file
- Name five problem-solving strategies
- Name two things you do if your screen is frozen
- What do you do if desktop icons are messed up
- What do you do if monitor is black
- What if you accidentally delete words/pictures
- What if your capitals are stuck on
- What if your computer doesn't work
- What if your mouse doesn't work
- What if your Start button disappears
- What if your volume doesn't work
- What is the name of the classroom printer
- What is the next thing you do if monitor is black

5th Grade Technology Curriculum: Teacher Manual

- What is the password to log-on the computer
- What is the user name to log-on the computer
- What keyboard shortcut auto-inserts current date
- What's the right mouse button for
- Why use a brainstorming tool

Spreadsheet

- Why use a spreadsheet?
- Name three spreadsheet projects you've done
- How do you build arrays in spreadsheets
- Decode spreadsheet formulas
- What must be at the start of every formula
- How do you enter data
- How do you graph data
- How do you alphabetize names
- How do you auto-sum
- How do you average numbers
- How do you add numbers
- How do you subtract numbers
- How do you multiply numbers
- How do you divide numbers
- How do you widen columns
- How to widen rows
- How do you format text
- How do you insert a picture
- How do you add the date
- How do you add the time
- How do you change the worksheet name
- How do you change the tab color
- How do you add a worksheet

Vocabulary

- .com
- .edu
- .net
- .org
- Active window
- Address bar
- Animation
- Auto-advance
- Auto-play
- Back button
- Back-up
- Browser
- Bullets
- Caps lock
- Cc
- Class exit ticket
- Class warm-up
- Clip art
- Clone
- Crop
- Cursor
- Data
- Default
- Desktop
- Dialogue box
- Digital locker
- Drill down
- Drop down menu
- Explorer
- Export
- F4
- Flash drive
- Folder
- Font
- Footer
- Format
- Forward button
- GIF
- Google (verb)
- Handles
- Hits
- Hue
- Hyperlink
- I-beam
- Icon
- Import
- Initialize
- Internet address
- JPG
- Jump drive
- Kilobyte
- Landscape
- Log-on
- Monitor
- Mouse over
- Multimedia
- Netiquette
- Network
- Numbered list
- Page Break
- PC
- Photoshopped
- Pixel
- Place saver
- Portrait
- Print preview
- Printkey
- Protocol
- Queue
- Recycle bin
- Right-click menu
- Saturation
- Scrollbar
- Search bar
- Search engine
- Select-do
- Shortcut
- Synonym
- Taskbar
- Thesaurus
- Thumbnail
- Toolbar
- Transition
- Upload
- USB port
- Washout
- Watermark
- Wizard
- Worksheet
- Wrap

Word Processing

- Why use word processing
- Compare/contrast WP and DTP
- What are three examples of projects you did
- How are grammar and formatting different
- What does the red squiggly line mean
- How do you clear a red squiggly line
- What does green squiggly line mean
- How do you clear a green squiggly line
- How do you change image background?
- How do you insert a page border
- How do you resize a picture
- How do you add a text box
- How do you spell-check a document?
- How do you add a watermark?
- How do you add a footer
- How do you double-space
- How do you share a Google Doc
- How do you collaborate on a Google Doc
- How do you include citations in a Google Doc

PS

If you teach technology, it's likely you're a geek. Even if you didn't start out that way–say, you used to be a first grade teacher and suddenly your Admin in their infinite wisdom, moved you to the tech lab—you became a geek. You morphed into the go-to person for computer quirks, crashes and freezes.

Overnight, your colleagues assumed you received an upload of data that allowed you to know the answers to their every techie question. It didn't matter that yesterday, you were one of them. Now, you are on a pedestal, their necks craned upward as they ask you, *How do I get the class screen to work?* Or *We need the microphones working for a lesson I'm starting in three minutes. Can you please-please-please fix them?*

Celebrate your cheeky geekiness. Flaunt it for students and colleagues. Play Minecraft. That's you now–you are sharp, quick-thinking. You tingle when you see an iPad. You wear a flash drive like jewelry. The first thing you do when you get to school is check your email.

It's OK. Here at Structured Learning and Ask a Tech Teacher, we understand. The readers understand. You're at home.

Classroom Posters

1. Backspace and Delete
2. Chromebooks shortkeys
3. Common Tech Problems
4. Digital Law
5. Email etiquette
6. Here's What We've Done
7. How to Save—4 Ways
8. How to solve problems
9. I Can't Find My File
10. Internet Research
11. iPad shortkeys
12. Keyboard Posture
13. K-5 Keyboarding Stages
14. Landscape
15. Netiquette Rules
16. Portrait
17. Save or Save-as
18. Save Early Save Often
19. Select-Do
20. Undo is Your Friend
21. What's a Mulligan

WHAT'S THE DIFFERENCE BETWEEN SAVE AND SAVE AS?

SAVE

- Save the first time
- Resave changes to the same location

SAVE AS

- Resave under a new name
- Resave to a new location

TWO WAYS TO DELETE

BACKSPACE

Deletes to the left, one character at a time

DELETE

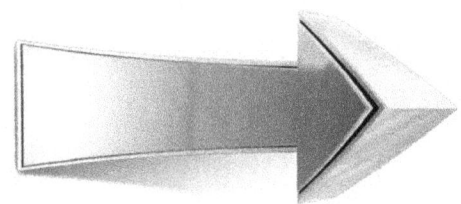

Deletes to the right, one character at a time

©AskaTechTeacher

EMAIL ETIQUETTE

1. Use proper formatting, spelling, grammar
2. CC anyone you mention
3. Subject line is what your email discusses
4. Answer swiftly
5. Re-read email before sending
6. Don't use capitals—THIS IS SHOUTING
7. Don't leave out the subject line
8. Don't attach unnecessary files
9. Don't overuse high priority
10. Don't email confidential information
11. Don't email offensive remarks
12. Don't forward chain letters or spam
13. Don't open attachments from strangers

©AskaTechTeacher

LANDSCAPE

PORTRAIT

UNDO

is your Friend

TROUBLESHOOTING COMPUTER PROBLEMS

#	Problem	Why	Solution
1.	Deleted a file	Deleted by accident	Open Recycle Bin—right-click--restore
2.	Can't exit a program	Can't find X or Quit	Alt+F4
3.	Can't find a program	Shortcut moved	Type 'Word' (or program name) into Search bar
4.	Keyboard doesn't work	Unplugged, lost file	Plug cord into back; reboot
5.	Mouse doesn't work	Unplugged, lost file	Plug cord into back, reboot
6.	Start button is gone	Task bar gone	Push Windows button
7.	No sound	Mute on	Unmute
		Volume down	turn volume up
		Unplugged headphones	plug headphones in
		Lost file	Reboot
8.	Can't find a file	Saved wrong, moved	Start button—Search
9.	Menu command grayed out	You're in another command	Push escape 3 times
10.	What's today's date?	You forgot!	Hover over the clock
11.	Taskbar gone	Student interference	Push Windows button
			Drag border up to expose
12.	Taskbar was moved	Student interference	Drag it to the bottom of screen
13.	Desktop icons messed up	Student interference	Right click on screen—arrange icons
			Too small? Highlight and Ctrl+ to enlarge
14.	Computer frozen	Mouse frozen	Reboot
15.	Program frozen	Dialog box open	Clear the dialog box
16.	I erased my document/text	Not selected on taskbar	Click program on taskbar
17.	Screen says "Ctrl-Alt-Del"	Ooops	Ctrl+Z
18.	Program closed down	You rebooted	Hold down Ctrl-Alt—push Delete
		Ooops	Is it open on the taskbar? If so—click on it
			Reopen program—see if it saved a back-up
19.	Tool bar missing on www	Pushing F11 key	Push F11 key
20.	Internet window too small	Hard to read	Ctrl+ to enlarge; Ctrl- to delarge (or Ctrl+mouse wheel)
21.	Double click doesn't work	Who knows?	Push enter
22.	Shift key doesn't work	Caps lock on	Push caps lock to disengage
23.	I can't remember how to...	So many skills...	Try a right click with the mouse
24.	When I type, it types over	I want to insert text	Push the 'insert' key
25.	The document is 'read only'	I didn't do anything	Just 'save-as' under a new name and all is fixed

K-5 Keyboarding Stages

- **K-1st:** Introduce mouse skills, keyboarding, key placement, posture
- **2nd:** Work on keyboarding, key placement, posture, two-hand position
- **3rd:** Reinforce basics, work on accuracy and technique
- **4th-5th:** Continue accuracy, technique. Begin work on speed

©AskATechTeacher

5th Grade Technology Curriculum: Teacher Manual

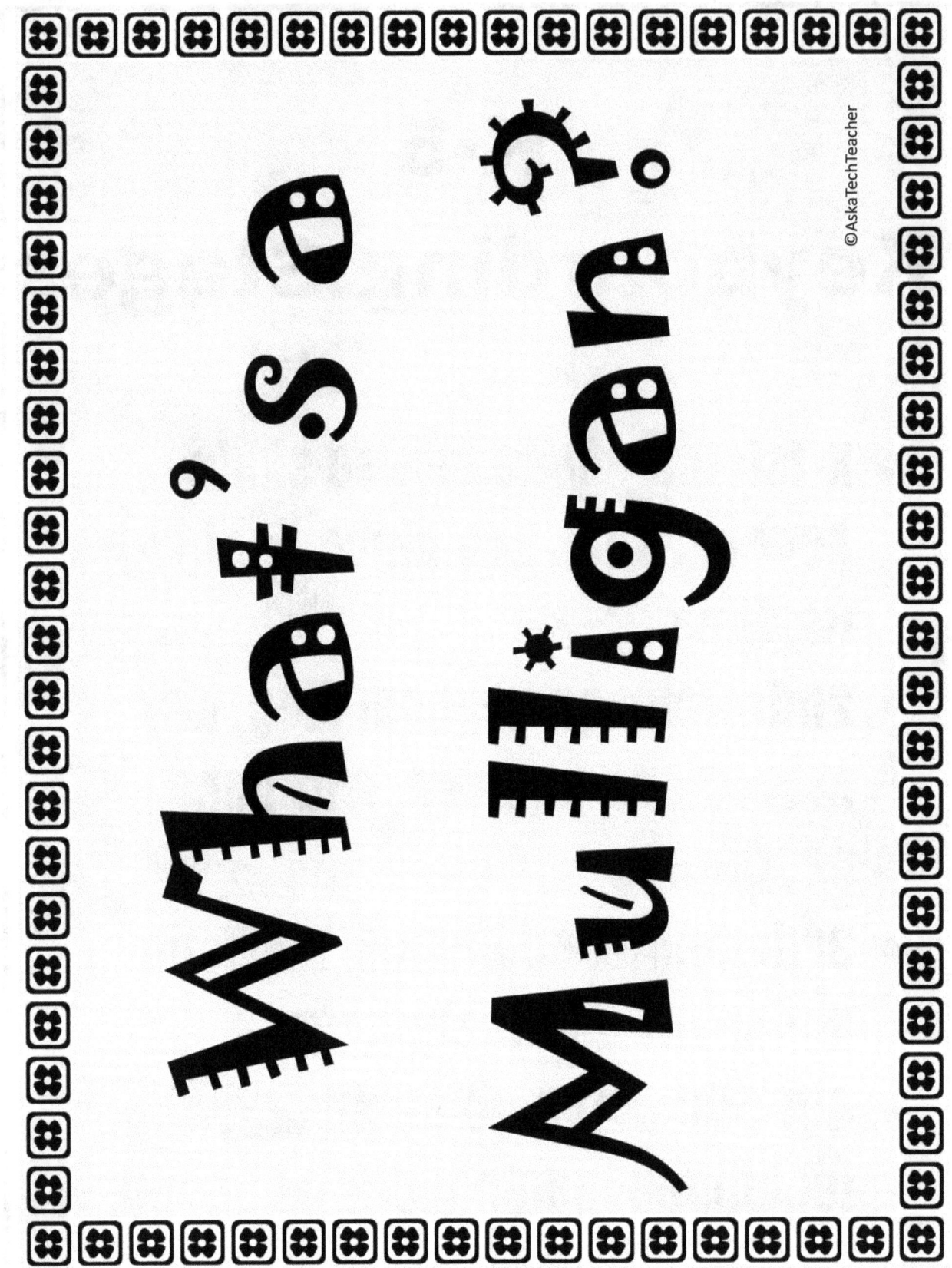

SAVE EARLY SAVE OFTEN

Netiquette Rules

- Be human
- Follow the same rules of behavior you follow in real life
- Be aware of your digital footprint
- Share your knowledge
- Help keep 'flame wars' under control
- Respect other's privacy
- Be forgiving of other's mistakes

The law states that works of art created in the U.S. after January 1, 1978, are automatically protected by copyright once they are fixed in a tangible medium (like the internet) BUT a single copy may be used for scholarly research (even if that's a 2nd grade life cycle report) or in teaching or preparation to teach a class.

5th Grade Technology Curriculum: Teacher Manual

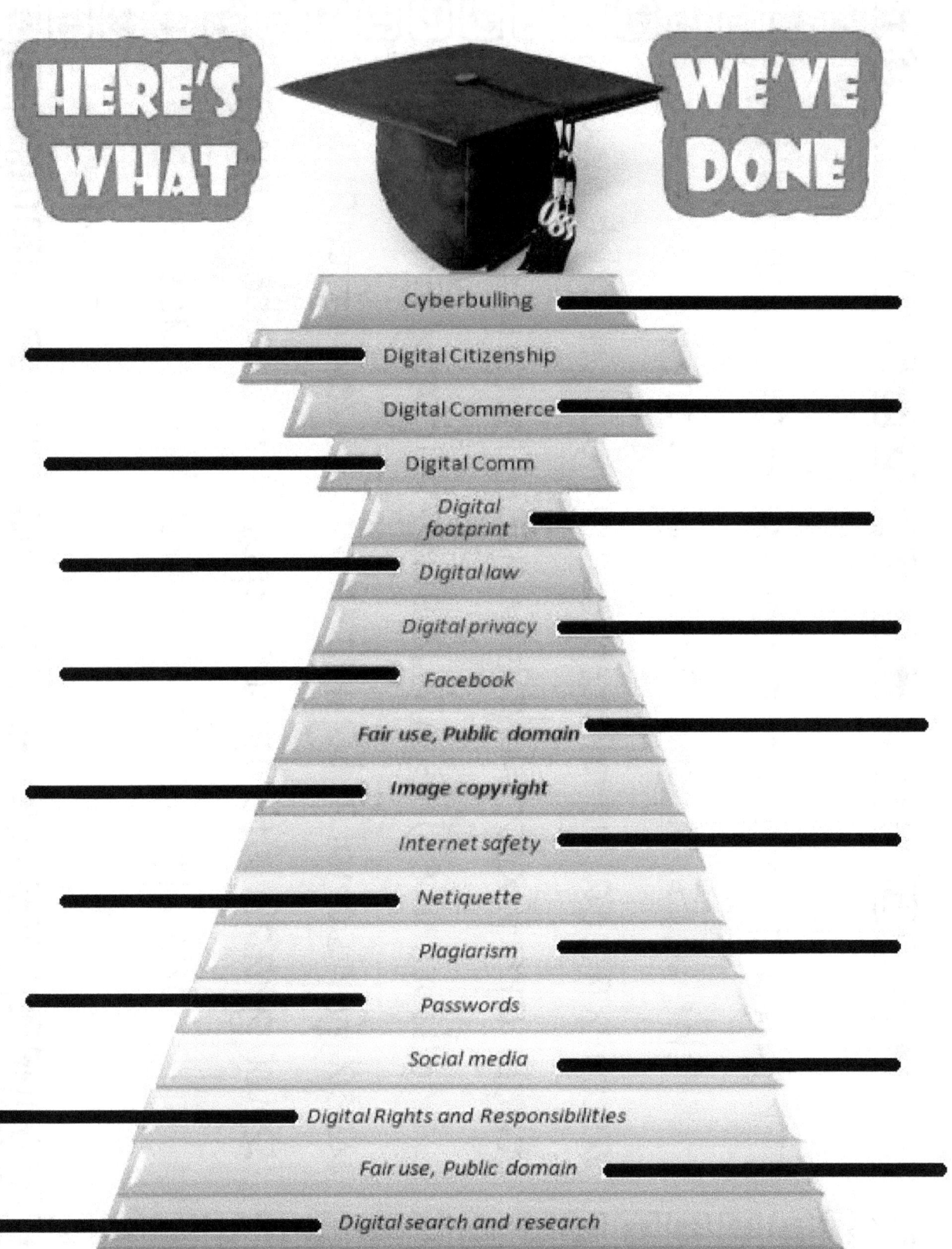

Here's What We've Done

- Cyberbullying
- Digital Citizenship
- Digital Commerce
- Digital Comm
- Digital footprint
- Digital law
- Digital privacy
- Facebook
- Fair use, Public domain
- Image copyright
- Internet safety
- Netiquette
- Plagiarism
- Passwords
- Social media
- Digital Rights and Responsibilities
- Fair use, Public domain
- Digital search and research

STEPS FOR INTERNET RESEARCH

Know Key Words — **General understanding of topic** — **Reliable site extensions** — **Read sidebars, headings, hyperlinks** — **Read pictures, insets, maps**

GET YOUR DUCKS IN A ROW

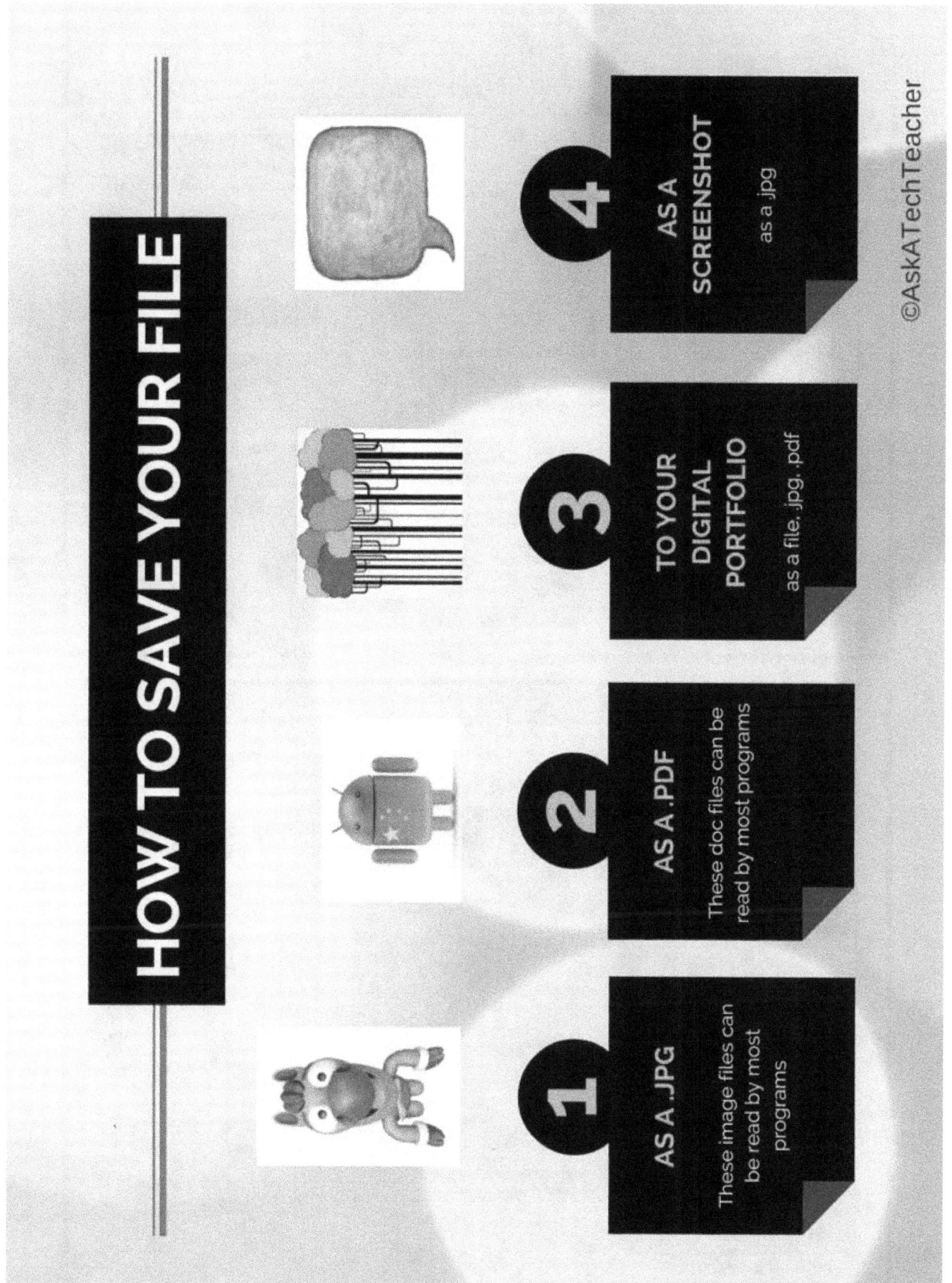

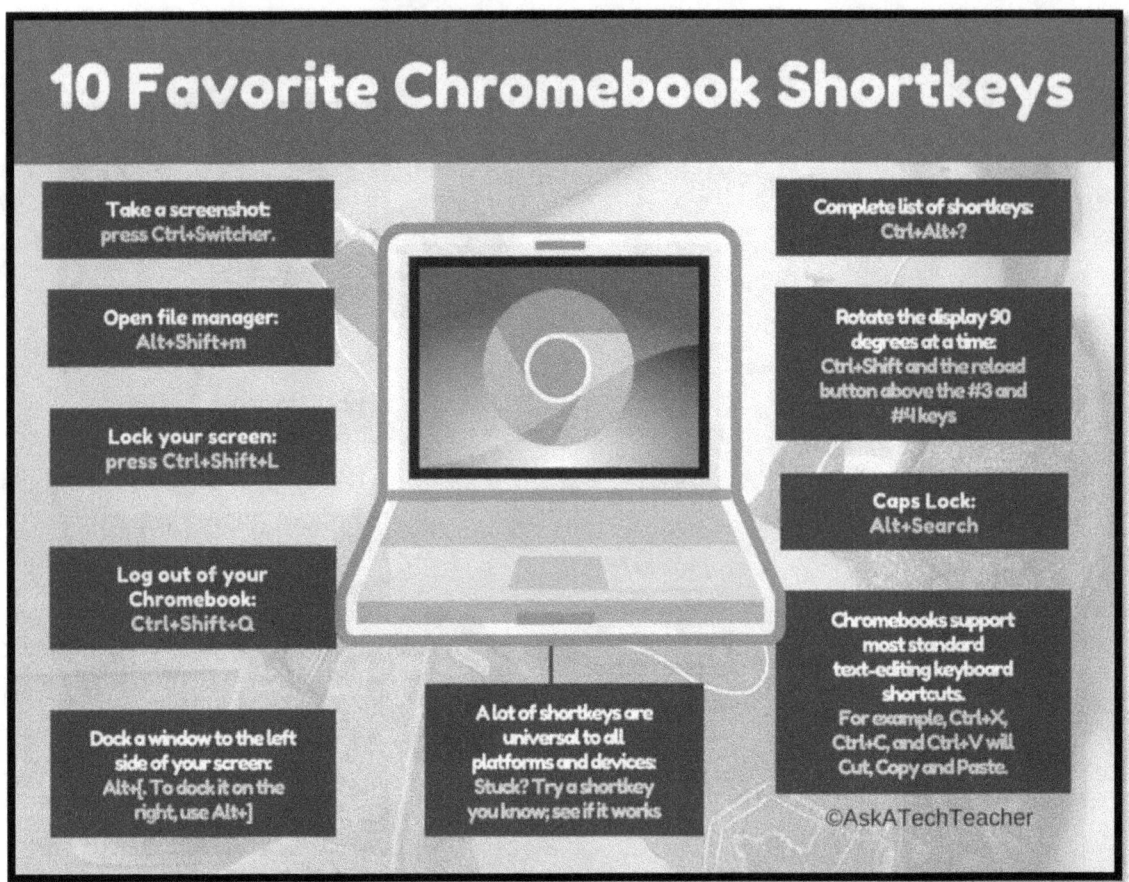
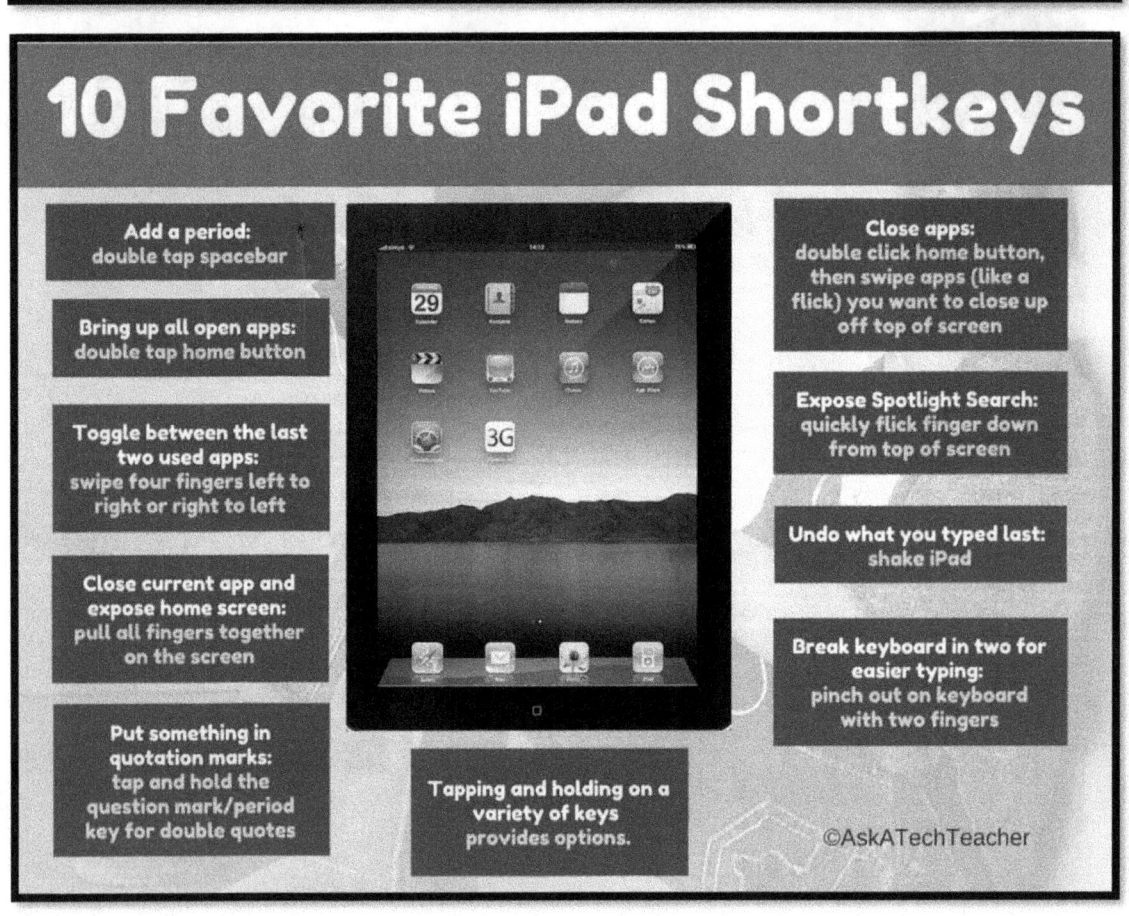

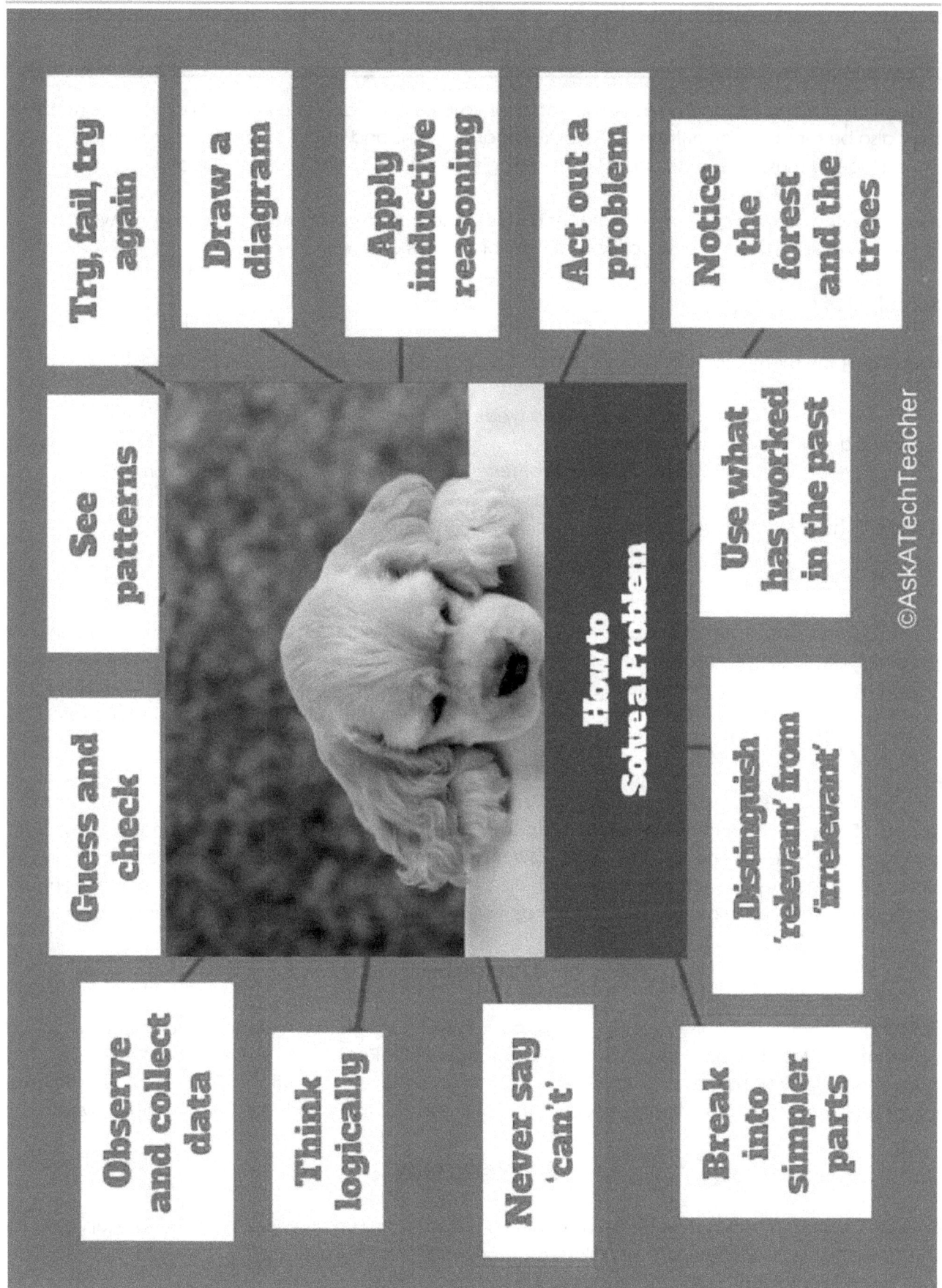

5th Grade Technology Curriculum: Teacher Manual

Homework

Homework may be optional, especially if many of your students don't have digital devices at home. It may also be replaced by authentic use of keyboarding skills and habits during class projects. In this case, students must focus on correct keyboarding habits while typing a class project.

Alternatively, you may offer two afternoons a week where students come in and do Homework at School while siblings are in after-school activities or parents chat with friends.

Submittal of homework:

Last day of the month, via a dropbox or email. Students write 3-5 sentences on the following:

- *Verify they typed 15 minutes 3 times a week (45 minutes a week) every week of month*
- *Share what was easy/difficult*
- *Reflect on how keyboarding affects other classes, homework assignments, life in general*

If students have student workbooks, this is included in their copies.

October

Spend 15 minutes, 3 times a week, on **Popcorn Typer** (Google for website) or another keyboard program that teaches one row at a time—**homerow keys only**. Repeat the exercise over and over. The goal: memorize key placement. When you can type home row without looking at your fingers, cover keys with a light cloth to hide your hands. For the rest of the month, type with hands covered.

November

Spend 15 minutes, 3 times a week, on **Popcorn Typer** (Google for website) or another keyboard program that teaches one row at a time—**QWERTY row only**. Repeat the exercise over and over. The goal: memorize key placement. When you can type QWERTY row without looking at your fingers, cover keys with a light cloth to hide your hands. For the rest of the month, type with hands covered.

December

Spend 15 minutes, 3 times a week, on **Popcorn Typer** (Google for website) or another keyboard program that teaches one row at a time—**Lower Row only**. Repeat the exercise over and over. The goal: memorize key placement. When you can type the lower row without looking at your fingers, cover keys with a light cloth to hide your hands. For the rest of the month, type with hands covered.

January-May

Spend 15 minutes, 3 times a week, on a keyboard program you use in your school. Try to keep eyes on the screen. The goal: memorize key placement. By mid-month, cover keys with a light cloth to hide your hands. For the rest of the month, type with hands covered.

Index

21st Century Lesson Plan 34
Acrobat 46
Address 144
Alt+F4 .... 107, 129
Annotation Tool 11, 46
Appointment Slots 72, 167
Arrays 154, 156
Articles 5
ASCII Art 68
Ask a Tech Teacher 14
Assessment... 5-7, 35, 52, 53, 54, 55, 62-66, 72, 73, 101, 106, 131, 132, 136, 137, 140, 142, 150, 153, 167, 168, 169, 170, 171, 172, 175, 176, 177, 206, 218
Automath 157
Autosum 163
avatar 75, 218
Axis 163
Background 97
Back-up 30
benchmark 62
Best Practices 14
Blank keyboard quiz 66, 88, 146
Blogging 71, 74
Blogs 9, 48, 74, 75, 79, 80
Board 13, 59, 114
Border 154
BrainPop 123
Brainstorming 81-84, 220
Bubbl.us 84
Building diagram 216
calendar 45, 46, 47, 72, 76, 130, 132, 137, 138, 139, 141, 167, 218
Canva 135, 214
card 128
Cell 154
Certificate of Completion 5
Chromebook 12, 44, 46, 55, 76, 84, 90, 99, 127, 218, 219
Citations 81, 181, 183
Class calendar 43, 46, 47
class internet start page 13, 45, 47, 122
Class warm-up..30, 39, 43, 59, 71, 81, 87, 97, 101, 109, 114, 122, 125, 130, 138, 144, 150, 154, 160, 163, 167, 173, 178, 181, 185, 193, 197, 199, 205, 207, 211, 213, 216, 220
class website 48
Cloud 48, 49
Coding 6, 9, 15, 109, 112, 218
Collaboration 6, 9, 34, 81, 130
Column 154
Common Core4, 5, 6, 14, 40, 48, 67, 74, 79, 82, 88, 91, 95, 110, 112, 182
Common Core State Standards 6
Common Tech Problems 22, 222
Compare-contrast 31, 133, 155, 160, 207, 209
Composition 101, 109, 122
Content Standards30, 43, 71, 81, 87, 97, 101, 109, 122, 125, 130, 138, 144, 150, 154, 160, 163, 167, 173, 178, 181, 185, 193, 197, 199, 205, 207, 211, 213, 216
Copyright 14, 37, 97, 108, 116, 125, 144, 150
Crop 122, 125, 178, 181
Ctr+P 145
Ctr+S 145, 183
Ctr+Z 150
curriculum map 5, 8, 9
Cyberbullying 114, 115
Dance Mat Typing 72, 87
Desktop 6, 85, 99
desktop publishing .... 132, 139, See DTP
Diagram 160
Dialogue box 130
Differentiation 5, 12, 35
Digital citizenship35, 43, 71, 81, 97, 114, 115, 122, 125, 178, 181, 185, 193, 197, 199, 205, 211
Digital Classroom 43
Digital commerce 115
Digital Communications 115
digital devices 6, 12
Digital footprint 114, 115, 116
Digital law 115
digital lockers 49
Digital Passport 122
Digital Portfolios 45, 49, 215
Digital privacy 114, 115, 116
Digital rights and responsibilities 114, 116
Digital search and research 115
Diigo 47
Discussion Board 49
Domain 122
domain-specific tech vocabulary 59
Drawing program 6
Drill down 150
Dropbox 45, 49
DTP6, 9, 15, 130, 132, 138, 139, 144, 146, 150, 153, 155, 218, 220
EasyBib 86
Email 6, 43, 114, 222
End-of-Year Challenge 15, 216, 218
Escape 43, 101
essential question 5
Etiquette 71
Evernote 47, 131, 211
Evidence Board .30, 32, 71, 74, 81, 82, 87, 97, 98, 101, 102, 109, 114, 122, 125, 130, 138, 144, 146, 150, 154, 160, 163, 173, 181, 182, 185, 193, 197, 199, 211
evidence of learning74, 82, 87, 98, 102, 114, 123, 125, 130, 138, 146, 151, 154, 163, 173, 178, 182, 185, 193, 197, 199, 211
Excel 155, 160, 163, 165
Exit Ticket 5, 6, 8, 11, 13, 39
F11 163
Failure 35
Fair use 97, 115, 116, 117, 150. 222

Favorites 193
Find My File 222
font 104
Format 122
Formatting 114, 144, 150, 152, 173
formulas 158
Games 9, 68
GIF 199, 207
Gimp 186
Gmail 48
Goodreader 11
Google Apps 48, 49
Google Calendar 46, 48, 72, 138, 139, 167
Google Docs ..48, 75, 85, 102, 103, 108, 134, 146, 147, 178, 179, 182
Google Draw 83, 98
Google Drive 48
Google Earth 6, 9, 15, 130, 131, 137, 138, 139, 144, 146, 150, 151, 154, 160, 163, 173, 174, 175, 177
Google Earth Board .130, 131, 137, 138, 144, 146, 150, 151, 154, 160, 163, 174, 175
Google Earth Tour 15, 139, 173, 177
Google Forms 39, 64, 70, 124, 184
Google Spreadsheet 124
Graphic arts 130
Graphic Organizers 15, 97-99
Graphics 9, 15, 97, 144, 178, 181, 219
Graphs 15, 154, 160, 163-166, 219, 220
Habits of Mind 6, 11, 35-38, 88
handles 199
Hardware 9, 44, 52, 53, 72
hardware problems 88
Help 216
higher order thinking 6
Hits 122
hoaxes 129
Homework 15, 31, 49, 102, 114, 243
Hotkeys 111
Hour of Code 6, 15, 109, 110, 111, 112
https 117
iAnnotate 11, 46, 72, 132, 133, 140
Image copyright 115
Image Editing 15, 185, 193, 197, 199
image editor 182, 185, 189, 190, 194, 198, 199, 200, 202, 205
important keys 63, 82
Inquiry 7, 11-13, 68
Internet Research 123, 222
Internet safety 115, 117
Internet Search 15, 75, 122
Internet Sources 124
Internet Start Page 57
iPads 6, 36, 44, 45, 62, 98, 102, 103, 127, 135, 139, 147, 155, 160, 163, 182
ISTE Standards 5
Journaling 48
Key signature 211
Keyboard 9, 59, 64, 68, 114, 141, 150, 178
keyboarding .4, 5, 10, 11, 13, 36, 40, 41, 42, 43, 59, 60, 61, 62, 72, 76, 79, 81, 85, 99, 103, 125, 127, 130, 138, 141, 144, 145, 149, 150, 152, 154, 163, 167, 173, 185, 193, 197, 199, 207, 208, 219, 243
Keyboarding certificate 151
keyboarding hints 145
Keyboarding Stages 222
keyboarding technique 61
Keyboarding technique checklist 61
Kidblog 71
Knowledge 207
laptop 12
Lemonade Stand 162
Lesson 13
line graph 165
link 211
literacy 4
LiveBinders 47
LucidPress 135
Lyrics 211
Mac ... 46, 76, 84, 99, 102, 127, 135, 139, 147, 155, 160, 163, 174, 219
Macros 111
Math 42, 70, 87, 91, 95, 109, 112, 154, 156, 158, 160, 163, 167
menu 30
Mindmapping 81--84
Minecraft 36, 88, 93, 94, 95, 96, 109, 221
MLA heading 111
models 155
monitor 81
mouse 9, 41, 44, 60, 142, 191, 203, 219, 220
MS Publisher 134
MS Word 98, 103, 107
Mulligan Rule 30, 71, 72, 82, 130, 137, 152, 170
Music 213
National Educational Technology Standards 4
Netiquette 114, 115, 117
Netiquette Rules 222
Newsletter 15, 130, 132-137
Notability 46
Notable 11
Office 365 48
Online presence 115
online tools 214
Outlining 76, 81, 84
Padlet 39, 43, 46, 72, 87, 97, 99, 124, 130, 167
PARCC/SBA 64, 69
Passwords 115-117
PBWorks 49
PC 12, 71, 81, 87, 97, 101, 122, 125, 130, 144, 150, 154, 160, 163, 178, 181, 185
Penzu 48
photo editing 186
Photoshop .. 15, 186, 188, 189, 196, 198, 202, 205, 206, 212
Photoshop Tennis 15, 205, 206
Photoshopped 185, 188, 193, 196, 197, 220
PicMonkey 179, 180
Placeholder 130
Plagiarism 114, 115, 117, 150
poll 13, 39, 64, 87, 90, 164
PORTRAIT 227

Posters 5, 12, 222
posture 41, 60, 82, 87, 141, 145, 154, 163, 178, 181, 185, 193, 218, 219
PowerPoint 34, 132, 134, 139, 189
Presentation Boards 72, 131, 167
Presentation Tools 6, 219
presentations 163
Presentations 10, 67, 130
Print preview 178, 183
Print Preview 180
Printkey 122
PrintMusic 212
Problem solving 7, 10, 30, 35, 43, 59, 71, 74, 81, 87, 88, 97, 101, 109, 114, 122, 125, 130, 138, 144, 150, 154, 160, 163, 167, 173, 178, 181, 185, 193, 197, 199, 205, 207, 211, 213, 216
Problem Solving Board 32, 33, 71, 72, 73, 97, 142
Protocol 43
Public domain 97, 115-117, 150
Publisher 132, 134, 135, 139, 141, 148
Question Board 146, 154
quotes 89, 123
QWERTY 114
Research 10, 42, 108, 122, 130, 222
Right-click 30, 199
risk takers 11
Row 154
rubric .. 114, 125, 131, 137, 140, 152, 154, 160, 163, 185, 193, 197, 199, 211
rules 116, 120
Scheme 197
Science 15, 62, 97, 112, 207
scientific method 207
Scope and Sequence 5
screen 130
search/research 117
sharing 6, 10, 34, 40, 42, 48, 71, 74, 75, 79, 132
Shortkeys 59, 71, 111, 219
Slideshows 9
smartphone 12
Social Media 115, 117
software 6, 12
Speak Like a Geek 43, 59, 71, 81, 87, 97, 101, 109, 114, 122, 125, 130, 138, 144, 150, 154, 160, 163, 167, 168, 173, 178, 181, 182, 185, 193, 197, 199, 211
speed quiz 43, 62, 74, 151, 161, 185, 208
spreadsheet 6, 34, 154, 155, 156, 158, 159, 160, 161, 162, 163, 164, 167, 169, 174, 184, 219, 220
Spreadsheet Formulae 15, 154, 160
Standards for Mathematical Practice 91, 92, 95, 112, 155
Stranger Danger 115
Student Blogs 15, 43, 49, 71
Student digital portfolios 49
student digital workbooks 10
Student email 50
student hands 60
Student workbooks 6, 12, 14, 45, 243
Summative 15, 167
Surface tablet 46, 99, 127
Symbaloo 47, 57
Tables 107, 122, 127, 163
Teacher Training 70
tech lab 13
Tech Problems 222
Tech Rules 218
Technology Curriculum 4, 5
Template 135, 139, 144, 150, 211
Text box 101, 149, 150
Texting 117, 121
Tomorrow's student 7
Transfer of knowledge 34
Trifold 15, 144, 147, 148, 150, 151, 153
Tutorial 216
Twitter 41, 49, 96, 117, 119, 120, 121
Type to Learn 145, 146, 163, 178, 181, 185, 197, 199
typing vs. handwriting speed 207
TypingTest.com 62, 145, 181
Venn Diagrams 104
Virtual Wall 39
visual learning 98
visual organizer 98, 100
Vocabulary. 9, 10, 30, 35, 40, 43, 50, 59, 71, 81, 87, 97, 101, 109, 114, 122, 125, 130, 138, 144, 150, 154, 160, 163, 167, 173, 178, 181, 185, 193, 197, 199, 205, 207, 211, 213, 216, 220
warm-up 6, 11, 13
Washout 178
watermark 104
webbased tools 213
website address 126
Website Evaluation 125
Weebly 48
Windows 46, 52, 99, 127
WinXP 71
Wix 48
Word 6, 10, 15, 40, 52, 83, 85, 98, 101, 102, 103, 107, 108, 111, 122, 127, 134, 139, 141, 143, 160, 165, 178, 179, 181, 212, 213, 220
word processing 34, 48, 68, 81, 84, 85, 97, 101, 102, 104, 114, 127, 132, 178, 179, 181, 182, 220
Wordpress 48
Writing 15, 71, 95, 181
writing skills 119, 121

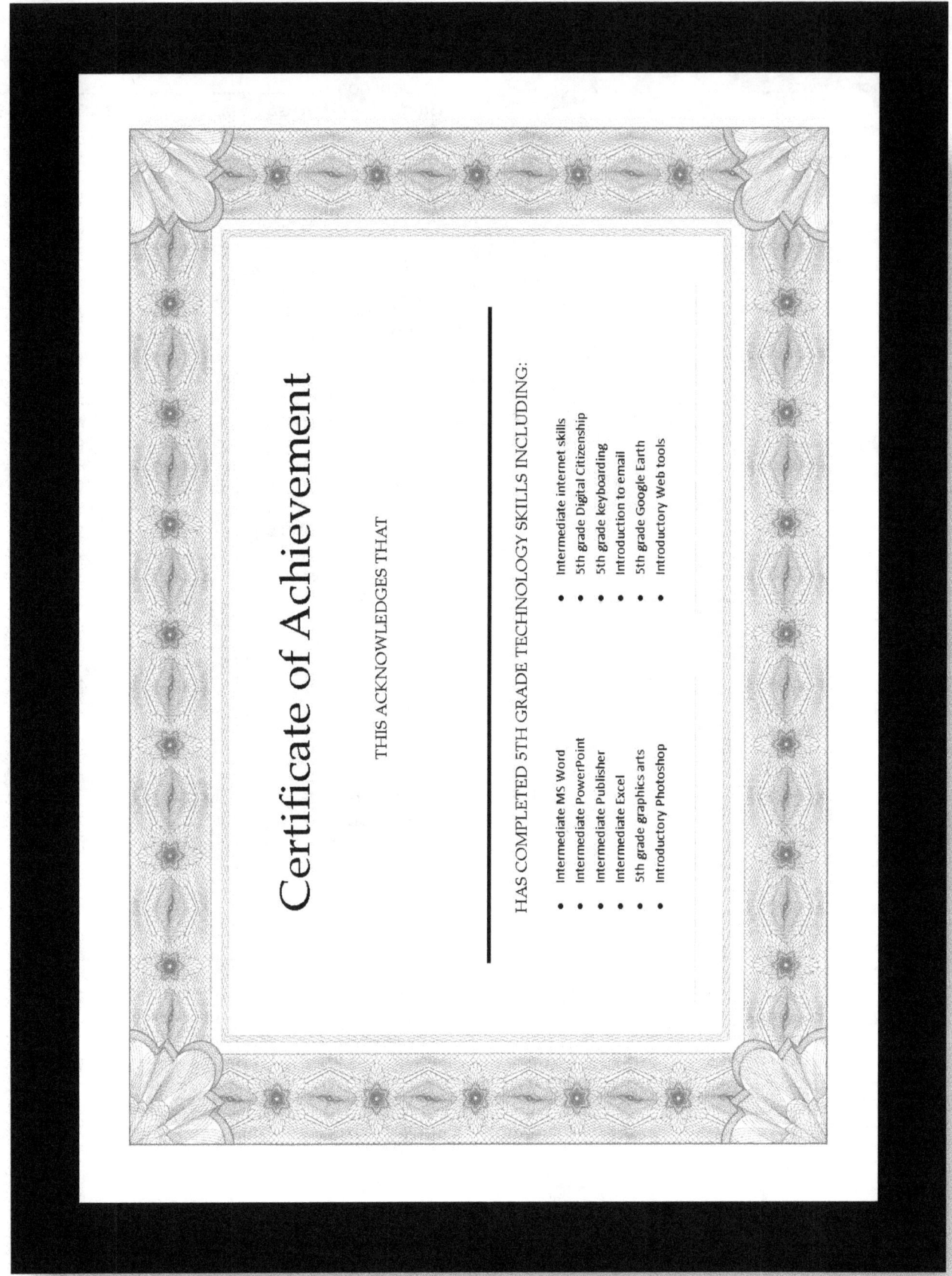

Which book	Price (print/digital/Combo)
K-8th Tech Textbook (each)	$25.99 + p&h
K-8 Combo (all 9 textbooks)	$248 and up + p&h
K-8 Student workbooks (license)	$199 per grade level and up
35 K-6 Inquiry-based Projects	$31.99/25.99/52.18 + p&h
55 Tech Projects	$18.99 and up–digital only
K-8 Keyboard Curriculum—3 options	$20 and up + p&h
K-8 Digital Citizenship Curriculum	$29.95 and up
CCSS—Math, Lang., Reading, Writing	$26.99 ea
K-5 Common Core Projects	$29.95/23.99/48.55 + p&h
Themed webinars	$8-30
PD classes (online—for groups)	$795
Summer tech camp for kids	$179 + p&h
College credit classes (online)	$497 and up
Digital Citizenship certificate class	Starts at $29.99
Classroom tech poster bundles	Start at $9.99
PBL lessons--singles	$1.99 and up
Bundles of lesson plans	$4.99 and up (digital only)
Tech Ed Scope and Sequence	$9.99 and up (digital only)
New Teacher Survival Kit	$285-620+ p&h
Homeschool Tech Survival Kit	$99 + p&h
Mentoring (30 min. at a time)	$50 and up/session
169 Tech Tips From Classroom	$9.99 (digital only)
Consulting/seminars/webinars	Call or email for prices

Free sample? Visit Structured Learning LLC website
Prices subject to change
Email Zeke.rowe@structuredlearning.net

Structured Learning
Premiere Provider of Technology Teaching Books to the Education Community

Pay via PayPal, Credit Card, Amazon, TPT, pre-approved school district PO